DATE DUE

LAWS OF FEAR

What is the relationship between fear, danger, and the law? Cass Sunstein attacks the increasingly influential Precautionary Principle – the idea that regulators should take steps to protect against potential harms, even if causal chains are uncertain and even if we do not know that harms are likely to come to fruition. Focusing on such problems as global warming, terrorism, DDT, and genetic engineering, Professor Sunstein argues that the Precautionary Principle is incoherent. Risks exist on all sides of social situations, and precautionary steps create dangers of their own. Diverse cultures focus on very different risks, often because social influences and peer pressures accentuate some fears and reduce others. Instead of adopting the Precautionary Principle, Professor Sunstein argues for three steps: a narrow Anti-Catastrophe Principle, designed for the most serious risks; close attention to costs and benefits; and an approach called "libertarian paternalism," designed to respect freedom of choice while also moving people in directions that will make their lives go better. He also shows how free societies can protect liberty amidst fears about terrorism and national security. *Laws of Fear* represents a major statement from one of the most influential political and legal theorists writing today.

CASS R. SUNSTEIN is Karl N. Llewellyn Distinguished Service Professor of Jurisprudence, Law School and Department of Political Science, University of Chicago.

The John Robert Seeley Lectures have been established by the University of Cambridge as a biennial lecture series in social and political studies, sponsored jointly by the Faculty of History and the University Press. The Seeley Lectures provide a unique forum for distinguished scholars of international reputation to address, in an accessible manner, themes of broad and topical interest in social and political studies. Subsequent to their public delivery in Cambridge the University Press publishes suitably modified versions of each set of lectures. Professor James Tully delivered the inaugural series of Seeley Lectures in 1994 on the theme of *Constitutionalism in an Age of Diversity*.

The Seeley Lectures include

(1) *Strange Multiplicity: Constitutionalism in an Age of Diversity*
JAMES TULLY
ISBN 0 521 47117 6 (hardback) 0 521 47694 1 (paperback)

(2) *The Dignity of Legislation*
JEREMY WALDRON
ISBN 0 521 65092 5 (hardback) 0 521 65883 7 (paperback)

(3) *Women and Human Development: The Capabilities Approach*
MARTHA NUSSBAUM
ISBN 0 521 66086 6 (hardback) 0 521 00385 7 (paperback)

(4) *Value, Respect, and Attachment*
JOSEPH RAZ
ISBN 0 521 80180 X (hardback) 0 521 00022 X (paperback)

(5) *The Rights of Others: Aliens, Residents and Citizens*
SEYLA BENHABIB
ISBN 0 521 83134 2 (hardback) 0 521 53860 2 (paperback)

(6) *Laws of Fear: Beyond the Precautionary Principle*
CASS R. SUNSTEIN
ISBN 0 521 84823 7 (hardback) 0 521 61512 7 (paperback)

LAWS OF FEAR

Beyond the Precautionary Principle

CASS R. SUNSTEIN

University of Chicago

CAMBRIDGE
UNIVERSITY PRESS

CAMBRIDGE UNIVERSITY PRESS
Cambridge, New York, Melbourne, Madrid, Cape Town, Singapore, São Paulo

Cambridge University Press
The Edinburgh Building, Cambridge CB2 2RU, UK

Published in the United States of America by Cambridge University Press, New York

www.cambridge.org
Information on this title: www.cambridge.org/9780521848237

© Cass R. Sunstein 2005

First published 2005
Reprinted 2005

A catalogue record for this publication is available from the British Library

ISBN-13 978-0-521-84823-7 hardback
ISBN-10 0-521-84823-7 hardback

ISBN-13 978-0-521-61512-9 paperback
ISBN-10 0-521-61512-7 paperback

Transferred to digital printing 2006

The publisher has used his best endeavours to ensure that the URLs for external websites
referred to in this publication are correct and active at the time of going to press. However,
the publisher has no responsibility for the websites and can make no guarantee that a site will
remain live or that the content is or will remain appropriate.

For Richard Thaler

Contents

Acknowledgments

This book grows out of the Seeley Lectures, delivered at Cambridge University in March 2004, under the shadow of many salient sources of fear: terrorism, the war in Iraq, global warming, crime, mad cow disease, water pollution, and genetic modification of food, among others. One of the particular benefits of my visit was the opportunity to see the large differences between American and European perspectives on risk and fear – and also some significant differences within Europe itself. I am most grateful for the multiple kindnesses I received while at Cambridge. For their hospitality, warmth, and help, special thanks to Gareth Stedman Jones, Tim Lewens, Miri Rubin, and David Runciman. During the visit, a workshop at University College, London, hosted by Ronald Dworkin and Stephen Guest, provided a good deal of help with the arguments in chapters 6 and 7. I am also grateful to my editor at Cambridge University Press, Richard Fisher, for wonderful suggestions on the manuscript. For superb research assistance, thanks to Viktoria Lovei, Rob Park, Andres Sawicki, Sarah Sulkowski, and Smita Singh.

I have been working on this book for several years, and preliminary versions of several chapters have appeared as Beyond the Precautionary Principle, 151 *U. Pa. L. Rev.* 1003 (2003); Probability Neglect: Emotions, Worst Cases, and the Law, 112 *Yale L.J.* 81 (2002); Fear and Liberty, *Social Reseach* (2004); Valuing Life: A Plea for Disaggregation, *Duke L.J.* (2004); and (with Richard H. Thaler), Libertarian Paternalism Is Not an Oxymoron, 70 *U. Chi. L. Rev.* 1159 (2003). Readers interested in more technical versions of several of the arguments here might consult those essays. In all cases, the preliminary versions have been substantially revised, in large part in response to comments and suggestions that I received in Cambridge and from multiple readers.

Parts of the manuscript have been presented at the University of Pennsylvania Law School, the John F. Kennedy School of Government at Harvard University, the New School for Social Research, and the University of Chicago Law School; I am thankful to audiences there for many valuable criticisms and suggestions. For helpful comments or discussions, I am particularly grateful to Cary Coglianese, Elizabeth Emens, Carolyn Frantz, Robert Goodin, Daniel Kahneman, Howard Margolis, Martha Nussbaum, Eric Posner, Richard Posner, Paul Slovic, David Strauss, Adrian Vermeule, W. Kip Viscusi, and Jonathan Wiener. Special thanks are due to Emens, Frantz, Nussbaum, E. Posner, R. Posner, Adam Samaha, Strauss, and Vermeule for comments on the manuscript as a whole.

This book is dedicated to Richard Thaler, a good friend and colleague who has taught me a lot about behavioral economics, rationality, and precautions.

Introduction

This is a book about fear, democracy, rationality, and the law. Sometimes people are fearful when they ought not to be, and sometimes they are fearless when they should be frightened. In democratic nations, the law responds to people's fears. As a result, the law can be led in unfortunate and even dangerous directions. The problem cuts across countless substantive areas, including global warming, genetic engineering, nuclear power, biodiversity, pesticides, blood transfusions, food safety, cloning, toxic chemicals, crime, and even terrorism and efforts to combat it. "Risk panics" play a large role in groups, cities, and even nations.

DELIBERATION AND THEORY

How should a democratic government respond to public fear? What is the connection between fear on the one hand and law and policy on the other? I suggest that these questions are best approached if we keep two general ideas in mind. The first is that well-functioning governments aspire to be *deliberative democracies*. They are accountable to the public, to be sure; they hold periodic elections and require officials to pay close attention to the popular will. Responsiveness to public fear is, in this sense, both inevitable and desirable. But responsiveness is complemented by a commitment to deliberation, in the form of reflection and reason giving. If the public is fearful about a trivial risk, a deliberative democracy does not respond by reducing that risk. It uses its own institutions to dispel public fear that is, by hypothesis, without foundation. Hence deliberative democracies avoid the tendency of populist systems to fall prey to public fear when it is baseless. They use institutional safeguards to check public panics.

The same safeguards come into play if the public is not fearful of a risk that is actually serious. When this is so, a deliberative democracy takes action, whether or not the public seeks it. In these respects, a well-functioning democratic system places a large premium on science and on what experts have to say. It rejects simple populism. Of course science may be inconclusive and experts may err. Of course the public's values should ultimately play a large role. Perhaps the public is especially opposed to risks that are concentrated in poor areas; perhaps citizens are particularly concerned about risks that are potentially catastrophic or uncontrollable. In a democracy, people's reflective values prevail. But values, and not errors of fact, are crucial.

My second point is that well-functioning democracies often attempt to achieve *incompletely theorized agreements.*[1] Especially when they are heterogeneous, such democracies attempt to solve social disputes by seeking agreements not on high-level theories about what is right or what is good, but on practices and low-level principles on which diverse people can converge. Citizens in free societies differ on the largest issues. They disagree about the nature and the existence of God; about the relationship between freedom and equality; about the place of utility and efficiency; about the precise nature of fairness. In the face of those differences, it is often best, if possible, to avoid committing a nation to a highly controversial view, and instead to seek solutions on which diverse people might agree. In a slogan: *Well-functioning societies make it possible for people to achieve agreement when agreement is necessary, and unnecessary for them to achieve agreement when agreement is impossible.*

The point has special relevance to the question of how to handle public fear. Sometimes that question is thought to require government to resolve large problems about its basic mission – to think deeply, for example, about the nature and meaning of human life. When people disagree about how to handle risks associated with genetic modification of food, or terrorism, or pesticides, or global warming, it is partly because of differences about the facts; but it is also because of differences about fundamental issues. To the extent possible, I suggest that those fundamental issues should be avoided. Deliberative

---

[1] I defend and elaborate this idea in Cass R. Sunstein, *Legal Reasoning and Political Conflict* (New York: Oxford University Press, 1996).

democracies do best if they abstract from the largest questions and try to obtain a consensus from people who disagree on, or are unsure about, how to resolve those questions. In the context of fear, I suggest, it is often possible to obtain just such a consensus.

But what counts as fear? Throughout this book, I understand fear to depend on some kind of judgment that we are in danger.[2] Some people are afraid of spending many hours in the sun, simply because they believe that doing so creates a risk of skin cancer. Other people are afraid of shaking hands with someone who has AIDS, because they think that shaking hands creates a risk of transmission. Still other people are frightened by the prospect of global warming, thinking that serious risks to human beings are likely to result. Of course the beliefs that underlie fear may or may not be justified.

Is some kind of "affect" a necessary or sufficient condition for fear? Many people think that without affect of some kind, people cannot really be afraid; perhaps human fear does not count as such in the absence of identifiable physiological reactions. It is generally agreed that the brain contains a distinctive region, the amygdala, that governs certain emotions and that is particularly involved in fear.[3] In fact these physiological reactions, and the relevant regions of the brain, permit extremely rapid responses to hazards, in a way that increases our chance to stay alive but that can also lead us to excessive fear about improbable dangers. Obviously these rapid responses have evolutionary advantages.

These points will turn out to be highly relevant to some of the arguments I shall be making, especially those that involve the human tendency to neglect the likelihood that bad outcomes will occur. But for the most part, my claims can be accepted without adopting a particularly controversial view about what fear really is.

PRECAUTIONS AND RATIONALITY

My point of departure is the Precautionary Principle, which is a focal point for thinking about health, safety, and the environment throughout Europe. In fact the Precautionary Principle is receiving

---

[2] See Martha C. Nussbaum, *Upheavals of Thought* (New York: Cambridge University Press, 2002).
[3] See Joseph E. LeDoux, *The Emotional Brain* (New York: Simon & Schuster, 1996).

increasing worldwide attention, having become the basis for countless international debates about how to think about risk, health, and the environment. The principle has even entered into debates about how to handle terrorism, about "preemptive war," and about the relationship between liberty and security. In defending the 2003 war in Iraq, President George W. Bush invoked a kind of Precautionary Principle, arguing that action was justified in the face of uncertainty. "If we wait for threats to fully materialize, we will have waited too long."[4] He also said, "I believe it is essential that when we see a threat, we deal with those threats before they become imminent. It's too late if they become imminent."[5] What is especially noteworthy is that this way of thinking is essentially the same as that of environmentalists concerned about global warming, genetic modification of food, and pesticides. For these problems, it is commonly argued that regulation, rather than inaction, is the appropriate course in the face of doubt.

The Precautionary Principle takes many forms. But in all of them, the animating idea is that regulators should take steps to protect against potential harms, even if causal chains are unclear and even if we do not know that those harms will come to fruition. The Precautionary Principle is worthy of sustained attention for two reasons. First, it provides the foundation for intensely pragmatic debates about danger, fear, and security. Second, the Precautionary Principle raises a host of theoretically fascinating questions about individual and social decision making under conditions of risk and uncertainty. For the latter reason, the principle is closely connected to current controversies about fear and rationality – about whether individuals and societies do, or should, follow conventional accounts of rational behavior.

My initial argument is that in its strongest forms, the Precautionary Principle is literally incoherent, and for one reason: There are risks on all sides of social situations. It is therefore paralyzing; it forbids the very steps that it requires. Because risks are on all sides, the Precautionary Principle forbids action, inaction, and everything in between. Consider the question of what societies should do about genetic engineering, nuclear power, and terrorism. Aggressive steps,

---

[4] See Complete Text of Bush's West Point Address (June 3, 2002), available at http://www. newsmax.com/archives/articles/2002/6/2/81354.shtml.
[5] See Roland Eggleston, Bush Defends War (Feb. 9, 2004), http://www.globalsecurity.org/ wmd/library/news/iraq/2004/02/iraq-040209-rferror.htm.

designed to control the underlying risks, seem to be compelled by the Precautionary Principle. But those very steps run afoul of the same principle, because each of them creates new risks of its own. It follows that many people who are described as risk averse are, in reality, no such thing. They are averse to *particular* risks, not to risks in general. Someone who is averse to the risks of flying might well be unconcerned with the risks of driving; someone who seeks to avoid the risks associated with medication probably disregards the risks associated with letting nature take its course; those who fear the risks associated with pesticides are likely to be indifferent to the risks associated with organic foods.

Why, then, is the Precautionary Principle widely thought to give guidance? I contend that the principle becomes operational, and gives the illusion of guidance, only because of identifiable features of human cognition. Human beings, cultures, and nations often single out one or a few social risks as "salient," and ignore the others. A central point here involves the *availability heuristic*, a central means by which people evaluate risks. When people lack statistical knowledge, they consider risks to be significant if they can easily think of instances in which those risks came to fruition. Individual and even cultural risk perceptions can be explained partly in that way. It follows that there can be no general Precautionary Principle – though particular, little precautionary principles, stressing margins of safety for certain risks, can and do operate in different societies. As I shall also suggest, the Precautionary Principle might well be reformulated as an Anti-Catastrophe Principle, designed for special circumstances in which it is not possible to assign probabilities to potentially catastrophic risks.

THE PLAN

This book is divided into two parts, one dealing with problems in individual and social judgments and the other with possible solutions. The first and second chapters elaborate the claims I have just summarized. The third and fourth extend the cognitive and cultural stories in two ways: first, by exploring human susceptibility to worst-case scenarios; and second, by developing an understanding of social influences on behavior and belief. The initial claim in chapter 3 is that a salient incident can make people more fearful than is warranted by reality. Well-publicized events – a terrorist attack, a case of mad cow disease, an apparent concentration of leukemia in an area with unusually high levels of cellphone use – can lead people to believe that the risk is much greater than it really is. But most of my discussion is devoted to the phenomenon of "probability neglect," by which people focus on the worst case, and neglect the probability that it will actually occur. Especially when emotions are intensely engaged, worst cases tend to crowd out an investigation of the actual size of the risk.

Chapter 4 emphasizes that fear does not operate in a social vacuum. It is spread through social interactions. Hence I explore, in the context of fear, the dynamics of two phenomena: *social cascades* and *group polarization*. Through social cascades, people pay attention to the fear expressed by others, in a way that can lead to the rapid transmission of a belief, even if false, that a risk is quite serious (or – at least equally bad – not at all serious). Fear, like many other emotions, can be contagious; cascades help to explain why. Through group polarization, social interactions lead groups to be more fearful than individuals. It is well established that members of deliberating groups often end up in a more extreme position in line with their predeliberation tendencies; hence groups can be far more fearful than their own members before deliberation began. An understanding of social cascades and group polarization helps to illuminate the much-discussed idea of "moral panics." Indeed, social fears, of the sort I am emphasizing here, often amount to moral panics; and a principle of precaution often operates when a moral panic is occurring.

Part II discusses some solutions to the problem of misplaced public fear. Chapter 5 extracts some positive lessons from the challenge to the Precautionary Principle. I sketch an Anti-Catastrophe Principle, specifically designed for situations of uncertainty and potentially severe harm. Outside of the context of catastrophe, I explore the relevance of irreversibility and also suggest the need for margins of safety, chosen on the basis of a wide rather than narrow understanding of what is at stake. I deal as well with the problem of public management of fear.

Chapters 6 and 7 investigate the uses and limits of cost-benefit analysis. I suggest that cost-benefit balancing has a significant advantage over the Precautionary Principle insofar as it uses a wide rather than narrow viewscreen for the evaluation of risks. But there is a serious problem with cost-benefit analysis: Understood in a certain way, it may neglect dangers that cannot be established with certainty. It follows that sensible cost-benefit analysts attend to speculative harms, not merely demonstrable ones. But how can risks be turned into monetary equivalents? How can it make sense to say that a mortality risk of 1/100,000 is worth $50, rather than twice that much or half that much? One of my major goals here is to sketch the theoretical underpinnings of cost-benefit analysis as it is currently practiced – to show that the assignment of monetary values to risks is far more plausible and intuitive than it might seem. But I also suggest that current practice has a major problem: it uses a *uniform* value for statistically equivalent risks, when the very theory that underlies current practice requires a wide range of values. The reason is that people care about qualitative distinctions among risks; they do not see statistically equivalent risks as the same.

Chapter 7 explores more fundamental questions about cost-benefit analysis. I suggest that in some cases, what is needed is democratic deliberation about what should be done, rather than an aggregation of costs and benefits – and that this point raises grave doubts about cost-benefit balancing in certain settings. I also suggest that in deciding what should be done, regulators must focus on who is helped and who is hurt – a question on which cost-benefit balancing says nothing. But these points should not be taken to mean that such balancing is to be rejected. They mean only that an assessment of costs and benefits tells us far less than we need to know.

Chapter 8 emphasizes cases in which people fail, foolishly, to take precautions. Here the problem is insufficient rather than excessive fear. I suggest the possibility of "libertarian paternalism," that is, an approach that steers people in directions that will promote their welfare without foreclosing their own choices. The chief theoretical claim is that often people do not have stable or well-ordered preferences. The chief practical claim is that it is possible to be libertarian (in the sense of respectful of private choices) while also accepting paternalism (through approaches that lead people in welfare-promoting directions). When people's fears lead them in the wrong directions, libertarian paternalism can provide a valuable corrective.

Chapter 9 explores the relationship between fear and liberty. In the context of terrorism and threats to national security, unjustified restrictions on civil liberties are a likely result, especially when the majority that favor those intrusions are not also burdened by them. Indeed, a kind of Precautionary Principle often produces indefensible limits on freedom. I argue that courts can reduce the risks posed by excessive fear in three ways. First, and most fundamentally, they should demand clear legislative authorization for any intrusions on liberty; they should not permit such intrusions simply because the executive favors them. Second, courts should give close scrutiny to intrusions on liberty that provide asymmetrical benefits and burdens by imposing restrictions on members of readily identifiable groups rather than the public as a whole. Third, courts should adopt rules or presumptions that reflect what might be called "second-order balancing," designed to counteract the risks of error that accompany ad hoc balancing.

APPROACHES AND POLICIES

I do not aim here to reach final conclusions about how to handle particular hazards. Of course I have views on many of them. I believe, for example, that electromagnetic fields pose little risk; people have been far more fearful of them than the evidence warrants. By contrast, countries all over the world should be taking far more aggressive steps to reduce tobacco smoking, which produces millions of preventable deaths each year (and nearly half a million in the United States alone). Far more should be done, especially in poor countries, to control the spread of HIV/AIDS. I also believe that significant steps should be taken to control the problem of global warming – and hence that the antiregulatory posture of the United States under George W. Bush has been worse than unfortunate. Global warming threatens to impose serious risks and wealthy nations have a particular obligation to reduce those risks – partly because they are largely responsible for the problem, partly because they have the resources to do something about it. A great deal of attention should be paid to the promise of alternative sources of energy, which pose lower risks than those associated with nuclear power and fossil fuels. A significant, and too often neglected, social risk comes from sun exposure, which causes skin cancer, a fact that has yet to provide sufficient changes in people's behavior.

In terms of general orientation, I do not believe that it makes the slightest sense to oppose government regulation as such, or to claim that "deregulation" is an appropriate response to the problem of excessive public fear. Of course overregulation can be found in many places, and of course it is a problem; but the problem of under-regulation is also serious. In many domains, government regulation is indispensable, particularly in the context of health, safety, and the environment. Nothing said here should be taken to suggest otherwise.

I also believe that an assessment of both costs and benefits is highly relevant to regulatory choices. For many problems, a form of cost-benefit balancing is far more helpful than the Precautionary Principle. But I do not believe that "economic efficiency" should be the exclusive foundation of regulatory decisions. On the contrary, that idea seems to me quite preposterous. Economic efficiency attempts to satisfy people's existing preferences, as measured by their "willingness to pay," and this is an inadequate basis for law and policy. Sometimes regulatory questions call for a reassessment of people's existing preferences, not for simple aggregation of those preferences; and distributional issues matter a great deal. In any case I shall raise questions about the idea of "willingness to pay," which is central to economic analysis of regulatory problems. If poor people are unable (and hence unwilling) to pay much to reduce a risk, it does not follow that private and public institutions should refuse to act. Special measures should be taken to assist those who are most in need.

All of these points will play a role in the discussion. But let us begin with the issue of precaution.

PART I

Problems

CHAPTER I

Precautions and Paralysis

All over the world, there is increasing interest in a simple idea for the regulation of risk: In case of doubt, follow the *Precautionary Principle*.[1] Avoid steps that will create a risk of harm. Until safety is established, be cautious; do not require unambiguous evidence. In a catchphrase: Better safe than sorry. In ordinary life, pleas of this kind seem quite sensible, indeed a part of ordinary human rationality. People buy smoke alarms and insurance. They wear seatbelts and motorcycle helmets, even if they are unlikely to be involved in an accident. Shouldn't the same approach be followed by rational regulators as well?

Many people, especially in Europe, seem to think so. In fact it has become standard to say that with respect to risks, Europe and the United States can be distinguished along a single axis: Europe accepts the Precautionary Principle, and the United States does not.[2] On this view, Europeans attempt to build a "margin of safety" into public

---

[1] The literature is vast. See, for general discussion, *The Precautionary Principle in the 20th Century: Late Lessons from Early Warnings*, ed. Poul Harremoës, David Gee, Malcolm MacGarvin, Andy Stirling, Jane Keys, Brian Wynne, and Sofia Guedes Vaz (London: Earthscan, 2002); Arie Trouwborst, *Evolution and Status of the Precautionary Principle in International Law* (The Hague: Kluwer Law International, 2002); *Interpreting the Precautionary Principle*, ed. Tim O'Riordan and James Cameron (London: Cameron May, 2002); *Precaution, Environmental Science and Preventive Public Policy*, ed. Joel Tickner (Washington, D.C.: Island Press, 2002); *Protecting Public Health and the Environment: Implementing the Precautionary Principle*, ed. Carolyn Raffensperger and Joel Tickner (Washington, D.C.: Island Press, 1999). A valuable discussion of problems with the Precautionary Principle in Europe is Giandomenico Majone, What Price Safety? The Precautionary Principle and Its Policy Implications, 40 *J. Common Mark. Stud.* 89 (2002).

[2] On some of the complexities here, see John S. Applegate, The Precautionary Preference: An American Perspective on the Precautionary Principle, 6 *Hum. & Ecol. Risk Assess.* 413 (2000); Peter H. Sand, The Precautionary Principle: A European Perspective, 6 *Hum. & Ecol. Risk Assess.* 445 (2000).

decisions, taking care to protect citizens against risks that cannot be established with certainty. By contrast, Americans are reluctant to take precautions, requiring clear evidence of harm in order to justify regulation. These claims seem plausible in light of the fact that the United States appears comparatively unconcerned about the risks associated with global warming and genetic modification of food; in those contexts, Europeans favor precautions, whereas Americans seem to require something akin to proof of danger. To be sure, the matter is quite different in the context of threats to national security. For the war in Iraq, the United States (and England) followed a kind of Precautionary Principle, whereas other nations (most notably France and Germany) wanted clearer proof of danger. But for most threats to safety and health, many people agree that Europe is precautionary and the United States is not.

I believe that this opposition between Europe and America is false, even illusory. It is simply wrong to say that Europeans are more precautionary than Americans. As an empirical matter, neither is "more precautionary." Europeans are not more averse to risks than Americans. They are more averse to particular risks, such as the risks associated with global warming; but Americans have their own preoc-cupations as well. In the early twenty-first century, for example, many Americans have been highly "precautionary" about the risks associated with aggressive regulation itself – fearing that costly steps, designed to combat global warming and other environmental problems, will lead to unemployment and excessive prices of energy, including gaso-line. Whether or not that fear is justified, it is, in its own way, highly precautionary.

My larger point, the central claim of this chapter, is conceptual. The real problem with the Precautionary Principle in its strongest forms is that it is incoherent; it purports to give guidance, but it fails to do so, because it condemns the very steps that it requires. The regulation that the principle requires always gives rise to risks of its own – and hence the principle bans what it simultaneously mandates. I therefore aim to challenge the Precautionary Principle not because it leads in bad directions, but because read for all it is worth, it leads in no direction at all. The principle threatens to be paralyzing, forbidding regulation, inaction, and every step in between. It provides help only if we blind ourselves to many aspects of risk-related situations and focus on a narrow subset of what is at stake. That kind of self-blinding is what makes the principle seem to give guidance; and I shall have a fair bit to say about why people and societies are selective in their fears.

Of course we have good reason to endorse the goals that motivate many people to endorse the Precautionary Principle. I will ultimately suggest that there are several domains in which refinements of the Precautionary Principle make sense, including the control of potentially catastrophic harms whose probability cannot be assessed with any confidence. Hence an Anti-Catastrophe Principle deserves public endorsement. Consider here a sensible and sober statement from the International Joint Commission's *Biennial Report on Scientific Priorities*: "The Precautionary Principle, sometimes called prudent avoidance, is an ethical imperative to prevent catastrophic damage which has a credible probability of resulting from current choice."[3] In Part II, I attempt to reconstruct the Precautionary Principle in these general terms. But the Anti-Catastrophe Principle is far narrower and more targeted than the general idea of precaution, which is what I mean to challenge here.

THE PRECAUTIONARY PRINCIPLE

I have said that the Precautionary Principle enjoys widespread international support.[4] Indeed, it has been a staple of regulatory policy for several decades.[5] The principle has been mentioned in an increasing number of judicial proceedings, including those in the International Court of Justice, the International Tribunal for the Law of the Sea, and the World Trade Organization Appellate Body, as well as in the courts of many nations, including the supreme courts of India and

---

[3] International Joint Commission, *Biennial Report on Scientific Priorities* 89 (1996), quoted in Carolyn Raffensperger and Peter L. DeFur, Interpreting the Precautionary Principle: Rigorous Science and Solid Ethics, 5 *Hum. & Ecol. Risk Assess.* 933, 935 (1999).

[4] See Trouwborst; *supra* note 1.

[5] For helpful discussion, see David Freestone and Ellen Hey, Origins and Development of the Precautionary Principle, in *The Precautionary Principle and International Law* 3, ed. David Freestone and Ellen Hey (The Hague: Kluwer Law International, 1996); Jonathan B. Wiener, Precaution, Risk, and Multiplicity (unpublished manuscript, 2004); Jonathan B. Wiener, Precaution in a Multirisk World, in *Human and Ecological Risk Assessment* 1509, ed. Dennis D. Paustenbach (New York: John Wiley & Sons, 2d ed., 2002).

Canada. Some people have gone so far as to claim that the Precautionary Principle is becoming a binding part of customary international
law.[6] In the United States, the Precautionary Principle received a
high-profile endorsement in the *New York Times Magazine*, which
listed the principle as one of the most important ideas of 2001.[7]
In a far less celebratory vein, the *Wall Street Journal* attacked
the Precautionary Principle as "an environmentalist neologism,
invoked to trump scientific evidence and move directly to banning
things they don't like – biotech, wireless technology, hydrocarbon
emissions."[8]

In law, the first use of a general Precautionary Principle appears
to be the Swedish Environmental Protection Act of 1969.[9] In the
same period, German environmental policy was founded on the
basis of *Vorsorgeprinzip*, a precursor of the Precautionary Principle.[10]
With respect to risks, German policy has been described as seeing
"precaution" as a highly interventionist idea, one that embodies "a
loose and open-ended interpretation of precaution."[11] In the United
States, federal courts, without using the term explicitly, have endorsed
a notion of precaution in some important cases, allowing or requiring
regulation on the basis of conservative assumptions.[12]

The Precautionary Principle has played a significant role in international agreements and treaties, to the point where it has become
ubiquitous. Variations on the notion can be found in at least four-
teen international documents.[13] In 1982, the United Nations World

---

[6] See Owen McIntyre and Thomas Mosedale, The Precautionary Principle as a Norm of
Customary International Law, 9 *J. Env. Law* 221 (1997); see generally Trouwborst, *supra*
note 1.

[7] Michael Pollan, The Year in Ideas, A to Z: Precautionary Principle, *New York Times*, Dec. 9,
2001, p. 92, col. 2.

[8] Quoted in Christian Gollier and Nicolas Treich, Decision-Making under Scientific Uncertainty: The Economics of the Precautionary Principle, 27 *J. Risk & Uncertainty* 77, 77
(2003).

[9] See Per Sandin, Dimensions of the Precautionary Principle, 5 *Hum. & Ecol. Risk Assess.* 889
(1999).

[10] Julian Morris, Defining the Precautionary Principle, in *Rethinking Risk and the Precautionary
Principle* 1, ed. Julian Morris (Oxford: Butterworth-Heinemann, 2000).

[11] See *Interpreting the Precautionary Principle, supra* note 1.

[12] See, e.g., *American Trucking Association v. EPA*, 283 F.3d 355 (D.C. Cir. 2002); *Lead Industries
v. EPA*, 647 F.2d 1130 (D.C. Cir. 1980).

[13] See Indur Goklany, *The Precautionary Principle: A Critical Appraisal of Environmental Risk Assessment* 3 (Washington, D.C.: Cato Institute, 2001). For a catalogue, see

Charter for Nature apparently gave the first international recognition to the principle, suggesting that when "potential adverse effects are not fully understood, the activities should not proceed."[14] European environmental legislation has increasingly shown the influence of the German version of the Precautionary Principle. The closing Ministerial Declaration from the United Nations Economic Conference for Europe in 1990 asserts, "In order to achieve sustainable development, policies must be based on the Precautionary Principle . . . Where there are threats of serious or irreversible damage, lack of full scientific certainty should not be used as a reason for postponing measures to prevent environmental degradation."[15] The Maastricht Treaty on the European Union, adopted in 1992, states that with respect to the environment, EU policy "shall be based on the Precautionary Principle."[16]

Between 1992 and 1999, no fewer than twenty-seven resolutions of the European Parliament explicitly referred to the principle.[17] The idea of precaution has been invoked in a number of high-profile disputes between Europe and the United States involving European prohibitions on genetically modified organisms and hormones in beef. In February 2000, the Precautionary Principle was explicitly adopted in a communication by the European Commission, together with implementing guidelines.[18] The Precautionary Principle even appears in the draft Constitution for the European Union:

http://www.biotech-info.net/treaties_and_agreements.html. Indeed there appears to be a cascade effect here, with informational and reputational influences leading to many casual uses of the Precautionary Principle, to the point where a failure to incorporate the principle would seem to be a radical statement. Simply because the Precautionary Principle has been used so often, those involved in international agreements are likely to believe that it is probably sensible to use it yet again. And because so many people identify the Precautionary Principle with a serious commitment to environmental protection (see, e.g., *Protecting Public Health and the Environment*, *supra* note 1), any nation that rejects the principle risks incurring international opprobrium. For a general treatment of informational cascades, in which decisions by others convey information about what it makes sense to do, see David Hirschleifer, The Blind Leading the Blind: Social Influence, Fads, and Informational Cascades, in *The New Economics of Human Behavior* 188–89, ed. Mariano Tommasi and Kathryn Ierulli (Cambridge: Cambridge University Press, 1995). On reputational pressures, see Timur Kuran, *Private Truths, Public Lies* (Cambridge, Mass.: Harvard University Press, 1995).

[14] Goklany, *supra* note 13, at 4. [15] *Id.* at 5.

[16] Treaty on European Union, Art. 174 (ex Art. 130r) (1997).

[17] David Vogel, *Risk Regulation in Europe and the United States* (Berkeley, Calif.: Haas Business School, 2002).

[18] http://europa.eu.int/comm/dgs/health_consumer/library/press/press38_en.html.

Union policy on the environment shall aim at a high level of protection taking into account the diversity of situations in the various regions of the Union. It shall be based on the precautionary principle and on the principles that preventive action should be taken, that environmental damage should as a priority be rectified at source and that the polluter should pay.[19]

WEAK AND STRONG

What exactly does the Precautionary Principle mean or require? There are twenty or more definitions, and they are not compatible with one another.[20] We can imagine a continuum of understandings. At one extreme are weak versions to which no reasonable person could object. At the other extreme are strong versions that would require a fundamental rethinking of regulatory policy.

The most cautious and weak versions suggest, quite sensibly, that a lack of decisive evidence of harm should not be a ground for refusing to regulate. Controls might be justified even if we cannot establish a definite connection between, for example, low-level exposures to certain carcinogens and adverse effects on human health. Thus the 1992 Rio Declaration states, "Where there are threats of serious or irreversible damage, lack of full scientific certainty shall not be used as a reason for postponing cost-effective measures to prevent environmental degradation."[21] The Ministerial Declaration of the Second International Conference on the Protection of the North Sea, held in London in 1987, is in the same vein: "Accepting that in order to protect the North Sea from possibly damaging effects of the most dangerous substances, a Precautionary Principle is necessary which may require action to control inputs of such substances even before a causal link has been established by absolutely clear scientific evidence."[22] Similarly, the United Nations Framework Convention on Climate Change offers cautious language:

---

[19] Draft EU Constitution, Art. III-129.

[20] See Morris, *supra* note 10, at 1–19; Wiener, Precaution, Risk, and Multiplicity, *supra* note 5.

[21] Quoted in Bjorn Lomborg, *The Skeptical Environmentalist* 347 (New York: Cambridge University Press, 2001).

[22] Quoted in Morris, *supra* note 10, at 3.

Where there are threats of serious or irreversible damage, lack of full scientific certainty should not be used as a reason for postponing [regulatory] measures, taking into account that policies and measures to deal with climate change should be cost-effective so as to ensure global benefits at the lowest possible cost.[23]

The widely publicized Wingspread Declaration, from a meeting of environmentalists in 1998, goes somewhat further: "When an activity raises threats of harm to human health or the environment, precautionary measures should be taken even if some cause and effect relationships are not established scientifically. In this context the proponent of the activity, rather than the public, should bear the burden of proof."[24] The first sentence just quoted is more aggressive than the Rio Declaration because it is not limited to threats of serious or irreversible damage. And in reversing the burden of proof, the second sentence goes further still. Of course everything depends on what those with the burden of proof must show in particular.

In Europe, the Precautionary Principle is sometimes understood in a still stronger way, suggesting that it is important to build "a margin of safety into all decision making."[25] According to one definition, the Precautionary Principle means "that action should be taken to correct a problem as soon as there is evidence that harm may occur, not after the harm has already occurred."[26] The word "may" is the crucial one here. In a comparably strong version, it is said that "the Precautionary Principle mandates that when there is a risk of significant health or environmental damage to others or to future generations, and when there is scientific uncertainty as to the nature of that damage or the likelihood of the risk, then decisions should be made so as to prevent such activities from being conducted unless and until scientific evidence shows that the damage will not occur."[27] The words "will not occur" seem to require proponents of an activity to demonstrate that there is no risk at all – often an impossible burden to meet.

---

[23] See Goklany, *supra* note 13, at 6.
[24] *Id.* A strong version is defended in Raffensperger and DeFur, *supra* note 3, at 934.
[25] See Lomborg, *supra* note 21, at 348.
[26] http://www.logophilia.com/WordSpy/precautionaryprinciple.asp.
[27] Testimony of Dr. Brent Blackwelder, President, Friends of the Earth, before the Senate Appropriations Committee, Subcommittee on Labor, Health and Human Services (Jan. 24, 2002).

The Cartagena Protocol on Biosafety to the Convention on Biological Diversity, adopted in 2000, appears to adopt a strong version as well.[28] The Final Declaration of the First European "Seas at Risk" Conference says that if "the 'worst case scenario' for a certain activity is serious enough then even a small amount of doubt as to the safety of that activity is sufficient to stop it taking place."[29]

PRECAUTION IN PRACTICE: A QUICK GLANCE AT EUROPE

As I have suggested, the official account in Europe is very much in favor of one or another version of the Precautionary Principle, with the European Commission having formally adopted it.[30] But European practice is quite complex.[31] To take just one example, "Europe has been more precautionary about hormones in beef, while the US has been more precautionary about mad cow disease (BSE) in beef and blood donations."[32] European nations have taken a highly precautionary approach to genetically modified foods,[33] but the United States has been more aggressive in controlling the risks associated with carcinogens in food additives.[34] In the context of occupational risk, American law is far more precautionary than Swedish law.[35]

---

[28] See Goklany, *supra* note 13, at 6.

[29] Final Declaration of the First European "Seas at Risk" Conference, Annex 1, Copenhagen, 1994.

[30] European Commission, Communication from the Commission on the Precautionary Principle, Brussels, Feb. 2, 2000, available at http://europa.eu.int/comm/dgs/health_consumer/library/press/press38_en.html.

[31] See the illuminating discussions in Wiener, Precaution, Risk, and Multiplicity, *supra* note 5; Jonathan B. Wiener and Michael D. Rogers, Comparing Precaution in the United States and Europe, 5 *J. Risk Research* 317 (2002).

[32] *Id.* at 323.

[33] See David Vogel and Diahanna Lynch, *The Regulation of GMOs in Europe and the United States: A Case-Study of Contemporary European Regulatory Politics* (Publication of the Study Group on Trade, Science and Genetically Modified Foods, Apr. 5, 2001), available at http://www.cfr.org/pub3937/david_vogel_diahanna_lynch/the_regulation_of_gmos_in_europe_and_the_united_states_a_casestudy_of_contemporary_european_regulatory_politics.php; Symposium, Are the US and Europe Heading for a Food Fight Over Genetically Modified Food? (2001), available at http://pewagbiotech.org/events/1024/; Tony Gilland, Precaution, GM Crops, and Farmland Birds, in *Rethinking Risk and the Precautionary Principle* 84, 84–88, ed. Julian Morris (Oxford: Butterworth-Heinemann, 2000).

[34] See Richard Merrill, FDA's Implementation of the Delaney Clause: Repudiation of Congressional Choice or Reasoned Adaptation to Scientific Progress? 5 *Yale J. on Reg.* 1 (1988).

[35] See Steven Kelman, *Regulating America, Regulating Sweden: A Comparative Study of Occupational Safety and Health Policy* (Cambridge, Mass.: MIT Press, 1981).

I do not venture a survey here, but it is reasonable to speculate that in actual practice, nations cannot plausibly be ranked along some continuum of precaution. Every nation is precautionary about some risks but not others, and a nation's claim to have adopted the Precautionary Principle will conceal this inevitable fact.[36] Nonetheless, the mounting importance of the principle in Europe deserves close attention, if only because the idea of precaution is playing such a large role in public debates. In fact the principle has been mentioned dozens of times in European Union courts, and it has often been a significant factor in the ultimate decision.[37] The advocate general of the European Court of Justice has stated, in a public opinion, that the Precautionary Principle applies "when no concrete threat . . . has yet been demonstrated but initial scientific findings indicate a possible risk";[38] he has also said that the principle requires risks to be reduced "to the lowest level reasonably imaginable."[39] But European tribunals have yet to choose between weak and strong versions of the Precautionary Principle. Traces of both can be found in judicial opinions, and indeed there has been a high degree of vacillation in the cases. Consider some representative examples.

The European Union banned the use of the antibiotic virginiamycin in animal feed because of the possibility that it would generate resistant bacteria that could infect human beings.[40] The ban was challenged as lacking supporting evidence in the European Court of First Instance. That Court nonetheless upheld the ban. It ruled that an additive could be prohibited "even when no risk assessment had been conducted, when there was limited or no evidence of such bacterial resistance arising, when there was no present need for the use of such antibiotics in human medicine," and when the EU's Scientific Committee for Animal Nutrition (SCAN) had recommended against

---

[36] See Wiener and Rogers, *supra* note 31.
[37] See Gary E. Marchant and Kenneth L. Mossman, *Arbitrary and Capricious: The Precautionary Principle in the European Union Courts* (Washington, D.C.: American Enterprise Institute, 2004), which offers many details about the actual operation of the Precautionary Principle.
[38] Case C-236/01, *Monsanto Agricoltura Italia v. Presidenza del Consiglio dei Ministri*, 2003 EC 0 (advocate general), ¶108.
[39] Case T-13/99, *Pfizer Animal Health S.A. v. Council*, 1999 ECR II-1961 (Celex No. 699 B 00113) (1999) (president of Court of First Instance), ¶76.
[40] Case T-13/99, *Pfizer Animal Health S.A. v. Council*, 2002 WL 31337, 2002 ECJ CELEX LEXIS 3613 (European Court of First Instance, Sept. 11, 2002).

the ban.[41] Invoking the idea of precaution, the Court insisted that conclusive evidence of the reality of the risk should not be required. In the particular case, there was no evidence that the bacterial resistance would develop or prove harmful to human beings. Nevertheless, the Court found the ban justified on precautionary grounds.

A similar decision dealt with bacitracin zinc, another antibiotic in animal feed.[42] The Court of First Instance reiterated that there is no need to conduct a formal risk assessment, even when the risk is highly speculative and SCAN recommended against a ban. "It is sufficient that the risk exists, that serious concerns have been expressed in scientific literature and in the reports of various conferences and bodies and that, if such transmission actually occurred, it could have serious consequences for human health."[43] The Court acknowledged that "a preventive measure cannot properly be based on a purely hypothetical approach to the risk, founded on mere conjecture which has not been scientifically verified."[44] But its own evidence consisted only of a World Health Organization report that recommended ending the use of antibiotics in animal feed if the antibiotic "might be used in human medicine."[45] Here, then, was precaution with a vengeance. More generally, the Court of First Instance has said that any regulatory choice must "comply with the principle that the protection of public health, safety and the environment is to take precedence over economic interests."[46] And the president of the Court of First Instance has said that it is appropriate to withdraw potentially harmful "products until it can be conclusively demonstrated that they pose no present or future risk to human health."[47]

The European Court of Justice has been more cautious about the Precautionary Principle than the Court of First Instance. Italy prohibited genetically modified maize that contained between 0.04 and 0.30 parts per million of transgenic protein,[48] even though the Italian

[41] J. Wiener, Whose Precaution after All? A Comment on the Comparison and Evolution of Risk Regulatory Systems, 13 *Duke J. Comp. & Int'l L.* 207, 217.

[42] Case T-70/99, *Alpharma Inc. v. Council*, 2002 WL 31338, 2002 ECJ CELEX LEXIS 3612 (European Court of First Instance, Sept. 11, 2002).

[43] *Id.* at ¶150.   [44] *Id.* at ¶156.   [45] *Id.* at ¶192.

[46] Case T-74/00, *Artegodan GmbH v. Commission*, 2002 ECR II-4945 (Court of First Instance).

[47] Case T-13/99, *Pfizer Animal Health S.A. v. Council*, 1999 ECR II-1961 (CELEX No. 699 B 00113) (1999) (president of Court of Instance), ¶76.

[48] Case C-236/01, *Monsanto Agricoltura Italia v. Presidenza del Consiglio dei Ministri*, 2003 ECJ CELEX LEXIS 359 (European Court of Justice, Mar. 13, 2003).

Istituto Superiore di Sanità had concluded that available evidence showed no health risk to people or animals.[49] The European Court of Justice ruled that for Italy's ban to be upheld, at least some evidence must show that consumption threatens human health. "The risk must be adequately sustained by scientific evidence."[50] The European Court of Justice is clear (and on this principle the Court of First Instance agrees) that the mere possibility of danger is not enough.

With respect to reduction of the risks associated with bovine spongiform encephalopathy (BSE), or "mad cow disease," there have been five European Union decisions; and they show no consistent pattern. Some of these decisions reject the idea of "risk-free" meat and insist that the Precautionary Principle is not intended "to achieve zero risk."[51] These decisions show a willingness to tolerate continuing risks so as not to disrupt ordinary trade relationships among nations. But other decisions suggest that no risk at all is acceptable.[52]

The real questions, not yet answered, are what, exactly, must be shown to justify regulation – and whether other risks, in the vicinity of the "target" risk, may or must be considered as part of the inquiry into what should be done. European courts have yet to resolve the question whether the Precautionary Principle must be applied in a way that is alert to the possibility that regulation of one risk will actually increase other risks.[53] On the key questions, European law remains to be settled. A central issue, relevant all over the world, is: How ought they to be settled?

SAFE AND SORRY?

I have suggested that the weak versions of the Precautionary Principle are unobjectionable and important.[54] Every day, people take steps to avoid hazards that are far from certain. We do not walk in moderately dangerous areas at night; we exercise; we buy smoke detectors; we

---

[49] *Id.* at ¶27.   [50] *Id.* at ¶138.

[51] Case C-241/01, *Nat. Farmers' Union v. Sec. General of the French Government*, 2001 OJ C245/7 (opinion of the advocate general).

[52] See Marchant and Mossman, *supra* note 37, at 54–63.   [53] See *id.* at 52–54.

[54] See W. David Montgomery and Anne E. Smith, Global Climate Change and the Precautionary Principle, 6 *Hum. & Ecol. Risk Assess.* 399 (2000).

buckle our seatbelts; we might even avoid fatty foods (or carbohydrates). Sensible governments regulate risks that, in individual cases or even in the aggregate, have a well under 100 percent chance of coming to fruition. An individual might ignore a mortality risk of 1/500,000, because that risk is awfully small, but if 100 million citizens face that risk, the nation had better take it seriously.

The weak versions of the Precautionary Principle state a truism – uncontroversial in principle and necessary in practice only to combat public confusion or the self-interested claims of private groups demanding unambiguous evidence of harm, which no rational society requires. This function should not be trivialized. Nearly a fifth of Americans, for example, have agreed with the following statement: "Until we are sure that global warming is really a problem, we should not take any steps that would have economic costs."[55] This is preposterous. Modest steps can certainly be justified before "we are sure that global warming is really a problem." Insofar as the Precautionary Principle counteracts the tendency to demand certainty, it should be approved.

Because the weakest versions are unobjectionable, even banal, I will not discuss them here. For the moment let us understand the principle in a strong way, to suggest that regulation is required whenever there is a possible risk to health, safety, or the environment, even if the supporting evidence remains speculative and even if the economic costs of regulation are high. To avoid absurdity, the idea of "possible risk" will be understood to require a certain threshold of scientific plausibility. To support regulation, no one thinks that it is enough if someone, somewhere, urges that a risk is worth taking seriously. But under the Precautionary Principle as I shall understand it, the threshold burden is minimal, and once it is met, there is something like a presumption in favor of regulatory controls.

I believe that this understanding of the Precautionary Principle fits with the understandings of some of its most enthusiastic proponents, and that with relatively modest variations, this understanding fits with many of the legal formulations as well. If the strongest versions reflect a position that no one is ultimately willing to hold, so be it. An understanding of its flaws will pave the way toward a more helpful

[55] See http://www.pipa.org/OnlineReports/GlobalWarming/buenos_aires_02.00.html#1.

understanding of how to proceed in the face of risk and fear, one that refines the Precautionary Principle in a way that satisfies the salutary goals of those who are drawn to it.

Why might the Precautionary Principle, understood in its strong sense, have such widespread appeal? At first glance, the answer is simple, for the principle contains some important truth. Certainly we should acknowledge that a small probability (say, 1 in 25,000) of a serious harm (say, 1,000,000 deaths) deserves extremely serious attention. It is worthwhile to spend a lot of money to eliminate that risk. An economically oriented critic might observe that our resources are limited and that if we spend large amounts of resources on highly speculative harms, we will not be allocating those resources wisely. In fact this is the simplest criticism of the Precautionary Principle.[56] If we take costly steps to address all risks, however improbable they are, we will quickly impoverish ourselves. On this view, the Precautionary Principle "would make for a dim future."[57] It would also eliminate technologies and strategies that make human lives easier, more convenient, healthier, and longer.

Consider in this light a 2003 survey of scientists, who were asked, "What are the most notable scientific, medical or technological discoveries and achievements that you believe would have been limited or prevented, if science at the time had been governed by the precautionary principle? Please list one or more."[58] The resulting list included airplanes, air conditioning, antibiotics, automobiles, chlorine, the measles vaccine, open-heart surgery, radio, refrigeration, the smallpox vaccine, and X-rays. A genetic statistician answered, "In their day, trains, planes, and antibiotics would have been prevented." A senior research fellow at King's College, London, responded, "For starters, X-rays; vaccination; blood transfusions; the Green Revolution." A professor in plant molecular genetics offered "Pasteurization; immunization; the use of chemicals and irradiation in crop variety development."

---

[56] See John D. Graham, Decision-Analytic Refinements of the Precautionary Prnciple, 4 *J. Risk Research* 127 (2001).

[57] See Morris, *supra* note 10, at 1, 17.

[58] See Sandy Starr, Science, Risk, and the Price of Precaution, available at http://www.spiked-online/Articles/00000006DD7A.htm.

Some version of this objection is surely convincing, but it is missing something about human behavior.[59] In some contexts, regulation is a form of insurance, or a way of placing special locks on a door. Consider the following choice. Would you rather have

a. A sure loss of $20, or

b. A 1 percent chance of losing $1,980?

In terms of expected value, (b), representing a statistical loss of $19.80, is a bit less bad than (a); but most people would gladly choose the sure loss of $20. People do not like to run a small risk of a large loss; this is why people buy insurance and take special precautions against serious harms, even if an analysis of expected value would not justify these steps. Prospect theory, an influential account of human behavior, emphasizes people's aversion to significant harms that have a low probability of occurring. If government follows the judgments of ordinary people, it will be risk averse in this sense as well. The willingness to incur sure losses, in preference to low-probability harms of lower expected value, helps explain decisions in a variety of domains, including foreign policy.

This point suggests that a democratic society, following popular views, will embody a form of risk aversion for low-probability risks that might result in serious harm. The result will be in the direction suggested by the Precautionary Principle. But neither prospect theory nor risk aversion can provide a defense of the principle in its strong form. I now explain why this is so.

WHY THE PRECAUTIONARY PRINCIPLE IS PARALYZING

It is tempting to object that the Precautionary Principle is hopelessly vague. How much precaution is the right amount of precaution? By itself, the principle does not tell us. It is also tempting to object, as I have suggested, that the principle is cost-blind. Some precautions simply aren't worthwhile. But the most serious problem lies elsewhere. The real problem is that the principle offers no guidance – not that it is wrong, but that it forbids all courses of action, including regulation. It bans the very steps that it requires. The scientists

---

[59] See Daniel Kahneman and Amos Tversky, Prospect Theory: An Analysis of Decision under Risk, in *Choices, Values, and Frames* 17, ed. Daniel Kahneman and Amos Tversky (Cambridge: Cambridge University Press, 2000).

who complained that the principle would forbid airplanes, antibiotics, refrigeration, and much more were quite wrong. They treated the principle as far more coherent than it actually is. If airplanes, antibiotics, and refrigeration reduce risks – as they clearly do – then isn't it clear the principle forbids, and does not mandate, regulatory prohibitions?

To understand the problem, it will be useful to anchor the discussion in some concrete problems:

1. Genetic modification of food has become a widespread practice.[60] The risks of that practice are not known with any precision. Some people fear that genetic modification will result in serious ecological harm and large risks to human health; others believe that genetic modification will result in more nutritious food and significant improvements in human health.

2. Scientists are not in accord about the dangers associated with global warming,[61] but there is general agreement that global warming is in fact occurring. It is possible that global warming will produce, by 2100, a mean temperature increase of 4.5° C (the high-end estimate of the International Panel on Climate Change); that it will result in $5 trillion or more in monetized costs; and that it will also produce a significant number of deaths from malaria. The Kyoto Protocol would require most industrialized nations to reduce greenhouse gas emissions to 92–94 percent of 1990 levels. A great deal of work suggests that significant decreases in such emissions would have large benefits; but skeptics contend that the costs of such decreases would reduce the well-being of millions of people, especially the poorest members of society.

3. Many people fear nuclear power, on the ground that nuclear power plants create various health and safety risks, including some possibility of catastrophe. But if a nation does not rely on nuclear power, it might well rely instead on fossil fuels, and in particular on coal-fired power plants. Such plants create risks of their own, including risks associated with global warming. China, for example, has relied

---

[60] Alan McHughen, *Pandora's Picnic Basket* (New York: Oxford University Press, 2000).
[61] For discussion, see Richard A. Posner, *Catastrophe: Risk and Response* (New York: Oxford University Press, 2004); Lomborg, *supra* note 21; William D. Nordhaus and Joseph Boyer, *Warming the World: Economic Models of Global Warming* 168 (Cambridge, Mass.: MIT Press, 2000).

on nuclear energy, in a way that reduces greenhouse gases and a range of air pollution problems.[62]

4. In the first years of the twenty-first century, one of the most controversial environmental issues in the United States involved the regulation of arsenic in drinking water. There is a serious dispute over the precise level of risks posed by low levels of arsenic in water, but on the "worst-case" scenario, over 100 lives might be lost each year as a result of the 50 parts per billion standard that the Clinton Administration sought to revise. At the same time, the proposed 10 parts per billion standard would cost over $200 million each year, and it is possible that it would save as few as six lives annually.

5. There is a possible conflict between the protection of marine mammals and military exercises. The United States Navy, for example, engages in many such exercises, and it is possible that marine mammals will be threatened as a result. Military activities in the oceans might well cause significant harm; but a decision to suspend those activities, in cases involving potential harm, might also endanger military preparedness, or so the government contends.[63]

In these cases, what kind of guidance is provided by the Precautionary Principle? It is tempting to say, as is in fact standard, that the principle calls for strong controls on arsenic, on genetic engineering of food, on greenhouse gases, on threats to marine mammals, and on nuclear power. In all of these cases, there is a possibility of serious harms, and no authoritative scientific evidence demonstrates that the possibility is close to zero. If the burden of proof is on the proponent of the activity or processes in question, the Precautionary Principle would seem to impose a burden of proof that cannot be met. Put

---

[62] See Ling Zhong, Note: Nuclear Energy: China's Approach Towards Addressing Global Warming, 12 *Geo. Int'l Envtl. L. Rev.* 493 (2000). Of course it is possible to urge that nations should reduce reliance on either coal-fired power plants or nuclear power, and move instead toward environmentally preferred alternatives, such as solar power. For general discussion, see *Renewable Energy: Power for a Sustainable Future*, ed. Godfrey Boyle (Oxford: Oxford University Press in association with the Open University, 1996); Allan Collinson, *Renewable Energy* (Austin, Tex.: Steck-Vaughn Library, 1991); Dan E. Arvizu, Advanced Energy Technology and Climate Change Policy Implications, 2 *Fl. Coastal L.J.* 435 (2001). But these alternatives pose problems of their own, involving feasibility and expense. See Lomborg, *supra* note 21, at 118–48.

[63] See Testimony of Vice Admiral Charles W. Moore, Deputy Chief of Naval Operations for Readiness and Logistics, before the House Resources Committee, Subcommittee on Fisheries Conservation, Wildlife and Oceans (June 13, 2002).

to one side the question whether the Precautionary Principle, understood to compel stringent regulation in these cases, is sensible. Let us ask a more fundamental question: Is that more stringent regulation therefore compelled by the Precautionary Principle?

The answer is that it is not. In some of these cases, it should be easy to see that in its own way, stringent regulation would actually run afoul of the Precautionary Principle.[64] The simplest reason is that such regulation might well deprive society of significant benefits, and hence produce serious harms that would otherwise not occur. In some cases, regulation eliminates the "opportunity benefits" of a process or activity, and thus causes preventable deaths. If this is so, regulation is hardly precautionary. Consider the "drug lag," produced whenever the government takes a highly precautionary approach to the introduction of new medicines and drugs onto the market. If a government insists on such an approach, it will protect people against harms from inadequately tested drugs; but it will also prevent people from receiving potential benefits from those very drugs. Is it "precautionary" to require extensive premarketing testing, or to do the opposite?

In the context of medicines to prevent AIDS, those who favor "precautions" have asked governments to reduce the level of premarketing testing, precisely in the interest of health. The United States, by the way, is more precautionary about new medicines than are most European nations. But by failing to allow such medicines on the market, the United States fails to take precautions against the illnesses that could be reduced by speedier procedures.

Or consider the continuing debate over whether certain antidepressants impose a (small) risk of breast cancer.[65] A precautionary approach might seem to caution against use of such antidepressants because of their carcinogenic potential. But the failure to use those antidepressants might well impose risks of its own, certainly psychological and possibly even physical (because psychological ailments are

---

[64] A good treatment is John D. Graham, Decision-Analytic Refinements of the Precautionary Prnciple, 4 *J. Risk Research* 127, 135–38 (2001).

[65] See Judith P. Kelly et al., Risk of Breast Cancer According to Use of Antidepressants, Phenothiazines, and Antihistamines, 150 *Am. J. Epidemiology* 861 (1999); C. R. Sharpe et al., The Effects of Tricyclic Antidepressants on Breast Cancer Risk, 86 *Brit. J. of Cancer* 92 (2002).

sometimes associated with physical ones as well). Or consider the decision, by the Soviet Union, to evacuate and relocate more than 270,000 people in response to the risk of adverse effects from the Chernobyl fallout. It is not clear that on balance this massive relocation project was justified on health grounds: "A comparison ought to have been made between the psychological and medical burdens of this measure (anxiety, psychosomatic diseases, depression and suicides) and the harm that may have been prevented."[66] More generally, a sensible government might want to ignore the small risks associated with low levels of radiation, on the ground that precautionary responses are likely to cause fear that outweighs any health benefits from those responses.[67]

Or consider a more general question about how to handle low-level toxic agents, including carcinogens. Do such agents cause adverse effects? If we lack clear evidence, it might seem "precautionary" to assume that they do, and hence to assume, in the face of uncertainty, that the dose-response curve is linear and without safe thresholds.[68] In the United States, this is the default assumption of the Environmental Protection Agency. But is this approach unambiguously precautionary? Considerable evidence suggests that many toxic agents that are harmful at high levels are actually beneficial at low levels.[69] Thus "hormesis" is a dose-response relationship in which low doses stimulate desirable effects and high doses inhibit them. When hormesis is involved, government use of a linear dose-response curve, assuming no safe thresholds, will actually cause mortality and morbidity effects. Which default approach to the dose-response curve is precautionary? To raise this question is not to take any stand on whether some, many, or all toxic agents are beneficial or instead harmful at very low doses. It is only to say that the simultaneous possibility of benefits at

---

[66] Maurice Tubiana, Radiation Risks in Perspective: Radiation-Induced Cancer among Cancer Risks, 39(1) *Radiat. Environ. Biophy.* 3, 8–10 (2000).

[67] *Id.* For some counterevidence in an important context, see Lennart Hardell et al., Further Aspects on Cellular and Cordless Telephones and Brain Tumours, 22 *Intl. J. Oncology* 399 (2003) (discussing evidence of an association between cellular telephones and cancer).

[68] For criticism of the linearity assumption, see Tubiana, *supra* note 66, at 8–9.

[69] See Edward J. Calabrese and Linda A. Baldwin, Hormesis: The Dose Response Revolution, 43 *Annu. Rev. Pharmacol. Toxicol.* 175 (2003); Edward J. Calabrese and Linda A. Baldwin, The Hormetic Dose-Response Model is More Common than the Threshold Model in Toxicology, 71 *Toxicol. Sciences* 246 (2003).

low levels and of harms at low levels makes the Precautionary Principle paralyzing. The principle requires use of a linear, non-threshold model; but it simultaneously condemns use of that very model. For this and other reasons, unreflective use of the Precautionary Principle, it has been argued, threatens to increase rather than decrease the risks associated with food.[70]

Or consider the case of genetic modification of food. Many people believe that a failure to allow genetic modification might well result in numerous deaths, and a small probability of many more. The reason is that genetic modification holds out the promise of producing food that is both cheaper and healthier – resulting, for example, in "golden rice," which might have large benefits in developing countries. My point is not that genetic modification will likely have those benefits, or that the benefits of genetic modification outweigh the risks. The claim is only that if the Precautionary Principle is taken literally, it is offended by regulation as well as by nonregulation.

Whatever the ultimate promise of such food, the use of the Precautionary Principle can produce palpably absurd results in terms of regulation. In 2002, the United States government donated thousands of tons of corn to the Zambian government, which refused the corn on the ground that it likely contained some GM kernels.[71] The Precautionary Principle lay at the foundation of the refusal. A group of Zambian scientists and economists had toured several American farms and grain elevators, concluding that the principle required the corn to be refused because of the inconclusiveness of studies on the health risks of genetically modified foods. Some representatives of the Zambian government were concerned that the aid recipients would plant the seeds, thereby "contaminating" exports to the European Union. The United States offered to mill the corn into flour (so that the seeds could not be planted), but the government rejected this offer. According to the United Nations Food and Agriculture Organization, the refusal left 2.9 million people at risk of starvation; a "conservative scenario" from the World Health Organization predicted that at least 35,000

[70] J. C. Hanekamp et al., Chloramphenicol, Food Safety, and Precautionary Thinking in Europe, 6 *Env. Liability* 209 (2003).

[71] John Bohannon, Zambia Rejects GM Corn on Scientists' Advice, 298 *Science* 1153 (Nov. 8, 2002), available online at http://www.bio.utexas.edu/courses/stuart/zambiareject.pdf.

Zambians would die of starvation if more corn could not be found. Was the refusal to accept the corn truly precautionary?

The example suggests that regulation sometimes violates the Precautionary Principle because it gives rise to *substitute risks*, in the form of hazards that materialize, or are increased, as a result of regulation.[72] Consider the case of DDT, often banned or regulated in the interest of reducing risks to birds and human beings. The problem with such bans is that in poor nations, they eliminate what appears to be the most effective way of combating malaria – and thus significantly undermine public health.[73] Or consider the Environmental Protection Agency's effort to ban asbestos,[74] a ban that might well seem justified or even compelled by the Precautionary Principle. The difficulty, from the standpoint of that very principle, is that substitutes for asbestos also carry risks. The problem is pervasive. In the case of arsenic, the Administrator of the Environmental Protection Agency expressed concern that aggressive regulation, by virtue of its cost, will lead people to cease using local water systems and to rely on private wells, which have high levels of contamination.[75] If this is so, stringent arsenic regulation violates the Precautionary Principle no less than less stringent regulation does. This is a common situation, for opportunity benefits and substitute risks are the rule, not the exception.[76]

It is possible to go much further. A great deal of evidence suggests the possibility that an expensive regulation can have adverse

---

[72] See the discussion of risk-risk tradeoffs in John Graham and Jonathan Wiener, *Risk vs. Risk* (Cambridge, Mass.: Harvard University Press, 1995); Cass R. Sunstein, Health-Health Tradeoffs, in Cass R. Sunstein, *Risk and Reason*, 133–52 (Cambridge: Cambridge University Press, 2002).

[73] See Goklany, *supra* note 13, at 13–27.

[74] See *Corrosion Proof Fittings v. EPA*, 947 F.2d 1201 (5th Cir. 1991).

[75] "But we have seen instances, particularly in the West and Midwest, where arsenic is naturally occurring at up to 700 and more parts per billion, where the cost of remediation has forced water companies to close, leaving people with no way to get their water, save dig wells. And then they are getting water that's even worse than what they were getting through the water company." Christine Todd Whitman, Administrator, US Environmental Protection Agency, in interview by Robert Novak and Al Hunt, CNN Evans, Novak, Hunt and Shields, Cable News Network (Apr. 21, 2001).

[76] Note also that some regulation will have ancillary *benefits*, by reducing risks other than those that are specifically targeted. For a valuable discussion, see Samuel J. Rascoff and Richard L. Revesz, The Biases of Risk Tradeoff Analysis, 69 *U. Chi. L. Rev.* 1763 (2002).

effects on life and health.[77] It has been urged that a statistical life can be lost for every expenditure of $7 million;[78] one study suggests that an expenditure of $15 million produces a loss of life.[79] Another suggests that poor people are especially vulnerable to this effect – that a regulation that reduces wealth for the poorest 20 percent of the population will have twice as large a mortality effect as a regulation that reduces wealth for the wealthiest 20 percent.[80] To be sure, both the phenomenon and the underlying mechanisms are disputed.[81] I do not mean to accept any particular amount here, or even to suggest that there has been an unambiguous demonstration of an association between mortality and regulatory expenditures. The only point is that reasonable people believe in that association. It follows that a multimillion dollar expenditure for "precaution" has – as a worst-case scenario – significant adverse health effects, with an expenditure of $200 million leading to perhaps as many as twenty to thirty lives lost.

This point makes the Precautionary Principle hard to implement not merely where regulation removes "opportunity benefits," or introduces or increases substitute risks, but in any case in which the regulation costs a significant amount. If this is so, the Precautionary Principle, for that very reason, raises doubts about many regulations. If the principle argues against any action that carries a small risk of imposing significant harm, then we should be reluctant to spend a lot of money to reduce risks, simply because those expenditures themselves carry risks. Here is the sense in which the Precautionary Principle, taken for all that it is worth, is paralyzing: It stands as an obstacle to regulation and nonregulation, and to everything in between.

It should now be easier to understand my earlier suggestion that despite their formal enthusiasm for the Precautionary Principle,

---

[77] Ralph Keeney, Mortality Risks Induced by Economic Expenditures, 10 *Risk Anal.* 147 (1990); Randall Lutter and John F. Morrall, III, Health-Health Analysis: A New Way to Evaluate Health and Safety Regulation, 8(1) *J. Risk & Uncertainty* 43, 49 table 1 (1994).

[78] See Keeney, *supra* note 77.

[79] See Robert W. Hahn et al., *Do Federal Regulations Reduce Mortality?* (Washington, D.C.: American Enterprise Institute, 2000).

[80] See Kenneth S. Chapman and Govind Hariharan, Do Poor People Have a Stronger Relationship between Income and Mortality than the Rich? Implications of Panel Data for Health-Health Analysis, 12 *J. Risk & Uncertainty* 51, 58–63 (1996).

[81] See Lutter and Morrall, *supra* note 77, at 49 table 1.

European nations are not "more precautionary" than the United States. Simply as a logical matter, societies, like individuals, cannot be highly precautionary with respect to all risks. Each society and each person must select certain risks for special attention. In these respects, the selectivity of precautions is not merely an empirical fact; it is a conceptual inevitability.

Comparing Europe to the United States, Jonathan Wiener and Michael Rogers have demonstrated this point empirically.[82] In the early twenty-first century, for example, the United States appears to take a highly precautionary approach to the risks associated with abandoned hazardous waste dumps and terrorism, but not to take a highly precautionary approach to the risks associated with global warming, indoor air pollution, poverty, poor diet, and obesity. It would be most valuable to attempt to see which nations are especially precautionary with respect to which risks, and also to explore changes over time. A nation-by-nation study commissioned by the German Federal Environmental Agency goes so far as to conclude that there are two separate camps in the industrialized world: "precaution countries" (Germany, Sweden, the Netherlands, and the United States) and "protection countries" (Japan, France, and the United Kingdom).[83]

This conclusion seems to me implausible. The universe of risks is far too large to permit categorizations of this kind. The most general point is that no nation is precautionary in general and costly precautions are inevitably taken against only those hazards that seem especially salient or insistent. The problem with the Precautionary Principle is that it wrongly suggests that nations can and should adopt a general form of risk aversion.

I do not contend that precautions are a mistake, or even that it is impossible to reconstruct the Precautionary Principle on sensible foundations. For now, my only claim is that the principle is a crude and sometimes perverse way of promoting desirable goals – and that if it is taken for all that it is worth, it is paralyzing, and therefore not helpful at all.

---

[82] See Wiener and Rogers, *supra* note 31.   [83] See Sand, *supra* note 2, at 448.

CHAPTER 2

Behind the Precautionary Principle

In practice, the Precautionary Principle is widely thought to provide concrete guidance. How can this be? I suggest that the principle becomes operational if and only if those who apply it wear blinders – only, that is, if they focus on some aspects of the regulatory situation but downplay or disregard others. But this suggestion simply raises an additional question: What accounts for the particular blinders that underlie applications of the Precautionary Principle? When people's attention is selective, why is it selective in the way that it is? I believe that much of the answer lies in an understanding of behavioral economics and cognitive psychology. Five points are especially pertinent:

- the availability heuristic, making some risks seem especially likely to come to fruition whether or not they actually are;
- probability neglect, leading people to focus on the worst case, even if it is highly improbable;
- loss aversion, making people dislike losses from the status quo;
- a belief in the benevolence of nature, making man-made decisions and processes seem especially suspect;
- system neglect, understood as an inability to see that risks are part of systems, and that interventions into those system can create risks of their own.

Politicians and interest groups exploit the underlying mechanisms, driving public attention in one or another direction. And taken together, these mechanisms show the sense in which the relevant blinders are not arbitrary or coincidental. They have an unmistakable structure. And while these features of human cognition are universal, they also have the advantage of explaining differences across cultures and even across nations. If, for example, salient examples of mad cow disease come to mind in London but not in New York, Londoners will be far more concerned about mad cow disease than New Yorkers. If illnesses from abandoned hazardous waste sites are known to have occurred in California but not in Berlin, then Californians will be far more worried about abandoned hazardous waste sites than Berliners. All this is so even if the risk is essentially identical in the various locales. Let us begin, then, with the availability heuristic.

THE AVAILABILITY HEURISTIC

It is well established that in thinking about risks, people rely on certain heuristics, or rules of thumb, which serve to simplify their inquiry.[1] Heuristics typically work through a process of "attribute substitution," in which people answer a hard question by substituting an easier one.[2] Should we be fearful of nuclear power, terrorism, abduction of young children, or pesticides? When people use the availability heuristic, they assess the magnitude of risks by asking whether examples can readily come to mind.[3] If people can easily think of such examples, they are far more likely to be frightened than if they cannot. The availability heuristic illuminates the operation of the Precautionary Principle, by showing why some hazards will be on-screen and why others will be neglected.

For example, "a class whose instances are easily retrieved will appear more numerous than a class of equal frequency whose instances are less retrievable."[4] Consider a simple study showing people a list of well-known people of both sexes, and asking them whether the list contains more names of women or more names of men. In lists in which the men were especially famous, people thought that there were

---

[1] See Daniel Kahneman, Paul Slovic, and Amos Tversky, *Judgment under Uncertainty: Heuristics and Biases* (Cambridge: Cambridge University Press, 1982).

[2] See Daniel Kahneman and Shane Frederick, Representativeness Revisited: Attribute Substitution in Intuitive Judgment, in *Heuristics and Biases: The Psychology of Intuitive Judgment*, 49, 53, ed. Thomas Gilovich, Dale Griffin, and Daniel Kahneman (Cambridge: Cambridge University Press, 2002).

[3] See Amos Tversky and Daniel Kahneman, Judgment under Uncertainty, in Daniel Kahneman, Paul Slovic, and Amos Tversky, *Judgment under Uncertainty: Heuristics and Biases* 3, 11–14 (Cambridge: Cambridge University Press, 1982).

[4] *Id.* at 11.

more names of men, whereas in lists in which the women were the more famous, people thought that there were more names of women.[5]

This is a point about how *familiarity* can affect the availability of instances. A risk that is familiar, like that associated with smoking, will be seen as more serious than a risk that is less familiar, like that associated with sunbathing. But *salience* is important as well. "For example, the impact of seeing a house burning on the subjective probability of such accidents is probably greater than the impact of reading about a fire in the local paper."[6] So, too, recent events will have a greater impact than earlier ones. The point helps explain much risk-related behavior, including decisions to take precautions. Whether people will buy insurance for natural disasters is greatly affected by recent experiences.[7] If floods have not occurred in the immediate past, people who live on flood plains are far less likely to purchase insurance. In the aftermath of an earthquake, insurance for earthquakes rises sharply – but it declines steadily from that point, as vivid memories recede. Note that the use of the availability heuristic, in these contexts, is hardly irrational.[8] Both insurance and precautionary measures can be expensive, and what has happened before seems, much of the time, to be the best available guide to what will happen again. The problem is that the availability heuristic can lead to serious errors, in terms of both excessive fear and neglect.

The availability heuristic helps to explain the operation of the Precautionary Principle for a simple reason: Sometimes a certain risk, said to call for precautions, is cognitively available, whereas other risks, including those associated with regulation itself, are not. For example, it is easy to see that arsenic is potentially dangerous; arsenic is well known as a poison, providing the first word of a classic movie about

---

[5] *Id.*   [6] *Id.*
[7] Paul Slovic, *The Perception of Risk* 40 (London: Earthscan, 2000).
[8] Kahneman and Tversky emphasize that the heuristics they identify "are highly economical and usually effective," but also that they "lead to systematic and predictable errors." See Tversky and Kahneman, *supra* note 3, at 20. Gerd Gigerenzer, among others, has emphasized that some heuristics can work extremely well: see Gerd Gigerenzer, P. M. Todd, and the ABC Group, *Simple Heuristics that Make Us Smart* (New York: Oxford University Press, 1999); Gerd Gigerenzer, *Adaptive Thinking: Rationality in the Real World* (New York: Oxford University Press, 2000); and he used this point as a rejoinder to those who stress the errors introduced by heuristics and biases. I do not mean to take a stand on the resulting debates. Even if many heuristics mostly work well in daily life, a sensible government can do much better than to rely on them.

poisoning, *Arsenic and Old Lace.* By contrast, there is a relatively complex mental operation in the judgment that arsenic regulation might lead people to use less safe alternatives. In many cases where the Precautionary Principle seems to offer guidance, the reason is that some of the relevant risks are available while others are barely visible.

Consider in this regard the finding that most of the time, public concern about risks tracks changes in the actual fluctuations of those risks – but that public concern outruns actual fluctuations in the case of "panics," bred by vivid illustrations that do not reflect changes in levels of danger.[9] At certain points in the 1970s and 1980s, there were extreme leaps, in the United States, in concern about teenage suicides, herpes, illegitimacy, and AIDS – leaps that did not correspond to changes in the size of the problem. Availability, produced by "a particularly vivid case or new finding that receives considerable media attention," played a major role in those leaps in public concern.[10] Sometimes the concern led to unjustified precautions, as in the behavior of some parents who refused to allow their children to attend classes having students with signs of herpes.

What, in particular, produces availability? An intriguing essay attempts to test the effects of ease of *imagery* on perceived judgments of risk.[11] The study asked subjects to read about an illness (Hyposcenia-B) that "was becoming increasingly prevalent" on the local campus. In one condition, the symptoms were concrete and easy to imagine – involving muscle aches, low energy, and frequent severe headaches. In another condition, the symptoms were vague and hard to imagine, involving an inflamed liver, a malfunctioning nervous system, and a general sense of disorientation. Subjects in both conditions were asked to imagine a three-week period in which they had the disease and to write a detailed description of what they imagined. After doing so, subjects were asked to assess, on a ten-point scale, their likelihood of contracting the disease. The basic finding was that likelihood judgments were very different in the two conditions, with

---

[9] See George Loewenstein and Jane Mather, Dynamic Processes in Risk Perception, 3 *J. Risk & Uncertainty* 155 (1990).

[10] *Id.* at 172.

[11] In Steven J. Sherman et al., Imagining Can Heighten or Lower the Perceived Likelihood of Contracting a Disease: The Mediating Effect of Ease of Imagery, in *Heuristics and Biases: The Psychology of Intuitive Judgment* 82, ed. Thomas Gilovich, Dale Griffin, and Daniel Kahneman (Cambridge: Cambridge University Press, 2002).

easily imagined symptoms making people far more inclined to believe that they were likely to get the disease.

To say the least, the availability heuristic does not operate in a social vacuum. What is readily "available" to some individuals, groups, cultures, and even nations will not be available to all. Many of those who favor gun control legislation have "available" a set of incidents in which such legislation would have avoided unnecessary deaths; many of those who reject such legislation are alert to incidents in which private gun ownership allowed people to fend off criminal violence.[12] I will return to this point in chapter 4. For present purposes, the key point is that the availability heuristic often underwrites the use of the Precautionary Principle, by suggesting the importance of taking precautions against some, but hardly all, of the risks involved.

PROBABILITY NEGLECT

The availability heuristic can produce an *inaccurate* assessment of probability. But sometimes people will attempt little assessment of probability at all, especially when strong emotions are involved. In such cases, large-scale variations in probabilities will matter little – even when those variations unquestionably should matter a lot. The point applies to hope as well as fear; vivid images of good outcomes will crowd out consideration of probability, too. Lotteries are successful partly for this reason. But for purposes of applying the Precautionary Principle, the topic is fear rather than hope. I suggest that sometimes the Precautionary Principle becomes workable because the issue of probability is neglected, and people focus on one emotionally gripping outcome among a large set of possibilities.

It should be easy to see the connection between probability neglect and the Precautionary Principle. If probabilities are neglected, especially when emotions are engaged, then the principle will operate through excessive public concern with certain low-probability hazards. Consider the familiar contrast between deaths from heat waves and deaths from airplane crashes. The latter triggers far more intense

---

[12] See Dan M. Kahan and Donald Braman, More Statistics, Less Persuasion: A Cultural Theory of Gun-Risk Perceptions, 151 *U. Pa. L. Rev.* 1291 (2003).

public attention, in part because of the availability heuristic, but in part because for some people, the outcome itself has such salience, and the probability much less so. In the context of genetic modification of food and global warming, the same phenomenon is at work, leading some people to focus on worst-case scenarios and thus to think that the Precautionary Principle, simply applied, calls for aggressive regulatory controls. Note that I am not urging that such controls are a mistake; in the context of global warming, they seem to be warranted. My claim is only that the Precautionary Principle appears to give guidance in part because the issue of probability is neglected.

For purposes of understanding the operation of the Precautionary Principle, it is important to see that visualization or imagery matters a great deal to people's reactions to risks.[13] When an image of a bad outcome is easily accessible, people will become greatly concerned about a risk, holding probability constant. Consider the fact that when people are asked how much they will pay for flight insurance for losses resulting from "terrorism," they will pay more than if they are asked how much they will pay for flight insurance from all causes.[14] The evident explanation for this peculiar result is that the word "terrorism" evokes vivid images of disaster, thus crowding out probability judgments. Note also that when people discuss a low-probability risk, their concern rises even if the discussion consists mostly of apparently trustworthy assurances that the likelihood of harm really is infinitesimal.[15] The reason is that the discussion makes it easier to visualize the risk and hence to fear it. I shall deal with this issue in some detail in chapter 3.

In many contexts, the law itself is a response to fear of bad outcomes without close attention to the question of probability – a version of the Precautionary Principle in action. Thus, for example, the European Community's ban on meat products treated with hormones has raised

---

[13] See Paul Slovic et al., Violence Risk Assessment and Risk Communication, 24 *Law Hum. Behav.* 271 (2000).

[14] See Eric J. Johnson et al., Framing, Probability Distortions, and Insurance Decisions, 7(1) *J. Risk & Uncertainty* 35 (1993).

[15] See A. S. Alkahami and Paul Slovic, A Psychological Study of the Inverse Relationship between Perceived Risk and Perceived Benefit, 14(6) *Risk Anal.* 1086, 1094 (1994).

large-scale issues about the role of public fear in risk regulation.[16] The Appellate Body of the World Trade Organization ruled[17] that the Community's ban ran afoul of Article 5.1 of the Agreement on Sanitary and Phytosanitary Measures (SPS Agreement), which requires members of the WTO to justify all health and safety regulations by reference to scientific risk assessments. In this way, the Appellate Body rejected the EC's effort to defend itself by reference to consumer fears about the safety of beef treated with hormones. In this context, such fears were real – but they neglected the issue of probability.

LOSS AVERSION AND FAMILIARITY

People tend to be loss averse, which means that a loss from the status quo is seen as more undesirable than a gain is seen as desirable.[18] When we anticipate a loss of what we now have, we can become genuinely afraid, in a way that greatly exceeds our feelings of pleasurable anticipation when we look forward to some supplement to what we now have. So far, perhaps, so good. The problem comes when individual and social decisions downplay potential gains from the status quo, and fixate on potential losses, in such a way as to produce overall increases in risks and overall decreases in well-being.

To see how loss aversion works, consider some classic experiments, which involve the *endowment effect*.[19] Some people were initially given (endowed with) certain goods – coffee mugs, chocolate bars, and binoculars – and were asked how much they would have to be paid to give them up. Other, similar people were not given these same

---

[16] For an illuminating discussion, see Howard Chang, Risk Regulation, Endogenous Public Concerns, and the Hormones Dispute: Nothing to Fear except Fear Itself?, 77 *So. Cal. L. Rev.* 743 (2004).

[17] Report of the Appellate Body, EC Measures Concerning Meat and Meat Products (Hormones), WT/DS48/AB/R, Jan. 16, 1998 (adopted Feb. 13, 1998), available in Westlaw, WTO-DEC file, 1998 WL 25520 (hereinafter Appellate Body).

[18] See Richard H. Thaler, The Psychology of Choice and the Assumptions of Economics, in *Quasi Rational Economics* 137, 143 (New York: Russell Sage Foundation, 1991) (arguing that "losses loom larger than gains"); Daniel Kahneman, Jack L. Knetsch, and Richard H. Thaler, Experimental Tests of the Endowment Effect and the Coase Theorem, 98(6) *J. Pol. Econ.* 1325, 1328 (1990); Colin Camerer, Individual Decision Making, in *The Handbook of Experimental Economics* 587, 665–70, ed. John H. Kagel and Alvin E. Roth (Princeton, N.J.: Princeton University Press, 1995).

[19] See Thaler, *Quasi Rational Economics, supra* note 18.

goods, and were asked how much they would pay to get them. The people initially given the goods valued them far more than those who were not initially given them. Interestingly, this effect was not observed for money tokens; people know that a dollar is worth a dollar. But with goods that are not readily turned into monetary equivalents, a substantial endowment effect is observed. The reason for this effect is loss aversion: People are much more displeased by the prospect of loss than they are pleased by the prospect of equivalent gain. An implication is that contrary to standard economic theory, people do not value out-of-pocket costs and opportunity costs the same. Opportunity costs, as forgone gains, seem to be far less bad than equivalent out-of-pocket costs.

In the context of fear and risk regulation, there is a clear implication: *People will be closely attuned to the losses produced by any newly introduced risk, or by any aggravation of existing risks, but far less concerned with the benefits that are forgone as a result of regulation.* I believe that loss aversion often helps to explain what makes the Precautionary Principle operational. The opportunity costs of regulation often register little or not at all, whereas the out-of-pocket costs of the activity or substance in question are entirely visible. In fact this is a form of status quo bias. The status quo marks the baseline against which gains and losses are measured, and a loss from the status quo seems much more bad than a gain from the status quo seems good.

If loss aversion is at work, we would predict that the Precautionary Principle would place a spotlight on the losses introduced by some risk and downplay the benefits forgone as a result of controls on that risk. Return to the scientists who believed that the Precautionary Principle would have banned airplanes, antibiotics, and refrigerators. They must have been thinking that the principle includes a form of loss aversion, assuring that it applies to risks that new processes create, but not to the reduction of risks caused by those same processes. Or recall the emphasis, in the United States, on the risks of insufficient testing of medicines as compared with the risks of delaying the availability of those medicines. If the "opportunity benefits" are off-screen, the Precautionary Principle will appear to give guidance notwithstanding the objections I have made. At the same time, the neglected opportunity benefits sometimes present a serious problem with the use of the Precautionary Principle. In the context of genetic engineering of food, this is very much the situation. We can find the same problem when the Precautionary Principle is invoked to support bans on nonreproductive cloning. For many people, the possible harms of cloning register more strongly than the potential therapeutic benefits that would be rendered unattainable by a ban on the practice.

But there is an evident problem with invoking loss aversion as a full explanation for the application of the Precautionary Principle: Regulation that seems required by the principle will often produce real losses from the status quo. In such cases, losses cannot be avoided. Consider global warming. Of course many people fear the associated risks, not only because they appear serious, but also because they represent losses from the current situation. At the same time, the expenditures necessary to control global warming will produce losses as well. Many of those who are skeptical about controls on greenhouse gas emissions emphasize the losses that such control would bring about; many who favor such controls emphasize the losses that will otherwise occur. What I am suggesting is that when the Precautionary Principle appears to give guidance, it is often because identifiable losses seem particularly salient.

Loss aversion is closely associated with another cognitive finding: *People are far more willing to tolerate familiar risks than unfamiliar ones, even if they are statistically equivalent.*[20] For example, the risks associated with driving do not occasion a great deal of concern, even though, in the United States alone, tens of thousands of people die from motor vehicle accidents each year. The relevant risks are simply seen as part of life. By contrast, many people are quite concerned about risks that appear newer, such as the risks associated with genetically modified foods, recently introduced chemicals, and terrorism. Part of the reason for the difference may be a belief that with new risks we cannot assign probabilities to the resulting dangers, and hence it makes sense to be cautious. But the individual and social propensity to focus on new risks outruns that belief. It makes the Precautionary Principle operational by emphasizing, for no sufficient reason, a mere subset of the hazards that are actually involved.

---

[20] See Paul Slovic, *The Perception of Risk* 140–43 (London: Earthscan, 2000).

THE (MYTHICAL?) BENEVOLENCE OF NATURE

Sometimes the Precautionary Principle operates by incorporating the belief that nature is essentially benign and that human intervention is likely to carry risks – as in the suggestion that the Precautionary Principle calls for stringent regulation of pesticides or genetically modified organisms. A belief that nature is benign overlaps with a commitment to loss aversion. Many people fear that any human intervention will create losses from the status quo and that those losses should carry great weight, whereas the gains should be regarded with some suspicion or at least be taken as less important. Often loss aversion and a belief in nature's benevolence march hand in hand: The status quo forms the baseline or reference state against which to assess deviations. Processes that interfere with nature seem, on the part of many, to be taken as troubling "degradation" – whereas gains or improvements seem, other things being equal, far less significant. But the commitment to nature's benevolence is quite general; it outruns loss aversion itself. For example, "[h]uman intervention seems to be an amplifier in judgments on food riskiness and contamination," even though "more lives are lost to natural than to man-made disasters in the world."[21] Studies show that people overestimate the carcinogenic risk from pesticides and underestimate the risks of natural carcinogens. People also believe that nature implies safety, so much so that they will prefer natural water to processed water even if the two are chemically identical.[22]

A belief in the benevolence of nature plays a major role in the operation of the Precautionary Principle, especially among those who see nature as harmonious or in balance. Many of those who endorse the principle seem to be especially concerned about new technologies. Most people believe that natural chemicals are more safe than man-made chemicals.[23] (Most toxicologists disagree.) On this view, the principle calls for caution when people are intervening in the natural world. Here of course we can find some sense: Nature often consists of systems, and interventions into systems can cause serious

---

[21] Paul Rozin, Technological Stigma: Some Perspectives from the Study of Contagion, in *Risk, Media, and Stigma: Understanding Public Challenges to Modern Science and Technology* 31, 38, ed. James Flynn, Paul Slovic, and Howard Kunverther (London: Earthscan, 2001).
[22] *Id.* [23] See Slovic, *supra* note 20, at 291.

problems. But there is a large problem with this understanding of the Precautionary Principle. What is natural may not be safe at all.[24]

Consider in this light the familiar idea that there is a "balance of nature." According to one account, this idea is "not true."[25] A scientific "revolution" has shown that nature "is characterized by change, not constancy," and that "natural ecological systems are dynamic," with desirable changes being "those induced through human action."[26] In any case, nature is often a realm of destruction, illness, killing, and death. Hence the claim cannot be that human activity is necessarily or systematically more destructive than what nature does. Nor is it clear that natural products are comparatively safe.[27] Organic foods, favored by many people on grounds of safety and health and creating annual revenues of $4.5 billion in the United States alone, are, according to one account, "actually riskier to consume than food grown with synthetic chemicals."[28] If the Precautionary Principle is seen to raise doubts about pesticides, but not about organic foods, it is probably because the health risks that come with departures from "nature" register as especially troublesome.

Of course, some of the most serious risks are a product of nature. Nothing is more natural than exposure to sunlight, which people rarely fear. But such exposure is associated with skin cancer and other harms, producing serious health problems that (unfortunately) have not been the occasion for invoking the Precautionary Principle. Tobacco smoking kills 400,000 Americans each year, even though tobacco is a product of nature. To say all this is not to resolve specific issues, which depend on complex questions of value and fact. But a false belief in the benevolence of nature helps to explain why the Precautionary Principle is thought, quite incorrectly, to provide a great deal of analytical help.

SYSTEM NEGLECT

The last point is, in a way, the largest. My suggestion is that much of the time, people neglect the systemic effect of one-shot interventions.

---

[24] See James P. Collman, *Naturally Dangerous* (Sausalito, Calif.: University Science Books, 2001).

[25] See Daniel B. Botkin, Adjusting Law to Nature's Discordant Harmonies, 7 *Duke Envtl. L. & Pol'y Forum* 25, 27 (1996).

[26] *Id.* at 33.   [27] See Collman, *supra* note 24.   [28] See Botkin, *supra* note 25, at 31.

They tend to assume that a change in a social situation would alter the part at issue but would not affect other parts. System neglect, thus understood, includes the general phenomenon of *tradeoff neglect*, by which people fail to see the frequent need to weigh competing variables against one another. But tradeoff neglect is only part of what is involved. When the Precautionary Principle appears to give guidance, and when it goes wrong, it is often because those who use it are falling victim to system neglect.

The clearest evidence comes from the German psychologist Dietrich Dorner, who has designed some ingenious experiments to see whether people can reduce social risks.[29] Dorner's experiments are run via computer. Participants are asked to reduce risks faced by the inhabitants of some region of the world. The risks may involve pollution, poverty, poor medical care, inadequate fertilization of crops, sick cattle, insufficient water, or excessive hunting and fishing. Through the magic of the computer, many policy initiatives are available – improved care of cattle, childhood immunization, drilling more wells. Participants are able to choose among them. Once particular initiatives are chosen, the computer projects, over short periods and then over decades, what is likely to happen in the region.

In these experiments, success is fully possible. Some initiatives will actually make for effective and enduring improvements. But many of the participants – even the most educated and professional – produce calamities. They do so because they fixate on isolated problems and do not see the complex, system-wide effects of particular interventions. They may appreciate the importance of increasing the number of cattle, but once they do that, they create a serious risk of overgrazing, and they fail to anticipate that problem. They may understand full well the value of drilling more wells to provide water, but they do not anticipate the energy and environmental effects of the drilling, which then endangers the food supply. Only the rare participant is able to see a number of steps down the road – to understand the multiple effects of one-shot interventions into the system, and to assess a wide range of consequences from those interventions. The successful participants seem to take small, reversible steps, or to see the full set of effects at once, and thus to protect themselves against major blunders. When people are not successful, it is because they fail to see that risks are parts of systems.

How would the Precautionary Principle operate if invoked in Dorner's experiments? It should be easy to see that while the weaker version might provide some assistance, the stronger versions offer no help at all. There are simply too many risks against which one might take precautions. Precautions cannot be taken against all risks, not for the important but less interesting reason that resources are limited, but simply because efforts to redress any set of risks might produce risks of their own. The real world of fear and risk offers countless analogues. To the extent that the Precautionary Principle appears to offer guidance, it is often because adverse systemic effects, and the need to take precautions against them, are simply being neglected.

Howard Margolis has used a related point to explain why experts have different risk judgments from ordinary people, and he has done so in a particular effort to explain why and when ordinary people will think, "Better safe than sorry."[30] Margolis thus offers some cognitive foundations for the Precautionary Principle, without explicitly discussing the idea. Margolis' goal is to cast light on some apparent anomalies in ordinary thinking about risks: Why do people believe that small risks from pesticides should be regulated, if comparatively small risks from X-rays are quite tolerable? Why are people so concerned about the risks of nuclear power, when many experts tend to believe that the risks are quite low – lower, in fact, than the risks from competing energy sources, such as coal-fired power plants, which produce relatively little public objection? When, exactly, does the idea of precaution seem so appealing – and when does it seem obsessive and unhelpful?

Margolis suggests that people are sometimes subject to a kind of optical illusion, in which they focus on the harms associated with some activity or process, but fail to see the benefits. If so, they will tend to think, "Better safe than sorry." If not, they will see some "fungibility" between both harms and benefits, and engage in the kind of tradeoff analysis that is more typical for experts. Margolis offers a wonderful example to support this suggestion. The removal

[30] See Howard Margolis, *Dealing with Risk* (Chicago: University of Chicago Press, 1996).

of asbestos from schools in New York City was initially quite popular, indeed demanded by parents, even though experts believed that the risks of leaving it were statistically small. (As it happens, the risk of a child getting cancer from asbestos insulation was about one-third the risk of being struck by lightning.) But when it emerged that the removal would cause schools to be closed for a period of weeks, and when the closing caused parents to become greatly inconvenienced, parental attitudes turned right around, and asbestos removal seemed like a really bad idea. As the costs of the removal came on-screen, parents thought much more like experts, and the risks of asbestos seemed tolerable: Statistically small, and on balance worth incurring. The Precautionary Principle often operates because of the visibility of only one side of the ledger, so that people think as parents do in advance of asbestos removal, seeing the possibility of danger without confronting the problems created by reducing it.

For an especially vivid example, consider the recorded views of Americans about environmental protection in the late 1990s. About 63 percent of Americans agreed with the following statement: "Protecting the environment is so important that requirements and standards cannot be too high and continuing environmental improvements must be made regardless of cost."[31] In the same general vein, 59 percent supported the Kyoto Treaty on global warming, with only 21 percent opposed.[32] But in the same period, 52 percent of Americans said that they would refuse to support the Kyoto Treaty on global warming if "it would cost an extra $50 per month for an average American household."[33] In fact, only 11 percent of Americans would support the Kyoto Treaty if the monthly expense were $100 or more.[34] How can we explain strong majority support for "environmental improvements . . . regardless of cost" and strong majority rejection of environmental improvements when the cost is high? The answer lies in the fact that people are not, in fact, willing to spend an infinite amount for environmental improvements. When the costs are squarely placed "on-screen," people begin to weigh both costs and benefits.

---

[31] See The Program on International Policy Attitudes, Americans on the Global Warming Treaty, available at http://www.pipa.org/OnlineReports/GlobalWarming/glob_warm_treaty.html at Box 15.

[32] *Id.*   [33] *Id.* at Box 16.   [34] *Id.*

There are many other examples. Many people are quite concerned about the risks associated with dioxin, a plausible candidate for use of the Precautionary Principle, but few are concerned about the statistically equivalent risks associated with aflatoxin, a carcinogen found in peanut butter. When aflatoxin does not trigger public concern, a large part of the reason is that the burdens of banning aflatoxin seem high and indeed unacceptable. Too many people would object to heavy regulation of peanut butter, a staple of school lunches and many diets for generations. Think in this light about steps designed to reduce risks of terrorism. It is both mildly counterintuitive and reasonable to predict that people would be willing to pay *less*, in terms of dollars and waiting time, to reduce low-probability risks of an airplane disaster if they are frequent travelers. An intriguing study finds exactly that effect.[35] It is also safe to predict that if people were told, by a reliable source, that eliminating pesticides would lead to serious health problems – for example, because pesticide-free fruits and vegetables carry special dangers – the perceived risk of pesticides would decline dramatically, and it would be difficult to invoke the Precautionary Principle as a basis for stringent regulation of pesticides. Indeed, I predict that if people were informed that eliminating pesticides would lead to a significant cost in the price of apples and oranges, the perceived risk would go down as well.

The conclusion is that the Precautionary Principle often seems helpful because analysts are focusing on the "target" risk, and not on the systemic, risk-related effects of being precautionary, or even on the risk-related consequences of risk reduction. Rational regulators, of course, think about systems, not snapshots. And once we see that risks are inevitably parts of systems, the Precautionary Principle will become far less helpful.

REJOINDERS AND SALUTARY GOALS

Proponents of the Precautionary Principle are unlikely to concede that the principle becomes workable only as a result of cognitive

[35] See Matthew Harrington, People's Willingness to Accept Airport Security Delays in Exchange for Lesser Risk 6–7 (Jan. 28, 2002) (unpublished manuscript, on file with author, describing how the twelve survey respondents who had experienced significant delays were less willing to pay for additional airport security than those twenty-four respondents who had not experienced such delays).

difficulties; there is a great deal that they might say in response. The imaginable responses can be placed in two categories. The first point to salutary and important goals, evidently held by proponents of the principle, to which the principle is crudely connected. Because of the crudeness of the connection, the principle cannot be supported by reference to those goals. The second and more promising set of responses points in the direction of refinements. Let us begin with salutary goals.

Distribution

Might the Precautionary Principle be defended on distributional grounds? In the United States, the Clean Air Act takes a highly precautionary approach, requiring an "adequate margin of safety" and hence regulation in the face of scientific uncertainty. At the same time, the Clean Air Act delivers large benefits to poor people and members of minority groups – larger benefits, on balance, than it gives to wealthy people.[36] In the international domain, aggressive action to combat climate change would be more beneficial to poor countries than to wealthy ones.[37] This is partly because wealthy countries are better able to adapt, simply because they are wealthier. It is partly because agriculture, highly vulnerable to climate change, is responsible for only 2 percent of the economy of wealthy nations, but 50 percent of the economy of poor nations. In the context of global warming, at least, the Precautionary Principle might be invoked to prevent especially severe burdens on those in the worst position to bear them.

It makes a great deal of sense to emphasize the distribution of domestic or international risks, and the distributional effects of global warming are among the strongest points in favor of aggressive regulation of greenhouse gases.[38] But in many cases, the Precautionary

---

[36] See Matthew E. Kahn, The Beneficiaries of Clean Air Act Regulation, 24(1) *Regulation* 34 (2001).

[37] See, e.g., Joseph Aldy, Peter Orszag, and Joseph Stiglitz, Climate Change: An Agenda for Global Collective Action (unpublished manuscript, 2001); Bjorn Lomborg, *The Skeptical Environmentalist* 291–302 (New York: Cambridge University Press, 2001).

[38] Note, however, that if the concern involves poor countries, it is not clear that global warming is an especially high priority, in light of the many needs of those countries, needs that might be addressed by wealthier nations. See Lomborg, *supra* note 37, at 322–23; Indur Goklany, *The Precautionary Principle: A Critical Appraisal of Environmental Risk Assessment* 71–88 (Washington, D.C.: Cato Institute, 2001).

Principle, as applied, would have unfortunate distributional effects. Consider the case of DDT. A ban on DDT, often supported by reference to the Precautionary Principle, is eminently justified in wealthy nations. But such a ban is likely to have – and is actually having – bad effects in at least some poor countries, where DDT is the cheapest and most effective way of combating serious diseases, most notably malaria.[39] In fact regulation of DDT is both compelled and prohibited by the Precautionary Principle, taken in its strong form; and distributional considerations argue strongly in favor of allowing its use. The case of genetic modification of food might be a similar example; according to some projections, the benefits are likely to be enjoyed by poor people, not the wealthy.[40]

The Precautionary Principle might seem to require stringent limits on aflatoxin, a known carcinogen, coming into Europe and America from Africa. But European Community standards are so stringent, in this regard, that they are projected to prevent only one death per year in the European Union. This is a small number in the abstract, and evidently trivial in light of the fact that 33,000 people die annually from liver cancer in the EU.[41] And this very precaution has real costs, imposing significant losses on African farmers, whose ability to export food is severely compromised by the EC requirements. Here, then, is a case in which the Precautionary Principle has perverse distributional consequences. Distributional issues should indeed be a part of a system of risk regulation, but the Precautionary Principle is a crude, indirect, and sometimes perverse way of incorporating distributional concerns.

Biases

Advocates of the Precautionary Principle might urge that environmental values are systematically disregarded in the regulatory process, or not given their due, and hence that the principle helps counteract systematic biases. David Dana, for example, has vigorously

---

[39] Cass R. Sunstein, *Risk and Reason* 14 (Cambridge: Cambridge University Press, 2002); Aaron Wildavsky, *But Is It True?* 61 (Cambridge, Mass.: Harvard University Press, 1995).

[40] See Goklany, *supra* note 38, at 55.

[41] See Giandomenico Majone, What Price Safety? The Precautionary Principle and its Policy Implications, 40 *J. Common Mark. Stud.* 89, 106 (2002).

defended the Precautionary Principle on the ground that it is well suited to overcoming cognitive biases that lead people to under-react to environmental risks.[42] On this view, it is oddly misleading to attack the principle as rooted in cognitive problems. On the contrary, the principle is best understood as a sensible response to those very problems.

For those who make this argument, the first problem is myopia: People often focus on the short term and neglect the long term, in a way that can harm their own interests. Government officials are often influenced by ordinary people; in any case such officials are not so different from ordinary people. If they are uninformed by the Precau-tionary Principle, such officials might fail to attend to risks that will not occur, or be seen to occur, in the short run. A second problem is that many people are unrealistically optimistic.[43] About 90 percent of drivers think that they are safer than the average driver and less likely to be involved in a serious accident.[44] People generally think that they are less likely than other people to be divorced, to have heart disease, to be fired from a job, and much more.[45] Professional finan-cial experts consistently overestimate likely earnings, and business school students overestimate their likely starting salary and the num-ber of offers that they will receive. In addition to believing that they are safer than most drivers, people tend to underestimate, in abso-lute terms, their likelihood of being involved in a serious automobile accident,[46] and their own failure to buy insurance for floods and earth-quakes is at least consistent with the view that people are excessively optimistic.[47]

As a result of excessive optimism, many low-level risks do not register at all. A related problem is that people tend to reduce cognitive

---

[42] See David Dana, A Behavioral Economic Defense of the Precautionary Principle, 97 *Nw. U.L. Rev.* 1315 (2003).

[43] See Shelley E. Taylor, *Positive Illusions: Creative Self-Deception and the Healthy Mind*, 9–12 (New York: Basic Books, 1989).

[44] See *id.* at 10.

[45] See Neil D. Weinstein, Unrealistic Optimism about Susceptibility to Health Problems, 10(5) *J. Behav. Med.* 481 (1987).

[46] Christine Jolls, Behavioral Economic Analysis of Redistributive Legal Rules, in *Behavioral Law and Economics* 291, ed. Cass R. Sunstein (Cambridge: Cambridge University Press, 2000).

[47] *Id.*

dissonance, sometimes by treating risks as if they are tiny, even worth ignoring.[48] When people think that they are "safe," even though they face a statistical risk, they might well be seeking to avoid the anxiety that comes from an understanding of the inevitability of risk. Nations are of course affected by the preferences and beliefs of their citizens. Perhaps nations neglect the long term and sometimes are excessively optimistic about genuine hazards. If so, the Precautionary Principle might be a sensible corrective.

For some risks, this pragmatic defense is not implausible, and the Precautionary Principle, applied with a narrow viewscreen, undoubtedly leads to some good results. But in the end, the principle cannot sensibly be defended in these terms. The reason is that the attempted defense ignores the central problem, which is that precautions against some risks almost always create other risks. Why don't the very cognitive arguments that support the war in Iraq, or aggressive regulation of genetic modification of food, also argue against the war in Iraq, or against aggressive regulation of genetic modification of food? Mightn't neglect of the long term, and excessive optimism, be responsible for that very war and that very regulation?

In short, the cognitive argument for the Precautionary Principle faces two problems. The first problem is that environmental values are often on both sides of the controversy. The same is certainly true of health and safety, as shown by the example of extensive premarket testing of pharmaceuticals, which reduces risks at the same time as it deprives people of access to potentially life-saving medicines. When risks and environmental values are on both sides, cognitive biases cannot possibly argue in favor of any particular course of action. The second problem is that even when environmental values are on only one side, the interests and values on the other side might also be ignored because of the human tendency to excessive optimism and to disregard the long term. As we shall see, cognitive biases are an extremely important part of the laws of fear, but they do not justify the Precautionary Principle.

[48] See George A. Akerlof and William T. Dickens, The Economic Consequences of Cognitive Dissonance, in George A. Akerlof, *An Economic Theorist's Book of Tales* 123, 124–28 (Cambridge: Cambridge University Press, 1984).

Democracy

It is tempting to defend the Precautionary Principle on democratic grounds, as a way of structuring democratic deliberation and ensuring a firm role for citizen values in risk regulation. For example, Carolyn Raffensperger and Katherine Barrett argue that "Above all, the precautionary principle is grounded firmly in democratic process." In their view,

lack of democratic process has been a primary source of contention surrounding GM crops and food. Under the precautionary principle, not only is this ethically unacceptable, it is an impoverished procedure for making decisions about a technology that now affects (voluntarily or not) millions of people and many other species throughout the world.[49]

Although risk assessment "can provide some guidance to the potential damage of a particular hazard," civil society is best equipped to weigh the "risks, benefits, and alternative options."[50] Thus Raffensperger and Barrett stress the "dialogue between science and society" that the Precautionary Principle inspires.[51]

   A European analyst has defended the principle from a related direction, contending that it provides a way to deal with the "problem of mass psychology."[52] The public has come to distrust science after the tragedies of thalidomide, mad cow disease, and Chernobyl. In each case, scientists insisted that there was no risk and the public believed them. In these circumstances, the Precautionary Principle provides a way to legitimate activities and processes that might otherwise be unacceptable. Even when public fear about new technologies is irrational, scientists and policymakers cannot ignore it. At least some version of the Precautionary Principle might seem to offer a compromise between science and democracy by assuring the public of the safety of a new technology and making it "harder for scaremongers to block a new technology."

[49] Carolyn Raffensperger and Katherine Barrett, In Defense of the Precautionary Principle, 19 *Nature Biotechnology* 811 (Sept. 2001).

[50] Lillian Auberson-Huang, The Dialogue between Precaution and Risk, 20 *Nature Biotechnology* 1076 (Nov. 2002).

[51] In the same vein, see Joel A. Tickner and Carolyn Raffensperger, The Precautionary Principle: A Framework for Sustainable Business Decision-Making, 5 *Env. Policy* 75 (1998).

[52] Maurizio Iaccarino, A Cost/Benefit Analysis about the Precautionary Principle, 6 *EMBO Reports* 454 (2000).

It is certainly correct to emphasize the centrality of democratic deliberation to risk regulation, and also to stress the need to respond to, rather than to trivialize, public concerns. A risk assessment, offering numbers about expected harms, is not a sufficient ground for democratic choice, even when accompanied by figures about expected costs as well as benefits. We need to know about the distribution of benefits and burdens; we also need to have the expected harms described in qualitative as well as quantitative terms. People legitimately care about whether risks are inequitably distributed, potentially catastrophic, and voluntarily incurred – a point to which I shall return. And if a reflective public would like to take special steps to counteract certain risks, it is entitled to do exactly that; margins of safety make a great deal of sense.

But none of these points provides a democratic defense of the Precautionary Principle. The problem with the principle is that it is too vague and abstract, and too incoherent, to provide a sensible basis for structuring democratic discussion. What if a democratic public chooses to run certain risks, on the ground that those are sensible risks to run? What if citizens decline to take precautions? Rather than pretending that it is possible to adopt a general attitude in favor of precaution, it is far better to insist on the importance of protecting against harms that most concern a reflective and informed public.

Rights

On one view, human beings have a right to be free from certain risks and harms. If a company imposes a significant risk of mortality on members of a community, there might well be a violation of their rights; if that risk comes to fruition, the claim of a rights violation is stronger still. For present purposes it is unnecessary to say anything about the foundation of rights. The only point is that the Precautionary Principle might seem defensible as a means of protecting those rights, whatever their source.

I shall explore this point from another direction in chapter 7. For the moment, notice only that there is a crude relationship between the Precautionary Principle and any account of rights. Suppose that the principle is invoked to forbid the use of DDT in poor countries, or to call for aggressive controls on electromagnetic fields, or to require preemptive wars against unfriendly nations that are credibly claimed to be aiding terrorists. In all these cases, that very use of the Precautionary Principle might count as a rights violation, certainly if risks and harms are on all sides. Arguments based on rights undoubtedly justify certain kinds of regulatory steps, including certain kinds of precautions. But they cannot justify the Precautionary Principle as such.

False negatives and false positives

Defenders of the principle sometimes insist that their real goal is to reverse "the preferred type of error."[53] They contend that scientists are typically concerned to avoid "false positives," finding harm when there is none. In their view, nations should err instead on the side of "false negatives," which come from finding safety when there is in fact harm. A central reason is that a false positive "is more easily corrected – through further testing – than a false negative, which may result in irreversible harm."[54] In one of the classic discussions of precaution, Talbot Page made a closely related argument, emphasizing that the social consequences of false negatives and false positives may not be symmetrical: The expected damage of risky technologies may well be far greater than the expected damage, or forgone benefits, of refusing to go forward with such technologies.[55] Hence Page argued for precautionary decisions, grounded on three intuitively appealing principles: (1) risk aversion toward uncertain but especially harmful outcomes; (2) a reluctance to make irreversible commitments foreclosing future courses of action; and (3) a concern for intergenerational equity when benefits are immediate but risks are imposed on those not yet born.

In some circumstances, it certainly makes sense to be concerned about false positives, and Page's three principles deserve serious consideration. The difficulty with this defense of the Precautionary Principle is that irreversible harm can be caused by false positives as well as false negatives – if, for example, the false positives lead government not to provide food, medicine, or energy sources that would save lives. Often irreversibility lies on all sides. Death itself is irreversible, and

---

[53] See Raffensperger and DeFur, *supra* note 3, at 937.   [54] *Id.*

[55] Talbot Page, A Generic View of Toxic Chemicals and Similar Risks, 7 *Ecology L.Q.* 207 (1978).

if government uses the idea of precaution to eliminate or reduce life-saving initiatives, then an emphasis on false positives, assuming harm when none exists, will cause irreversible losses. There is no reason to think that as a rule, new technologies pose greater potential harms than potential benefits. Sometimes they do; sometimes they don't.

REJOINDERS AND REFINEMENTS

Perhaps the Precautionary Principle can be refined and reconstructed in a way that meets the objections I have made, and that captures some important insights that have given the idea of precaution its widespread appeal. In Part II, I will attempt a reconstruction of just that sort. For the moment, consider three possible refinements, designed as general defenses of the principle.

Balancing, risk aversion, and insurance: certain costs vs. uncertain benefits

Perhaps the Precautionary Principle does not really eschew balancing. Perhaps it can be taken to call for a form of balancing, but with an emphasis on risk aversion. Perhaps the point of the principle is to build a "margin of safety" into decisions affecting health, safety, and the environment – to go beyond existing evidence of harm in order to protect people against dangers that are possible though not demonstrable. Suppose, for example, that a monetary expenditure, large but not huge, would prevent a risk that, on the best case, would be less than large, but on the worst case would be huge. A large expenditure, ventured in the name of precaution, might well be justified in that circumstance.

If this claim is meant to defend the weak version of the Precautionary Principle, there is nothing wrong with it. Indeed it points to a true and important point. But if it is meant more ambitiously, it misses the central problem. A "margin of safety" can be used to protect some risks or some aspects of risk-related situations. But it cannot be used to defend against all risks for the reason I have emphasized: Risks are on all sides. The Precautionary Principle cannot plausibly be defended as a form of balancing alongside risk aversion, simply because it is possible to be averse only to some risks, not to the full universe of risks. What emerges, from an understanding of risk aversion, is not the Precautionary Principle, but a more mundane willingness to purchase "regulatory insurance" in the form of margins of safety against risks whose magnitude cannot be established. As those risks approach the catastrophic, the extent of the margin of safety increases – a point to which I shall return in chapter 5.

Irreversible losses, options, and two types of error

Some of the most sophisticated defenses of the Precautionary Principle emphasize irreversibility, drawing in particular on the theory of options in the stock market.[56] In that context, there are several methods that a prospective investor can use to place a value on his ability to purchase a stock for a given price at a later date if he chooses. This situation contrasts with the typical stock purchase decision, in which a prospective investor must place a value on a projected revenue stream. The idea of buying an option is that, over time, the ability to project the revenue stream will improve and hence there is a value to being able to make the decision later in time rather than earlier.[57] Quite plausibly, there is a similar value in the regulatory context. When making a regulatory decision, we are trying to project a revenue stream of costs and benefits. If we will be able to do so more accurately later on, then there is a (bounded) value to putting the decision off to a later date.[58] This (bounded) degree of precaution, freezing the status quo while more information is obtained over time, appears to be justified in principle.[59]

---

[56] See Christian Gollier and Nicolas Treich, Decision-Making under Scientific Uncertainty: The Economics of the Precautionary Principle, 27 *J. Risk & Uncertainty* 77, 84 (2003), for the definition of irreversibility used in the real options approach. See also *id.* at 87–91 for distinctions between stock externalities, environmental irreversibility, and capital irreversibility.

[57] Chan S. Park and Hemantha S. B. Herath, Exploiting Uncertainty – Investment Opportunities as Real Options: A New Way of Thinking in Engineering Economics, 45 *Engineering Economist* 1, 3–4 (2000).

[58] Gollier and Treich, *supra* note 56, at 88. "The basic insight is that the prospect to [sic] receive information in the future leads to adopt [sic] a more flexible position today. The intuitive reasoning is clear: choosing an inflexible position undermines the value of information. Hence, as the informativeness increases the incentive to remain flexible and take advantage of it also increases."

[59] Scott Farrow and Hiroshi Hayakawa, Investing in Safety: An Analytical Precautionary Principle, 33 *J. Safety Research* 165, 166–67 (2002). "However, a new type of analysis from the private sector – real options analysis – suggests a bounded degree of precaution" (citations omitted).

The key point of the options analysis of the Precautionary Principle is that uncertainty and irreversibility should lead to a sequential decision-making process. Suppose the question is whether to preserve a wildlife area when we lack information about the value of that area. If better information will emerge, we might seek an approach that biases decisions in favor of greater flexibility. If development "involves some irreversible transformation of the environment, hence a loss in perpetuity of the benefits from preservation," there is some reason to wait for more "information about the costs and benefits of" the relevant alternatives.[60] On reasonable assumptions, a policy that preserves the area, if its destruction would be irreversible, would be justified if it created greater flexibility for posterity.

In some contexts, this argument does justify special steps to protect the environment; global warming may be an example. But the argument does not support the Precautionary Principle. At most, it suggests that in certain cases, involving irreversible losses on one side and reversible ones on another, regulators, like ordinary people, should be willing to pay a certain amount to ensure that specified options remain available. If the idea of irreversible losses is adequately specified, then the idea makes sense and justifies "precautions" under the specified conditions. But the Precautionary Principle has a far broader reach; it is not limited to cases in which irreversible losses lie on one side and reversible ones on another. In any case, irreversible losses are often on both sides. Consider the war in Iraq, a highly precautionary approach to allowing new medicines on the market, and genetic modification of food. In all of these cases, irreversibility is everywhere.

Risk, uncertainty, and ignorance

Thus far I have been speaking as if environmental and other risk-related problems involve hazards of ascertainable probability – as if we can say that the risk of death, from a certain activity, is 1/100,000, or at least that it ranges from (say) 1/20,000 to 1/500,000, with an exposed population of (say) 10 million. But we can imagine instances in which analysts cannot specify even a range of probability. Hence

---

[60] See Kenneth Arrow and Anthony Fischer, Environmental Preservation, Uncertainty and Irreversibility, 88 *Q.J. Economics* 312, 313–14 (1974).

regulators, and ordinary people, are often acting in a situation of *uncertainty* (where outcomes can be identified but no probabilities can be assigned) rather than *risk* (where outcomes can be identified and probabilities assigned to various outcomes).[61] And they are sometimes acting under conditions of *ignorance*, in which regulators are unable to specify either the probability of bad outcomes or their nature – where regulators do not even know the magnitude of the harms that they are facing.[62] In circumstances of uncertainty, a more subtle defense of the Precautionary Principle is possible.

When existing knowledge allows regulators to identify outcomes, but does not permit them to assign probabilities to each, it is standard to follow the maximin principle: Choose the policy with the best worst-case outcome.[63] Perhaps the Precautionary Principle can be seen as a form of the maximin principle, asking officials to identify the worst case among the various options, and to select that option whose worst case is least bad. Perhaps the maximin principle would support many proposed applications of the Precautionary Principle by, for example, urging aggressive steps to combat global warming. Suppose that such steps would impose various hardships, but that even in the worst case, these are not nearly so bad as the worst cases associated with global warming. Oughtn't governments to combat the worst of the worst cases? In fact, President George W. Bush defended the war in Iraq in terms of exactly this sort: "Imagine those 19 hijackers [involved in the 9/11 attacks] with other weapons and plans, this time armed by Saddam Hussein. It would take one vial, one canister, one crate slipped into this country to bring a day of horror like none we have ever known." On this view, costly steps toward risk reduction are defensible if they eliminate the most serious of the worst-case scenarios.

[61] See Frank H. Knight, *Risk, Uncertainty, and Profit* (Boston, Mass.: Houghton Mifflin Co., 1933); Paul Davidson, Is Probability Theory Relevant for Uncertainty? A Post-Keynesian Perspective, 5(1) *J. of Econ. Perspectives* 129 (1991). Some people object that uncertainty does not exist, because it is always possible for decision makers to produce probability assignments by proposing a series of lotteries over possible outcomes; but such assignments have no epistemic credentials if not rooted in either theory or repeated experiences, and many risk-related problems, such as those involving global warming, are that sort of case.

[62] On ignorance and precaution, see Poul Harremoes, Ethical Aspects of Scientific Incertitude [*sic*] in Environmental Analysis and Decision Making, 11 *Journal of Cleaner Production* 705 (2003).

[63] See Jon Elster, *Explaining Technical Change* 185–207 (Cambridge: Cambridge University Press, 1983), for a helpful discussion.

This is not an implausible suggestion; sometimes it is best to identify and to respond to the worst-case scenario. I shall have much more to say about this point in Part II. But as a defense of the Precautionary Principle, the response suffers from three problems. The first and most fundamental is that the Precautionary Principle is not the maximin principle. If the latter principle is what is meant, then we should be discussing that principle directly, and evaluating it against the alternatives. The Precautionary Principle obscures those issues. The second problem is that so defended, the Precautionary Principle might well prevent rational priority setting, simply because it leads government to spend its resources on activities whose risks are uncertain at the expense of activities whose risks are better understood. The third problem is that risks that are now in the realm of uncertainty will often move, over time, into the realm of risk, simply because knowledge grows over time. Indeed, one of the principal goals of a well-functioning system of environmental protection is to produce more information about potential hazards, information that includes the probability of harm. In some circumstances, acquiring information is far better than responding to the worst-case scenario, at least when that response itself creates dangers in the realm of both uncertainty and risk.

My conclusion is that the Precautionary Principle cannot be defended by reference to situations posing unquantifiable risks of catastrophe. But an understanding of such situations does justify taking particular precautions when they arise. In the context of terrorist threats, it makes sense to adopt a kind of Precautionary Principle against dangers whose probability cannot be assessed but that would be devastating if they materialized. In the context of global warming, the risk of catastrophe, if it cannot be ruled out as insignificant, might similarly justify costly precautions. We might well adopt a specialized form of maximin, a kind of Anti-Catastrophe Principle, specifically designed to handle potentially catastrophic risks under conditions of uncertainty. But even here it is important to be careful. Some steps, intended to reduce risks of catastrophe, will simultaneously increase risks of just that kind. Many people so argued about the war in Iraq. And even if the relevant steps pose no risk of catastrophe, it is important to know their costs. A nation would not want to spend all its resources to avert potentially catastrophic risks.

TOWARD WIDER VIEWSCREENS

I have not suggested any particular substitute for the Precautionary Principle. But none of the arguments here supports the argument of Aaron Wildavsky, an influential political scientist with a special interest in risk regulation, who also rejects the Precautionary Principle.[64] In Wildavsky's view, the notion of "precaution" should be abandoned and replaced with a principle of "resilience," based on an understanding that nature, and society, are quite able to incorporate even strong shocks, and that the ultimate dangers are therefore smaller than we are likely to fear. It would follow from Wildavsky's "resilience" principle that people should be less concerned than they now are with the risks associated with (for example) arsenic, global warming, and destruction of the ozone layer.

Unfortunately, the principle of "resilience" is no better than that of "precaution." Some systems are resilient, but many are not. Whether an ecosystem, or a society, is "resilient" cannot be decided in the abstract. In any case resilience is a matter of degree. Everything depends on the facts. The "resilience principle" should be understood as a heuristic, one that favors inaction in the face of possibly damaging technological change. Like most heuristics, the resilience principle will work well in many circumstances, but it can also lead to systematic and even deadly errors.

A better approach would acknowledge that a wide variety of adverse effects may come from inaction, regulation, and everything between. Such an approach would attempt to consider all of those adverse effects, not simply a subset. Such an approach would pursue distributional goals directly by, for example, requiring wealthy countries – the major contributors to the problem of global warming – to pay poor countries to reduce greenhouse gases or to prepare themselves for the relevant risks. When societies face risks of catastrophe, even risks whose likelihood cannot be calculated, it is appropriate to act, not to stand by and merely to hope. A sensible approach would attempt to counteract, rather than to embody, the various cognitive limitations that people face in thinking about risks. An effort to produce a fair

---

[64] See Wildavsky, *supra* note 39, at 433.

accounting of the universe of dangers should also help to diminish the danger of interest-group manipulation.

To be sure, public alarm, even if ill informed, is itself a harm, and it is likely to lead to additional harms, perhaps in the form of large-scale "ripple effects."[65] A sensible approach to risk will attempt to reduce public fear even if it is baseless. My goal here has been not to deny that point, but to explain the otherwise puzzling appeal of the Precautionary Principle and to isolate the strategies that help make it operational. At the individual level, these strategies are hardly senseless, especially for people who lack much information or who do the best they can by focusing on only one aspect of the situation at hand. But for governments, the Precautionary Principle is not sensible, for the simple reason that once the viewscreen is widened, it becomes clear that the principle provides no guidance at all. Rational nations should certainly take precautions. But they should not adopt the Precautionary Principle. In Part II, we will see what they should do instead. For the moment, let us explore the special power of worst-case scenarios, which often underlie excessive precautions.

---

[65] See the discussion of the social amplification of risk in Slovic, *supra* note 7, and *Social Amplification of Risk*, ed. Roger Kasperson et al. (Cambridge: Cambridge University Press, 2003).

CHAPTER 3

Worst-Case Scenarios

Consider the following problems:
- People live in a community near an abandoned hazardous waste site. The community appears to suffer from an unusually high number of deaths and illnesses. Many members of the community fear that the hazardous waste site is responsible for the problem. Government officials attempt to offer reassurance that the likelihood of adverse health effects, as a result of the site, is extremely low. The reassurance is met with skepticism and distrust.
- An airplane, carrying people from London to Paris, has recently crashed. Though the source of the problem is unknown, many people suspect terrorism. For the next weeks, many people are taking trains, or staying home, who would otherwise fly. Some of those same people acknowledge that the statistical risk is exceedingly small. Nonetheless, they refuse to fly, in part because they do not want to experience the anxiety that would come from flying.
- An administrative agency is deciding whether to require labels to be placed on genetically modified food. According to experts within the agency, genetically modified food, as such, poses insignificant risks to the environment and to human health. But many consumers disagree. Knowledge of genetic modification triggers strong emotions, and the labeling requirement is thought likely to have large effects on consumer choice, notwithstanding expert claims that the danger is trivial.

How should we understand human behavior in cases of this sort? My principal answer, the thesis of this chapter, is that when intense emotions are engaged, people tend to focus on the adverse outcome, not on its likelihood. They are not closely attuned to the probability that harm will occur. They emphasize worst-case scenarios. The result is to produce serious distortions for both individuals and societies.

At the individual level, the phenomenon of probability neglect results in indifference to small but statistically real risks, excessive worry, and unjustified behavioral changes. Probability neglect also creates problems for law and regulation. As we shall see, governments, no less than individuals, may neglect the issue of probability, in a way that can lead to either indifference to real risks or costly expenditures for little or no gain. As we shall also see, an understanding of probability neglect helps show how governments and others can heighten or dampen public concern about hazards. Terrorists exploit probability neglect; so do environmentalists and corporate executives. Public-spirited political actors, not less than self-interested ones, use probability neglect so as to promote attention to problems that may or may not deserve public concern. It will be helpful to begin, however, with some general background on individual and social judgments about risks.

COGNITION

On the conventional view of rationality, probabilities matter a great deal to reactions to risks, and emotions, as such, are not assessed independently; they are not taken to play a distinctive role. Of course people might be risk averse or risk inclined. It is possible, for example, that people will be willing to pay $100 to eliminate a 1/10,000 risk of losing $9,000 – a clear case of risk aversion, because people are paying $100 to eliminate a risk with a value of merely $90. Many people are willing to gamble, and such people might be willing to pay $101 for a 1/1,000 chance of winning $100,000. But most people believe that variations in probability should matter, so that there would be a serious puzzle if people were willing to pay *both* $100 to eliminate a 1/1,000 risk of losing $900 *and* $100 to eliminate a 1/100,000 risk of losing $900. And for many purposes it does not much matter whether risk-related dispositions are a product of emotions or something else.

I have emphasized that when lacking statistical information, people rely on certain heuristics, or rules of thumb, which serve to simplify their inquiry; the availability heuristic is probably the most important for purposes of understanding fear. For purposes of law and regulation, the problem is that the availability heuristic can lead to serious errors of fact, in terms of both excessive reactions to small risks that are cognitively available and insufficient reactions to large risks that are not. When people use heuristics to simplify their inquiry into the existence of danger, errors are likely, but no emotions need be involved.

Cognition is also the focus of prospect theory, a departure from expected utility theory that is meant to explain decision under risk.[1] For present purposes, what is most important is that prospect theory offers an explanation for simultaneous gambling and insurance. When given the choice, most people reject a certain gain of X in favor of a gamble with an expected value below X, *if the gamble involves a small probability of riches*. At the same time, most people prefer a certain loss of X to a gamble with an expected value less than X, *if the gamble involves a small probability of catastrophe*. If expected utility theory is taken to define rationality, then people depart from rationality in giving excessive weight to low-probability outcomes when the stakes are high. Indeed we might easily see prospect theory as emphasizing a form of probability neglect. But in making these claims about human behavior, prospect theory does not set out a special role for emotions.

EMOTION

No one doubts, however, that in many domains, people do not think much about variations in probability and that emotions have a large effect on judgment and decision making.[2] With some low-probability events, anticipated and actual emotions, triggered by the best-case or worst-case outcome, help to determine choice. Those who buy lottery tickets often fantasize about the goods associated with a lucky outcome. With respect to risks of harm, many of our ordinary ways of speaking suggest strong emotions: panic, hysteria, terror. People might refuse to fly, for example, not because they are currently frightened, but because they anticipate their own anxiety, and they

---

[1] See Daniel Kahneman and Amos Tversky, Prospect Theory: An Analysis of Decision under Risk, in *Choices, Values, and Frames* 17, ed. Daniel Kahneman and Amos Tversky (Cambridge: Cambridge University Press, 2000).

[2] George Loewenstein et al., Risk as Feelings, 127 *Psych. Bull.* 267 (2001); Eric Posner, Law and the Emotions, 89 *Geo. L.J.* 1977, 1979–84 (2001).

want to avoid it. People often decide as they do because they anticipate their own regret. The same is true for fear. Knowing that they will be afraid, people may refuse to travel to Israel or South Africa, even if they would much enjoy seeing those nations and even if they believe, on reflection, that their fear is not entirely rational. Social science evidence is quite specific.[3] It suggests that people are especially likely to neglect significant differences in probability when the outcome is "affect rich" – when it involves not simply a serious loss, but one that produces strong emotions, including fear.

To be sure, the distinction between cognition and emotion is complex and contested.[4] In the domain of risks, and most other places, emotional reactions are usually based on thinking; they are hardly cognition free. When a negative emotion is associated with a certain risk – pesticides or nuclear power, for example – cognition is playing a central role.[5] For purposes of the analysis here, it is not necessary to say anything especially controversial about the emotion of fear. The only suggestion is that when emotions are intense, calculation is less likely to occur, or at least that form of calculation that involves assessment of risks in terms of not only the severity but also the probability of the outcome.

---

[3] See Yuval Rottenstreich and Christopher Hsee, Money, Kisses, and Electric Shocks: On the Affective Psychology of Risk, 12 *Psych. Sci.* 185, 186–88 (2001); Loewenstein et al., *supra* note 2, at 276–78.

[4] For varying views, see Ronald De Sousa, *The Rationality of Emotion* (Cambridge, Mass.: MIT Press, 1987); Jon Elster, *Alchemies of the Mind* (Cambridge: Cambridge University Press, 1999); Martha C. Nussbaum, *Upheavals of Thought* (New York: Cambridge University Press, 2001).

[5] Some research suggests that the brain has special sectors for emotions, and that some types of emotions, including some fear-type reactions, can be triggered before the more cognitive sectors become involved at all: Joseph LeDoux, *The Emotional Brain* (New York: Simon & Schuster, 1996). Those who hear sudden, unexplained noises are fearful before they are able to identify the source of the noise: Robert B. Zajonc, On the Primacy of Affect, 39 *Am. Psych.* 117 (1984); Robert B. Zajonc, Feeling and Thinking: Preferences Need No Inferences, 35 *Am. Psych.* 151 (1980). People who have been given intravenous injections of procaine, which stimulates the amygdala, report panic sensations: David Servan-Schreiber and William M. Perlstein, Selective Limbic Activation and its Relevance to Emotional Disorders, 12 *Cognition & Emotion* 331 (1998). In research with human beings, electrical stimulation of the amygdala leads to reported feelings of fear and foreboding, even without any reason for these things, leading people to say, for example, that they feel as if someone were chasing them: Jaak Panksepp, Mood Changes, in *Handbook of Clinical Neurology* vol. 45, ed. Pierre J. Vinken, G. W. Bruyn, H. L. Klawans, and J. A. M. Frederiks (New York: Elsevier, 1985). It is not true, however, that fear in human beings is generally precognitive or noncognitive, and even if it is in some cases, it is not clear that noncognitive fear would be triggered by most of the risks faced in everyday human lives.

Problems

Drawing on and expanding the relevant evidence, I will explore a general phenomenon: In many domains, people often focus on the goodness or badness of the outcome in question, and pay (too) little attention to the probability that a good or bad outcome will occur. Probability neglect is especially large when people focus on the worst possible case or otherwise are subject to strong emotions. When such emotions are at work, people do not give sufficient consideration to the likelihood that the worst case will occur. This is a problem because it is not fully rational to treat a 1 percent chance that a bad event will occur as equivalent, or nearly equivalent, to a 99 percent chance that a bad event will occur, or even a 10 percent chance that it will occur. Because people suffer from probability neglect, and because neglecting probability is not fully rational, the phenomenon I identify raises questions about the widespread idea that with respect to risk, ordinary people have a kind of "richer rationality" superior to that of experts.[6] Most of the time, experts are concerned principally with the number of lives at stake, and for that reason they will be closely attuned, as ordinary people are not, to the issue of probability.

We should think of probability neglect in light of "dual process" approaches of the sort that have received considerable recent attention in psychology.[7] According to such approaches, people use two cognitive systems. System I is rapid, intuitive, and error prone; System II is more deliberative, calculative, slower, and more likely to be error free. Heuristic-based thinking is rooted in System I; it is subject to override, under certain conditions, by System II.[8] System I is thus

---

[6] See Clayton P. Gillette and James E. Krier, Risk, Courts, and Agencies, 138 *U. Pa. L. Rev.* 1027, 1061–85 (1990) (defending the idea of competing rationalities). I do not mean to deny that some of the time, ordinary people care, rationally, about values that experts disregard. All I mean to suggest is that insofar as people focus on the badness of the outcome but not on its likelihood, they are thinking less clearly than experts, who tend to focus on the statistical outcomes at stake.

[7] See generally *Social Judgments*, ed. Joseph P. Forgas, Kipling D. Williams, and William Von Hippel (New York: Cambridge University Press, 2003); *Dual-Process Theories in Social Psychology*, ed. Shelly Chaiken and Yaacov Trope (New York: Guildford Press, 1999); Daniel Kahneman and Shane Frederick, Representativeness Revisited: Attribute Substitution in Intuitive Judgment, in *Heuristics and Biases: The Psychology of Intuitive Judgment* 49, ed. Thomas Gilovich, Dale Griffin, and Daniel Kahneman (Cambridge: Cambridge University Press, 2002).

[8] See Kahneman and Frederick, *supra* note 7. The two systems need not be seen as occupying different physical spaces; they might even be understood as heuristics (!), see *id*. There is,

involved in the use of the availability heuristic, as when people make a quick, intuitive judgment that a risk is serious because they can think of an instance in which it came to fruition. This intuitive judgment might be corrected by a more deliberative assessment, suggesting that the risk is actually quite low. So, too, for probability neglect: When people fixate on the outcome without considering the question of probability, they are using System I, in a way that demands System II correction.

By drawing attention to probability neglect, I do not mean to suggest that most people, most of the time, are indifferent to large variations in the probability that a risk will come to fruition. Large variations can and often do make a difference – but when emotions are engaged, the difference is far less than might be expected. Nor do I suggest that probability neglect is impervious to circumstances. If the costs of neglecting probability are placed "on-screen," then people will be more likely to attend to the question of probability. Market forces can dampen the effect of probability neglect, making it likely that (say) risks of 1/10,000 are "priced" differently from risks of 1/1,000,000, even if individuals, in surveys, show relative insensitivity to such differences.

Acknowledging all this, I emphasize two central points. First, differences in probability will often affect behavior far less than they should, especially when emotions are intensely engaged. Second, the public's demand for government intervention can be greatly affected by probability neglect, so that regulators may end up engaging in extensive regulation precisely because intense emotional reactions are making people relatively insensitive to the (low) probability that dangers will ever come to fruition. When a bad outcome is highly salient and triggers strong emotions, government will be asked to do something about it, even if the probability of the bad outcome is low. Political participants of various stripes, focusing on the "worst case," are entirely willing to exploit probability neglect.

however, some evidence that different sectors of the brain can be associated with Systems I and II. See the discussion of fear in LeDoux, *The Emotional Brain* 106–32, *supra* note 5, and the more general treatment in Matthew Lieberman, Reflexive and Reflective Judgment Processes: A Social Cognitive Neuroscience Approach, in *Social Judgments*, ed. Joseph P. Forgas, Kipling D. Williams, and William Von Hippel (New York: Cambridge University Press, 2003).

PROBABILITY NEGLECT: THE BASIC PHENOMENON

Do people care about probability at all? Of course they do; a risk of 1/100,000 is far less troublesome than a risk of 1/100. But much of the time, people show a remarkable unwillingness to attend to the question of probability. Several studies demonstrate that when people are seeking relevant information, they often do not try to learn about probability at all. One study, for example, finds that in deciding to purchase warranties for consumer products, people do not spontaneously point to the probability of needing repair as a reason for the purchase.[9] Another study finds that those making hypothetical risky managerial decisions rarely ask for data on probabilities.[10] Or consider a study involving children and adolescents,[11] in which the following question was asked:

Susan and Jennifer are arguing about whether they should wear seat belts when they ride in a car. Susan says that you should. Jennifer says that you shouldn't . . . Jennifer says that she heard of an accident where a car fell into a lake and a woman was kept from getting out in time because of wearing her seat belt . . . What do you think about this?

In answering that question, many subjects did not think about probability at all. One exchange took the following form:[12]

A: Well, in that case I don't think you should wear a seat belt.
Q: (interviewer): How do you know when that's gonna happen?
A: Like, just hope it doesn't!
Q: So, should you or shouldn't you wear seat belts?
A: Well, tell-you-the-truth we should wear seat belts.
Q: How come?
A: Just in case of an accident. You won't get hurt as much as you will if you didn't wear a seat belt.
Q: Ok, well what about these kinds of things, where people get trapped?
A: I don't think you should, in that case.

---

[9] Robin M. Hogarth and Howard Kunreuther, Decision Making under Ignorance, 10 *J. Risk & Uncertainty* 15 (1995).

[10] Oswald Hober et al., Active Information Search and Complete Information Presentation in Naturalistic Risky Decision Tasks, 95 *Acta Psychologica* 15 (1997).

[11] See the summary in Jonathan Baron, *Thinking and Deciding* 246–47 (Cambridge: Cambridge University Press, 3d ed., 2001).

[12] *Id.* at 246–47.

These answers might seem odd and idiosyncratic, but we might reasonably suppose that some of the time, both children and adults alternate between bad scenarios, without much thinking about the question of probability.

Many studies find that significant differences in low probabilities have little impact on decisions. This finding is in sharp conflict with the standard view of rationality, which suggests that people's willingness to pay for small risk reductions ought to be roughly proportional to the size of the reduction.[13] Perhaps these findings reflect people's implicit understanding that in these settings, the relevant probability is "low, but not zero," and that finer distinctions are unhelpful, partly because they are too complicated to try to unpack. (What does a risk of 1 in 100,000 really mean? How different is it, for an individual, from a risk of 1 in 40,000, or 1 in 600,000?) In an especially striking study, Howard Kunreuther and his coauthors found that people did not distinguish among risks of 1 in 100,000, 1 in 1,000,000, and 1 in 10,000,000.[14] In the same study, they found little difference in perceptions of riskiness for hazards ranging from 1 in 650, to 1 in 6,300, to 1 in 68,000. In an illuminating paper,[15] Kunreuther and his coauthors find that people's estimates of the likelihood that an event will occur have essentially no relationship to their willingness to pay (WTP) for insurance protection, even in a realistic setting in which real money is involved. The study finds a relationship between people's stated level of "concern" and their WTP; but neither of these is affected by large differences in the probability of loss.

The studies just described had a "between subjects" design; subjects in these studies considered only one risk, and the same people were not asked to consider several risks at the same time. When low-probability risks are being seen in isolation, and are not being assessed together, we have a problem of "evaluability."[16] A low probability, taken by

---

[13] Phaedra S. Corso et al., Valuing Mortality-Risk Reduction: Using Visual Aids to Improve the Validity of Contingent Valuation, 23(2) *J. Risk & Uncertainty* 165, 166–68 (2001).

[14] Howard Kunreuther et al., Making Low Probabilities Useful, 23(2) *J. Risk & Uncertainty* 103, 107 (2001).

[15] See Howard Kunreuther et al., Probability Neglect and Concern in Insurance Decisions with Low Probabilities and High Stakes (unpublished manuscript).

[16] See Christopher Hsee, Attribute Evaluability: Its Implications for Joint-Separate Evaluation and Beyond, in *Choices, Values, and Frames*, 543, 547–49, ed. Daniel Kahneman and Amos Tversky (Cambridge: Cambridge University Press, 2000).

itself, is not terribly meaningful to most people; but almost everyone would know that a 1/100,000 risk is worse than 1/1,000,000 risk. For most people, most of the time, isolated decisions, focusing on one low-probability risk at a time, will show little variation among people's assessments of quantitatively different risks.

But several studies have a "within subjects" design, exposing people simultaneously to risks of different probabilities, and even here, the differences in probabilities have little effect on decisions. An early study examined people's willingness to pay (WTP) to reduce travel fatality risks. The central finding was that the mean WTP to reduce fatality risk by 7/100,000 was merely 15 percent higher than the mean WTP to reduce the risk by 4/100,000.[17] A later study found that for serious injuries, WTP to reduce the risk by 12/100,000 was only 20 percent higher than WTP to reduce the same risk by 4/100,000.[18] These results are not unusual. Lin and Milon attempted to elicit people's willingness to pay to reduce the risk of illness from eating oysters.[19] People were quite insensitive to variations in probability of illness. A similar study found only modest changes in WTP across significant variations in the probability of harm from exposure to pesticide residues on fresh produce.[20] A similar anomaly was found in a study involving hazardous wastes, where WTP actually decreased as the stated fatality risk reduction increased![21]

There is much to say about people's insensitivity to significant variations within the category of low-probability events. It would be difficult to produce a rational explanation for this insensitivity; the standard view is that WTP for small risk reductions should be roughly proportional to the size of the reduction.[22] Why don't people think in this way? A reasonable explanation is that in the abstract, most

---

[17] Michael W. Jones-Lee et al., The Value of Safety: Results of a National Sample Survey, 95 *Ec. J.* 49 (1985).

[18] Michael W. Jones-Lee et al., Valuing the Prevention of Non-Fatal Road Injuries, 47 *Oxford Economic Papers* 676 (1995).

[19] C. T. Jordan Lin and J. Walter Milon, Contingent Valuation of Health Risk Reductions for Shellfish Products, in *Valuing Food Safety and Nutrition* 83, ed. Julie A. Caswell (Boulder, Colo.: Westview Press, 1995).

[20] Young Sook Eom, Pesticide Residue Risk and Food Safety Valuation: A Random Utility Approach, 76 *Am. J. of Agric. Economics* 760 (1994).

[21] V. Kerry Smith and William H. Desvouges, An Empirical Analysis of the Economic Value of Risk Changes, 95 *J. Polit. Econ.* 89 (1987).

[22] Corso et al., *supra* note 13, at 166–68.

people simply do not know how to evaluate low probabilities. A risk of 7/100,000 seems "small"; a risk of 4/100,000 also seems "small." True, these figures can be evaluated better if they are placed in the context of one another; everyone would prefer a risk of 4/100,000 to a risk of 7/100,000, and simultaneous assessment of the two improves evaluability. But even when the preference is clear, both risks seem "small," and hence it is not at all clear that a *proportional* increase in WTP will follow.

Some imaginative studies attempt to overcome probability neglect through visual aids[23] or through providing a great deal of information about comparison scenarios located on a probability scale.[24] Without these aids, it is not so surprising that differences in low probabilities do not greatly matter to people. For most of us, most of the time, the relevant differences – between, say, 1/100,000 and 1/1,000,000 – are not pertinent to our decisions, and by experience we are not well equipped to take those differences into account.

SAFE OR UNSAFE? OF THRESHOLDS AND CERTAINTY

A form of probability neglect can also be seen in the fact that people seem to treat situations as "safe" or "unsafe," without seeing that the real question is the likelihood of harm. Consider this discussion of the effects of natural disasters:

One of the bargains men make with one another in order to maintain their sanity is to share an illusion that they are safe, even when the physical evidence in the world around them does not seem to warrant that conclusion. The survivors of a disaster, of course, are prone to overestimate the perils of their situation, if only to compensate for the fact that they underestimated those perils once before; but what is worse, far worse, is that they sometimes live in a state of almost constant apprehension because they have lost the human capacity to screen the signs of danger out of their line of vision.[25]

What is most remarkable here is the sharp division between ordinary people, who "share an illusion that they are safe," and those subject to

---

[23] See Corso et al., *supra* note 13.
[24] Kunreuther et al., *supra* note 14.
[25] Kai T. Erikson, *Everything in its Path: Destruction of Community in the Buffalo Creek Flood* 234 (New York: Simon & Schuster, 1976).

a natural disaster, who "sometimes live in a state of almost constant apprehension." Of course being "safe" is a question of degree. There is no simple point at which situations switch from "safety" to "danger." If ordinary people "share an illusion that they are safe," part of the reason is that many low-level risks do not register at all. As we have seen, human beings sometimes tend to be unrealistically optimistic; they also try to reduce cognitive dissonance, by treating certain risks as if they are tiny, even worth ignoring.[26] When people think that they are "safe," even though they face a statistical risk, they might well be responding to actual and anticipated emotions, seeking to avoid the anxiety that comes from an understanding of the inevitability of risk.

At the individual level, a decision to disregard low-level risks is far from irrational. We lack the information that would permit fine-grained risk judgments, and when the probability really is very low, it is sensible to treat it as if it were zero. The category of "being safe" is far too crude, but for most people, most of the time, it makes sense to ignore low-probability risks and worst cases, and to act as if that category is the relevant one. Of course regulators should do better, if only because they are typically dealing with large populations, and a risk that is best ignored at the individual level (1/500,000, say) might deserve a good deal of attention if it is faced by 200 million people.

As the passage also suggests, risks can suddenly come "on-screen," making people believe that where they once were "safe," they are now "unsafe." In the United States, the terrorist attacks of 9/11 are an obvious case in point, making people think, for a short time, that airports and other public spaces were "not safe," and continuing to make people worry that the nation is essentially "at risk." Indeed, the attacks of 9/11 seem to have elevated people's concern about many mortality risks, not simply those from terrorism. Among American teenagers, terrorism created a large-scale increase in judgments about the riskiness of daily life.[27] Of course a form of probability neglect is at work whenever risks are placed into the two categories of "safe" and

---

[26] See George A. Akerlof and William T. Dickens, The Economic Consequences of Cognitive Dissonance, in George A. Akerlof, *An Economic Theorist's Book of Tales* 123, 124–28 (Cambridge: Cambridge University Press, 1984).

[27] See Bonnie L. Halpern-Felsher and Susan G. Millstein, The Effects of Terrorism on Teens' Perception of Dying, 30 *J. Adolescent Health* 308 (2002).

"unsafe." The desire to feel "safe" is often responsible for probability neglect when people are treating statistical risks as if they were zero.

Experimental work strongly supports this conclusion. With respect to the decision whether to insure against low-probability hazards, people show bimodal responses.[28] When a risk is below a certain threshold, people treat the risk as essentially zero, and are willing to pay little or nothing for insurance in the event of loss. But when the risk is above a certain level, people are willing to pay a significant amount for insurance, indeed an amount that greatly exceeds the expected value of the risk. Such bimodal responses connect well with the intuitive suggestion that some risks are simply "off-screen," whereas others, statistically not much larger, can come "on-screen" and produce behavioral changes. And indeed, one study finds that when told that the probability of being killed in an accident is only .00000025 per trip, 90 percent of people said that they would not wear seat belts – a finding apparently based on the (understandable) judgment that so small a probability is equivalent to zero.[29]

The role of thresholds is connected with an aspect of prospect theory, emphasizing the great importance of *certainty* to people's decisions.[30] People are willing to pay relatively little for a small increment in safety, but they will pay far more when the additional increment is the last one, eliminating any risk at all. A change in a risk from .04 to .03 will produce far less enthusiasm than a change from .01 to zero; and hence people are willing to pay and to do much less for the former reduction than for the latter. This finding, commonly described as the "certainty effect," is in line with the suggestion that people are insensitive to variations among low probabilities and instead ask, much of the time, whether they are in the domain of the "safe" or the "unsafe."

I now turn from the general neglect of differences in low probabilities to the particular role of strong emotions in crowding out attention to the issue of probability, both low and less low. My central claim is that when strong emotions are involved, large-scale

[28] See Donald L. Coursey et al., Insurance for Low Probability Hazards: A Bimodal Response to Unlikely Events, 7 *J. Risk & Uncertainty* 95 (1993).
[29] See Baron, *supra* note 11, at 255.
[30] See Kahneman and Tversky, *supra* note 1; Howard Margolis, *Dealing With Risk* 83–84 (Chicago: University of Chicago Press, 1996).

variations in probabilities will matter surprisingly little – even when the variations unquestionably matter if emotions are not triggered. The general point is that probability neglect is dramatically heightened when emotions are involved; it is partly for this reason that worst-case scenarios have tremendous power. The point applies to hope as well as fear. Vivid images of best-case outcomes will crowd out consideration of probability too. Lotteries are successful partly for this reason. Consider this account:

> They didn't really know what the odds – 1 in 76 million – mean. Big dreams are easier than big odds; to be precise, in the 11 p.m. drawing, there is only one possible winning combination out of 76,275,360 . . . Clarence Robinson, a manager at Macy's, said: "One in 76 million people right? It's just a number. I'll win."[31]

But the subject here is fear rather than hope.

A SIMPLE DEMONSTRATION

The basic point has received its clearest empirical confirmation in a striking study of people's willingness to pay to avoid electric shocks.[32] The central purpose of the study was to explore the relevance of probability in "affect-rich" decisions. The experiment tested whether varying the probability of harm would matter more, or less, in settings that trigger strong emotions than in settings that seem relatively emotion free. In the "strong emotion" setting, participants were asked to imagine that they would participate in an experiment involving some chance of a "short, painful, but not dangerous electric shock." In the relatively emotion-free setting, participants were told that the experiment entailed some chance of a $20 penalty. Participants were asked to say how much they would be willing to pay to avoid participating in the relevant experiment. Some participants were told that there was a 1 percent chance of receiving the bad outcome (either the $20 loss or the electric shock); others were told that the chance was 99 percent; and still others were told that the chance was 100 percent.

---

[31] Ian Shapira, Long Lines, Even Longer Odds, Looking for a Lucky Number? How About 1 in 76,275,360? *Washington Post*, Apr. 12, 2002, p. B1.

[32] Rottenstreich and Hsee, *supra* note 3, at 176–88.

The central result was that variations in probability aff
facing the relatively emotion-free injury (the $20 penalty
than they affected people facing the more emotionally evc
come of an electric shock. For the cash penalty, the differen~~ between
the median payment for a 1 percent chance and the median payment
for a 99 percent chance was predictably large and indeed consistent
with the standard model: $1 to avoid a 1 percent chance, and $18 to
avoid a 99 percent chance. For the electric shock, by contrast, the
difference in probability made little difference to median willingness
to pay: $7 to avoid a 1 percent chance, and $10 to avoid a 99 percent
chance! Apparently people will pay a significant amount to avoid
a small probability of a hazard that is emotionally gripping – and
the amount that they will pay will not vary greatly with changes in
probability.

A MORE COMPLEX DEMONSTRATION

To investigate the role of probability and emotions in responses to risk,
I conducted an experiment asking eighty-three University of Chicago
law students to describe their maximum willingness to pay to reduce
levels of arsenic in drinking water. The questions had a high degree
of realism. They were based on actual choices confronting the Environmental Protection Agency, involving cost and benefit information
within the ballpark of actual figures used by the agency itself.

Participants were randomly sorted into four groups, representing
the four conditions in the experiment. In the first condition, people
were asked to state their maximum willingness to pay to eliminate a
cancer risk of 1 in 1,000,000. In the second condition, people were
asked to state their maximum willingness to pay to eliminate a cancer
risk of 1 in 100,000. In the third condition, people were asked the
same question as in the first, but the cancer was described in vivid
terms, as "very gruesome and intensely painful, as the cancer eats
away at the internal organs of the body." In the fourth condition,
people were asked the same question as in the second, but the cancer
was described in the same terms as in the third condition. In each
condition, participants were asked to check off their willingness to
pay among the following options: $0, $25, $50, $100, $200, $400,
and $800 or more. Notice that the description of the cancer, in the

Table 3.1. *Willingness to Pay (in dollars) for Elimination of Arsenic Risks**

Probability	Unemotional description	Emotional description	Overall
1/1,000,000	$71.25 (25)	$132.95 (100)	$103.57 (50)
1/100,000	$194.44 (100)	$241.30 (100)	$220.73 (100)
Overall	$129.61 (50)	$188.33 (100)	$161.45 (100)

*means (medians in parentheses)

"highly emotional" conditions, was intended to add little information, consisting simply of a description of many cancer deaths, though admittedly some participants might well have thought that these were especially horrific deaths.

My central hypothesis was that the probability variations would matter far less in the highly emotional conditions than in the less emotional conditions. More specifically, it was predicted that differences in probability would make little or no difference in the highly emotional conditions – and that such variations would have real importance in the less emotional conditions. This prediction was meant to describe a substantial departure from expected utility theory, which predicts that an ordinary, risk-averse person should be willing to pay at least 10X to eliminate a risk that is ten times more likely than a risk that he is willing to pay X to eliminate. It was also expected that the tenfold difference in probabilities – between 1/100,000 and 1/1,000,000 – would not, in either condition, generate a tenfold difference in willingness to pay. The results are set out in Table 3.1.

The results for the first hypothesis are in the predicted direction.[33] With an unemotional description, increasing the probability by a factor of 10 produced a statistically significant increase in mean WTP, from $71.25 to $194.44. But in the highly emotional condition, the increase in probability produced a much smaller relative increase in WTP, from $132.95 to $241.30, which did not reach statistical significance. Thus, while increasing the probability by a factor of ten increased WTP in both conditions, the effect was more than *twice* as

[33] The data were analyzed using a 2 × 2 ANOVA (Probability × Emotionality of description) for overall means, and by t-tests within cells.

large in the less emotional condition (a 173 percent increase in mean WTP) compared to the emotional condition (an 81 percent increase). Because of the small sample, the difference between these increases is not statistically significant, but the result is nonetheless highly suggestive, especially because of its consistency with other similar findings.

The second hypothesis was also supported. The increase in probability did produce a significant overall difference in mean WTP, from $103.57 to $220.73. Consistent with other work on probability neglect, however, varying the probability had a relatively weak effect on WTP. Most dramatically, the *tenfold* increase in the risk produced barely more than a doubling of mean WTP (a 113 percent increase). It is noteworthy that in this experiment, the quite sophisticated University of Chicago law students showed far more sensitivity to probability information than in some of the studies; but even so, the sensitivity was far less than conventional theory would predict.

From this experiment, there is one other potentially noteworthy result. All by itself, making the description of the cancer more emotional appeared to have an effect on mean WTP, raising it from $129.61 to $188.33. *Indeed, the effect of merely making the description of the outcome more emotional was about half as large as a tenfold increase in actual risk.* My principal emphasis, however, is on the fact that when the question was designed to trigger especially strong emotions, variations in probability had little effect on WTP – far less of an effect than when the question was phrased in less emotional terms. This is the kind of probability neglect that I am emphasizing here.

OTHER EVIDENCE

Probability neglect, when strong emotions are involved, has been confirmed in many studies.[34] Consider, for example, experiments designed to test levels of anxiety in anticipation of a painful electric shock of varying intensity, to be administered after a "countdown period" of a specified length. In these studies, the stated intensity of the shock had a significant effect on physiological reactions. But the

---

[34] For an overview, see Loewenstein et al., *supra* note 2, at 276.

probability of the shock had no effect. "Evidently, the mere thought of receiving a shock was enough to arouse subjects, and the precise likelihood of being shocked had little impact on their arousal level."[35] A related study asked people to provide their maximum buying prices for risky investments, which contained different stated probabilities of losses and gains of different magnitudes.[36] Happily for the standard theory of rationality, maximum buying prices were affected by the size of losses and gains and also by probabilities. (Note that for most people, this experiment did not involve an affect-rich environment, because money was all that was at stake.) But – and this is the key point – reported feelings of *worry* were not much affected by probability levels. In this study, then, probability did affect behavior, but it did not affect emotions. The point has independent importance: Worry isn't much fun to experience, even if it does not affect behavior. And in most of the cases dealt with here, intense emotions drive out concern with probability, and hence both behavior and worry are affected.

Several studies have attempted to ask whether variations in probability matter more for emotionally evocative risks than for others.[37] Here it is hypothesized that certain low-probability risks, such as those associated with nuclear waste radiation, produce *outrage*, whereas other low-probability risks, such as those associated with radon exposure, do not. A key finding is consistent with what I am emphasizing here: a large difference in probability had no effect in the "high outrage" condition, with people reacting the same way to a risk of 1 in 100,000 as to a risk of 1 in 1,000,000.[38] In the "low outrage" condition, by contrast, differences in probabilities mattered significantly to people's perception of the threat and their intention to act to avoid it. More striking still: Even when the statistical risk was *identical* in the nuclear waste (high outrage) and radon (low outrage) cases, people in the nuclear waste case reported a much greater perceived threat and a much higher intention to act to reduce that threat.[39]

[35] *Id.*   [36] *Id.*

[37] Peter Sandman et al., Communications to Reduce Risk Underestimation and Overestimation, 3 *Risk Decision & Policy* 93 (1998); Peter Sandman et al., Agency Communication, Community Outrage, and Perception of Risk: Three Simulation Experiments, 13 *Risk Anal.* 589 (1993).

[38] See Sandman et al., Communications to Reduce, *supra* note 37, at 102.

[39] *Id.* at 106.

Indeed, "the effect of outrage was practically as large as the effect of a 4000-fold difference in risk between the high-risk and low-risk conditions."[40]

Efforts to communicate the meaning of differences in risk levels, by showing comparisons to normal risk levels, did reduce the effect of outrage. But even after those efforts, outrage had nearly the same effect as a 2,000-fold increase in risk. A great deal of information appears to be necessary to counteract the effects of strong emotions. People are not impervious to such information. But when emotions are involved, careful work has to be done to make people take account of probabilities.[41] Recall here that visualization or imagery matters a great deal to people's reactions to risks.[42] Recall as well that when people are asked how much they will pay for flight insurance for losses resulting from "terrorism," they will pay more than if they are asked how much they will pay for flight insurance from all causes.[43]

When probability neglect is involved, we are not dealing with the availability heuristic, which leads people not to neglect probability, but to *answer* the question of probability by substituting a hard question (What is the statistical risk?) with an easy question (Do salient examples readily come to mind?). My point here is not that visualization makes an event seem more probable (though this is also often true), but that visualization makes the issue of probability seem less relevant or even irrelevant. In theory, the distinction between use of the availability heuristic and probability neglect should not be obscure. In practice, of course, it will often be hard to know whether the availability heuristic or probability neglect is driving behavior. In either case, worst-case scenarios are having an excessive effect on both thought and behavior.

[40] *Id.*

[41] *Id.* at 106–7. Consider in particular the following suggestion: "When people are upset about a high-outrage, low-risk situation, explanations coming from the distrusted source of the trouble may not help much; merely providing risk probability data also may not help much, even if the source is trusted. But considerable reductions in threat perception and action intentions are possible when a trusted, neutral source offers a comparison to background or a chat with a risk ladder, risk comparisons, and an action standard." *Id.*

[42] See Paul Slovic et al., Violence Risk Assessment and Risk Communication, 24 *Law Hum. Behav.* 271 (2000).

[43] See Eric J. Johnson et al., Framing, Probability Distortions, and Insurance Decisions, 7(1) *J. Risk & Uncertainty* 35 (1993).

Emotional reactions to risk, and probability neglect, also account for "alarmist bias."[44] When presented with competing accounts of danger, people tend to move toward the more alarming account. In the key study, W. Kip Viscusi presented subjects with information from two parties, industry and government. Some subjects were given low-risk information from government and high-risk information from industry; other subjects were given high-risk information from government and low-risk information from industry. The basic result was that people treated "the high risk information as being more informative."[45] This pattern held regardless of whether the low-risk information came from industry or from government. Thus people show "an irrational asymmetry: respondents overweight the value of a high risk judgement."[46] A central reason is that the information, whatever its content, makes people focus on the worst case. (It is also possible that people distrust both industry and government, and believe that the situation is likely to be a "worst-case" version of what either suggests.) There is an unambiguous lesson for policy here: It might not be helpful to present people with a wide range of information, containing both assuring and less assuring accounts. The result of such presentations will be to scare people.

The most sensible conclusion is that with respect to risks of harm, vivid images and concrete pictures of disaster can "crowd out" other kinds of thoughts, including the crucial thought that the probability of disaster is really small. "If someone is predisposed to be worried, degrees of unlikeliness seem to provide no comfort, unless one can prove that harm is absolutely impossible, which itself is not possible."[47] With respect to hope, those who operate gambling casinos and state lotteries are well aware of the underlying mechanisms. They play on people's emotions in the particular sense that they conjure up palpable pictures of victory and easy living. With respect to risks, insurance companies and environmental groups do exactly the same. The point explains "why societal concerns about hazards such as nuclear power and exposure to extremely small amounts of toxic

---

[44] W. Kip Viscusi, Alarmist Decisions with Divergent Risk Information, 107 *Ec. J.* 1657, 1657–59 (1997).

[45] *Id.* at 1666.   [46] *Id.* at 1668.

[47] See John Weingart, *Waste Is a Terrible Thing to Mind* 362 (Trenton, N.J.: Center for Analysis of Public Issues, 2001).

chemicals fail to recede in response to information about the very small probabilities of the feared consequences from such hazards."[48]

If probability neglect characterizes individual judgment under certain circumstances, government and law are likely to neglect probability under those same circumstances. Public officials respond to the public demand for law. If people insist on government protection against risk, government is likely to provide that protection. If people show unusually strong reactions to low-probability catastrophes, government is likely to act accordingly. Of course interest groups are involved as well. When their self-interest is at stake, we should expect them to exploit people's emotions, in particular by stressing the worst case. And government's own self-interest is far from irrelevant. If officials will be more likely to be elected when they downplay risks, saying that people are essentially "safe," then probability neglect will be exploited in the interest of inaction. If the likelihood of reelection is increased when risks are foremost in people's minds, then officials will emphasize risks. Some critics of President George W. Bush have argued that his administration exaggerated the need for a "war on terrorism" in part because the exaggeration served its political interests.

However that question might be resolved, a good deal of legislation and regulation can be explained partly by reference to probability neglect. Consider a few examples:

1. In the aftermath of the adverse health effects allegedly caused by abandoned hazardous waste in Love Canal, New York, the government responded with an aggressive program for cleaning up abandoned hazardous waste sites, without examining the probability that illness would actually occur. In fact almost nothing was accomplished by early efforts to assure people of the low probability of harm.[49] When the local health department publicized controlled studies showing little evidence of adverse effects, the publicity did not dampen concern, because the numbers "had no meaning."[50] The numbers seemed to aggravate fear: "One woman,

---

[48] See Paul Slovic et al., The Affect Heuristic, in *Heuristics and Biases: The Psychology of Intuitive Judgment*, ed. Thomas Gilovich, Dale Griffin, and Daniel Kahneman (Cambridge: Cambridge University Press, 2002).

[49] See Timur Kuran and Cass R. Sunstein, Availability Cascades and Risk Regulation, 51 *Stan. L. Rev.* 683, 691–98 (1999) (discussing the growth of fear of health risks at Love Canal).

[50] Lois Marie Gibbs, *Love Canal: The Story Continues* 25 (Stony Creek, Conn.: New Society Publishers, 1998).

divorced and with three sick children, looked at the piece of paper
with numbers and started crying hysterically: 'No wonder my children are sick. Am I doing to die? What's going to happen to my
children?'"[51] Questions of this sort contributed to the enactment
of new legislation to control abandoned hazardous waste sites –
legislation that did not embody careful consideration of the probability of significant health or environmental benefits. Even now,
the American government does not take much account of the
probability of significant harm in making clean-up decisions.[52]

2. During a highly publicized campaign designed to show a connection between Alar, a pesticide, and cancer in children, the public
   demand for action was not much affected by the EPA's cautionary
   notes about the low probability of getting that disease.[53]

3. In the fall of 2001, vivid images of shark attacks in the United
   States created a public outcry about new risks for ocean swim-
   mers.[54] A computer search found no fewer than 940 references
   to shark attacks between August 4, 2001, and September 4, 2001,
   with 130 references to "the summer of the shark." This was so
   notwithstanding the exceedingly low probability of a shark attack
   and the absence of any reliable evidence of an increase in shark
   attacks in the summer of 2001. Predictably, there was considerable
   discussion of new legislation to control the problem, and eventually such legislation was enacted, in the form of statutory bans on
   shark feeding. Public fear seemed relatively impervious to the fact
   that the underlying risk was tiny.

4. Terrorist incidents create a severe risk of probability neglect. Consider, for example, the American anthrax scare of October, 2001,

---

[51] *Id.*

[52] See James T. Hamilton and W. Kip Viscusi, *Calculating Risks? The Spatial and Political Dimensions of Hazardous Waste Policy* 91–108 (Cambridge, Mass.: MIT Press, 1999) (discussing lack of government interest in size of population affected).

[53] See Robert V. Percival et al., *Environmental Regulation: Law, Science, and Policy* 524 (New York: Aspen Publishers, 4th ed., 2003).

[54] See Howard Kurtz, Shark Attacks Spark Increased Coverage, *Washington Post On-Line*, Sept. 5, 2001, available at http://www.washingtonpost.com/wp-dyn/articles/A44720-2001Sep5.html: "A maritime expert said on last night's 'NBC Nightly News' that more people die from bees, wasps, snakes or alligators than from shark attacks. But there's no ratings in bees. Unpleasant little critters, but not scary-looking enough. With 'Jaws' music practically playing in the background, the media have turned this into the Summer of the Shark. Never mind that the number of attacks has actually dropped since last year. They're here, they're nasty and they could be coming to a beach near you."

which was based on exceedingly few incidents. Only four people died of the infection; only about a dozen others fell ill. The probability of being infected was extremely low. Nonetheless, fear proliferated, with people focusing their attention on the outcome rather than the low probability of the harm. The government responded accordingly, investing massive resources in protecting against anthrax infections. Private institutions reacted the same way, asking people to take extraordinary care in opening the mail even though the statistical risks were tiny. To say this is not to suggest that extensive precautions were unjustified in this case. Private and public institutions faced an unknown probability of a major health problem, and it was appropriate to respond. My point is that public fear was disproportionate to its cause, and that the level of response was disproportionate, too.

PROBABILITY NEGLECT, "RIVAL RATIONALITY," AND DUAL PROCESSING

When it comes to risk, why do experts disagree with ordinary people? Many people think that the reason lies in the fact that ordinary people have a "rival rationality."[55] On this view, experts are concerned with statistics, and above all with the number of lives at stake. By contrast, ordinary people are concerned with a range of qualitative factors that can make certain risks a special cause of concern. People care, for example, about whether risks are voluntarily incurred, potentially controllable, inequitably distributed, especially dreaded, and so forth. For those who believe that ordinary people display a rival rationality, experts seem obtuse, fixated as they are on the "bottom-line" numbers.[56] On this view, suggested most eloquently by risk theorist Paul Slovic, experts and ordinary people display "rival rationalities" and each "side must respect the insights and intelligence of the other."[57]

There is much truth in Slovic's claim that ordinary people consider factors that the numbers alone will obscure. People do care about whether risks come with special pain and suffering, or whether they are inequitably distributed. It makes sense to focus on whether risks

---

[55] See Paul Slovic, *The Perception of Risk* 219–23 (London: Earthscan, 2000).
[56] See Gillette and Krier, *supra* note 6, at 1071–85.   [57] Slovic, *supra* note 55, at 231.

are faced voluntarily and whether they are controllable. If the costs of risk avoidance are especially high, government should make special efforts to reduce the relevant risk; if a risk is concentrated among poor people, or members of a disadvantaged group, government should be particularly concerned. It would indeed be obtuse to focus only on the number of lives at stake. But the idea of rival rationality cannot explain all of the disagreement between experts and ordinary people. Often experts are aware of the facts and ordinary people are not. And when people are far more (or for that matter less) concerned than experts about shark attacks, or nuclear power, or terrorism, probability neglect is a large part of the reason. Hence a form of irrationality, not a different set of values, often helps explain the different risk judgments of experts and ordinary people.

This point is closely connected with Slovic's important suggestion that an "affect heuristic" accounts for people's concern, or lack of concern, with certain risks.[58] When people have a strong negative affect toward a process or product – for example, nuclear power, genetically modified organisms, arsenic, DDT – they are not likely to think much about the question of probability, and hence they will overreact. Here there is irrationality, not a rival rationality. And when people have a strong positive affect toward a process, activity, or product – in some communities, for example, alcohol, sunbathing, cigarettes, herbal cures, or organic foods – they are not likely to think of the risks, even though the probability of harm is not low. Here, too, there is irrationality. In fact, an "affect heuristic" helps to explain much of human evaluation, involving products and activities and also politicians, teachers, job candidates, investment possibilities, and automobiles. My suggestion here is that probability neglect offers a partial explanation for the division between experts and ordinary people in thinking about social hazards – one that raises fresh doubts about how ordinary people evaluate risks.

Of course it is true that experts use their own heuristics and have their own biases;[59] they are hardly immune to the cognitive

---

[58] See Slovic et al., *supra* note 48.
[59] See Sheldon Rampton and John Stauber, *Trust Us, We're Experts!* (New York: Jeremy P. Tarcher/Putnam, 2001), and in particular the authors' especially alarming accounts of the link between corporate funding sources and purportedly objective research outcomes, e.g., *id.* at 216–21; see also Slovic, *supra* note 48, at 311, for findings of affiliation bias.

problems faced by all human beings in thinking about risks. The point is not that experts are always right, but that when ordinary people disagree with experts, it is often not because of competing value judgments, but because ordinary people are more likely to fall prey to probability neglect.

I have said that probability neglect should be seen in light of the idea of "dual processing," of much recent interest in psychology, including the psychology of fear and moral judgment. Recall that according to dual-process theories, some cognitive operations, involving "System I," are rapid, associative, and intuitive, whereas others, involving "System II," are slow, complex, and often calculative or statistical. In many circumstances, rapid processing of this sort works extremely well, as, for example, when someone is confronted with a bear in the forest or a large man with a knife in an alley (and immediately runs away). But governments, and people making decisions under circumstances that permit deliberation, can do a lot better.

NOTES ON THE MEDIA AND ON HETEROGENEITY

From what has been said thus far, it should be clear that news sources do a great deal to trigger fear, simply by offering examples of situations in which the "worst case" has actually come to fruition. For crime, the point is well established.[60] Media coverage of highly unusual crimes makes people fearful of risks that they are most unlikely to face. When newspapers and magazines are emphasizing deaths from terrorism or mad cow disease, we should expect a significant increase in public concern, not only because of the operation of the availability heuristic, but also because people will not naturally make sufficient adjustments from the standpoint of probability. There is a large warning here. If newspapers, magazines, and news programs are stressing certain harms from remote risks, people's concern is likely to be out of proportion to reality. Significant changes should therefore be expected over time. Across nations, it is also easy to imagine substantial differences in social fear if small initial differences are magnified as a result of media influences. I will return to this point shortly.

---

[60] See Joel Best, *Random Violence: How We Talk about New Crimes and New Victims* (Berkeley: University of California Press, 1999).

It is also true that individuals and even societies differ in their susceptibility to probability neglect. Some people take probability information into account even when the context engages human emotions. It is also clear that other people neglect probability information much of the time, focusing insistently on the worst case (or for that matter the best). My arsenic experiment displays a great deal of individual heterogeneity in taking account of probability. Those who are peculiarly insensitive to probability information are likely to do poorly in many domains, including markets; those who are unusually attentive to that information are likely to make money for just that reason. Perhaps there are demographic differences here; it is well known that some groups are less concerned about certain health risks than are others, with women and African-Americans showing special fear of environmental hazards in particular.[61] The difference in concern may stem, in part, from the fact that some groups are less likely to neglect probability.

On the social level, institutions can make a lot of difference in decreasing or increasing susceptibility to probability neglect. A deliberative democracy would attempt to create institutions that have a degree of immunity from short-term public alarm. I will turn to this possibility in Part II. For now, let us investigate another aspect of the problem.

[61] See Slovic, *supra* note 55, at 396–402.

CHAPTER 4

Fear as Wildfire

Human cognition does not take place in a social vacuum. When a particular incident is cognitively "available," it is usually because of social influences. When emotions lead people to probability neglect, the alarm shown by others is highly likely to be playing a role. When citizens fixate on a worst-case scenario, social processes are probably ensuring that they do so.

Obviously both government and the media make some risks appear particularly salient. Return to President George W. Bush's plea: "Imagine those 19 hijackers [involved in the 9/11 attacks] with other weapons and plans, this time armed by Saddam Hussein. It would take one vial, one canister, one crate slipped into this country to bring a day of horror like none we have ever known." Environmentalists, in and out of government, operate in the same way, focusing public attention on potentially catastrophic harms. Well-organized private groups play a central role in activating public concern. But to say this is to get ahead of the story. Begin with an example.

SNIPERS

In fall 2002, a pair of snipers killed ten people in the Washington, D.C. area. The victims were randomly chosen. They included men and women, young and old, whites and African-Americans. Each of these murders was a tragedy, of course; but the actions of the snipers affected millions of others as well. Many citizens were afraid that they could be next. Fear, sometimes dull and sometimes very sharp, gripped the nation's capital. Behavior changed dramatically.

Ever since a sniper began picking off people one-by-one, daily tasks like shopping, pumping gas and mowing lawns have become potentially deadly. Desperate to stay out of the fatal crosshairs, Washington, D.C.-area residents are adjusting where they buy groceries, when they fill their cars, how they exercise. Some even wear bullet-proof vests . . . It's hard for residents to know what to do to protect themselves.[1]

Numerous people drove to Virginia to buy gasoline. Consider the following examples of the Precautionary Principle in action:

- Many school districts placed their classes under a "code blue," which means that students must stay inside school buildings and cannot leave campus for lunches or outdoor activities. Nearly one million children were affected.
- At several schools, October testing for college aptitude tests was canceled.
- Recreation league soccer for six-year-olds, high school girls' tennis, field hockey, and baseball were all canceled or postponed.
- In Winchester, Virginia, all school field trips were canceled.
- About fifty area Starbucks stores removed their outside seating.
- The Prince George's County school system canceled all athletic events indefinitely.
- A Washington, D.C. soccer league, with more than 5,000 players aged 4 to 19, called off games, and youth leagues in Maryland and Virginia were told to follow the lead of the school systems, most of which canceled outdoor events.
- Many people stopped going to health clubs with large front windows, and some took to wearing body armor while pumping gas or shielding themselves with a car door to keep safe.

But there is something very odd about the extraordinary effects of the snipers' actions. For people in the area, the snipers caused a minuscule increase in risk. About five million people live in that area. If the snipers were going to kill one person every three days, the daily statistical risk was less than one in one million, and the weekly statistical risk was less than three in one million. These are trivial risks, far lower than the risks associated with many daily activities about which people do not express even the slightest concern. The daily risk was smaller than the one in one million risk from drinking thirty

[1] http://www.jondube.com/resume/msnbc/snipersshadow.htm.

diet sodas with saccharin, driving 100 miles, smoking two cigarettes, taking ten airplane trips, living in a home with a smoker for two weeks, living in Denver rather than Philadelphia for forty days, and eating thirty-five slices of fresh bread.[2] Some of the precautionary steps, such as driving to Virginia to purchase gasoline, almost certainly posed risks in excess of those associated with the snipers' attacks. The drivers were far more likely to be injured or killed in an accident than to be shot by the snipers.

To be sure, it would be possible to quibble with my assessment of the statistical risk. Perhaps some people at the time were at particular risk, rationally thinking that the risk was somewhat higher than I have suggested. But even if so, the real risk could not possibly have been sufficient to justify the high levels of anxiety and fear, which, for many people, bordered on hysteria. Perhaps some of the defensive behavior was rational, given the fact that the behavior itself was not terribly costly. But the extent of the alarm could not possibly be justified by the extent of the risk.

Why, then, did so many people in Washington feel fear, and alter their behavior, in the midst of the snipers' attacks? The discussion thus far provides some clues. The relevant incidents were highly publicized and readily available, undoubtedly leading many people to think that the risk was higher than it actually was. Recall that public fears often suddenly "spike," even with no change in the actual level of risk, when vivid cases capture public attention.[3] And to say the least, the idea of being killed by a sniper, at a gas station or on a playground, is affect-rich, especially in a period in which newspapers and television stations are giving a great deal of attention to actual murders. It is therefore reasonable to explain the effects of the sniper attacks by reference to some combination of the availability heuristic and probability neglect.

But an account of this kind, focusing solely on individual cognition, is missing something important. Countless risks are, in principle, "available"; and countless risks might, in principle, have the kind of salience that would lead to probability neglect. Obviously

---

[2] Richard Wilson and Edmund A. C. Crouch, *Risk-Benefit Analysis* 208–9 (Cambridge, Mass.: Harvard Center for Risk Analysis, 2001). The risk of living in Denver comes from slightly elevated radiation levels; the risk from eating fresh bread comes from formaldehyde.

[3] See George Loewenstein and Jane Mather, Dynamic Processes in Risk Perception, 3 *J. Risk & Uncertainty* 155 (1990).

the availability of risks, and the risks to which probability neglect attaches, are variable from place to place. In many communities, the risks associated with unsafe sex (which kills tens of thousands of Americans each year) lack much salience. But in some communities, those risks are salient indeed. The risks associated with nuclear power are available to Americans, but less so to citizens of France, who are less concerned about those risks. Americans do not much fear the risks associated with genetic modification of food, even though in principle, such risks might be (made) "available."

Or consider the problem of gun violence. We can find cases in which the presence of guns led to many deaths – and also cases in which the presence of guns allowed law-abiding citizens to protect themselves against criminals.[4] Or consider the question whether women, facing a risk of sexual violence, increase or decrease their risks if they engage in aggressive self-defense. In some cases, resistance prevented the assault. In other cases, resistance led to murder.[5] Which cases are especially available? Even expert judgments appear to be driven by one or another set of available instances.[6] Abandoned hazardous waste sites were not a salient source of risk in the United States until about 1980, when the Love Canal controversy suddenly converted such sites into a strong basis of concern. Availability varies radically over time. In any case, some statistically large risks do not cause a great deal of fear. In many communities, the risks associated with tobacco smoking (a killer of hundreds of thousands of Americans annually) are not salient at all. Why is this?

The question suggests the need to attend to the social and cultural dimensions of fear and risk perception.[7] This is most obviously true for availability. In many cases of high-visibility, low-probability dangers, such as sniper attacks, shark attacks, and the kidnapping of young girls, the sources of availability are not obscure. The mass media focus on those risks; people communicate their fear and concern to

---

[4] See Dan M. Kahan and Donald Braman, More Statistics, Less Persuasion: A Cultural Theory of Gun-Risk Perceptions, 151 *U. Pa. L. Rev.* 1291 (2003).

[5] See Baruch Fischoff, Heuristics and Biases in Application, 730, 733–34, in *Heuristics and Biases: The Psychology of Intuitive Judgment*, ed. Thomas Gilovich, Dale Griffin, and Daniel Kahneman (Cambridge: Cambridge University Press, 2002).

[6] *Id.*

[7] On the cultural issues, see Mary Douglas and Aaron Wildavsky, *Risk and Culture* (Berkeley: University of California Press, 1982).

one another; the widespread fact of fear and concern increases media attention; and the spiral continues until people move on. (Hence the "risk of the month" syndrome, familiar in many societies, stems from the interaction between availability and social influences.) Much of the time, however, what is available and salient to some is not available and salient to all. For example, many of those who endorse the Precautionary Principle focus on cases in which the government failed to regulate some environmental harm, demanding irrefutable proof, with the consequence being widespread illness and death. To such people, the available incidents require strong precautions in the face of uncertainty. But many other people, skeptical of the Precautionary Principle, focus on cases in which the government overreacted to weak science, causing large expenditures for little gain in terms of health or safety. To such people, the available incidents justify a measure of restraint in the face of uncertainty. Which cases will be available and to whom?

In any case people have different *predispositions*. These predispositions play a large role in determining which, of the numerous possibilities, is salient. If you are predisposed to be fearful of genetic modification of food, you are more likely to seek out, and to recall, incidents in which genetic modification was said to cause harm. If you are predisposed to fear electromagnetic fields, you will pay attention to apparent incidents in which electromagnetic fields have produced an elevated incidence of cancer. If you are predisposed to believe that most media scares are false or trumped-up, you will find cases in which public fears have been proved baseless. Availability helps to determine beliefs, to be sure; but beliefs help to determine availability as well. Both beliefs and availability are endogenous to one another. When social and cultural forces interact with salience to produce concern about one set of problems but not another, predispositions are crucial.

In order to predict behavior, to see how law can accomplish shared goals, and to analyze the legitimate role of paternalism, it is necessary to know something about how social forces interact with individual cognition. Indeed, law can sometimes accentuate the relevant effects – as, for example, through a rapid, aggressive response to an available and salient risk, a response that makes the risk more available and salient still. If public officials focus on a risk, they can use the underlying cognitive processes to increase social concern. In emphasizing these points, I mean to suggest the importance of seeing fear in the context of social dynamics, including self-conscious manipulations of the flow of information.

CASCADES

Sometimes availability and salience spread through social bandwagons or cascades, in which apparently representative anecdotes and gripping examples move rapidly from one person to another.[8] In fact a process of this sort played a large role in the Washington area sniper attacks, the Love Canal scare, the debate over mad cow disease, and many other sets of social processes producing fear and sometimes law.

Consider a stylized example. Andrew hears of a dangerous event, which he finds to be revealing or illustrative. (The event might involve crime, terrorism, pesticides, environmental hazards, or threats to national security.) Andrew tells Barry, who would be inclined to see the event as not terribly informative, but who, learning Andrew's reaction, comes to believe that the event does indeed reveal a great deal, and that a serious threat exists. Carol would tend to discount the risk, but once she hears the shared opinion of Andrew and Barry, she is frightened as well. Deborah will have to have a great deal of private information to reject what has become the shared opinion of Andrew, Barry, and Carol.[9] Stylized though it is, the example shows that once several people start to take an example as probative, many people may come to be influenced by their opinion, giving rise to cascade effects. It is partly for this reason that vivid examples, alongside social interactions, account for decisions to purchase insurance against natural disasters.[10]

---

[8] Chip Heath et al., Emotional Selection in Memes: The Case of Urban Legends, 81 *J. Personality & Soc. Psych.* 1028 (2001); Chip Heath, Do People Prefer to Pass Along Good or Bad News? Valence and Relevance as Predictors of Transmission Propensity, 68 *Organizational Behavior & Human Decision Processes* 79 (1996).

[9] See David Hirschleifer, The Blind Leading the Blind: Social Influence, Fads, and Informational Cascades, in *The New Economics of Human Behavior* 188, 193–94, ed. Mariano Tommasi and Kathryn Ierulli (Cambridge: Cambridge University Press, 1995).

[10] See Jacob Gersen, Strategy and Cognition: Regulating Catastrophic Risk (unpublished manuscript, 2001).

Among doctors dealing with risks, cascades are common. "Most doctors are not at the cutting edge of research; their inevitable reliance upon what colleagues have done and are doing leads to numerous surgical fads and treatment-caused illnesses."[11] Thus an article in the prestigious *New England Journal of Medicine* explores "bandwagon diseases" in which doctors act like "lemmings, episodically and with a blind infectious enthusiasm pushing certain diseases and treatments primarily because everyone else is doing the same."[12] Some medical practices, including tonsillectomy, "seem to have been adopted initially based on weak information," and extreme differences in tonsillectomy frequencies (and other procedures) provide good evidence that cascades are at work.[13]

A distinctive feature of social cascades is that the people who participate in them are simultaneously amplifying the very social signal by which they are being influenced. By their very participation, those who join the cascade increase its size, making it more likely that others will join too. Unfortunately, cascades can lead people in mistaken directions, with a few "early movers" spurring social fear that does not match reality. In the example I have given, Andrew is having a large influence on the judgments of our little group, even though he may not, in fact, have accurate information about the relevant event. Barry, Carol, and Deborah might have some information of their own, perhaps enough to show that there is little reason for concern. But unless they have a great deal of confidence in what they do, they are likely to follow those who preceded them. The irony is that if most people are following others, then little information is provided by the fact that some or many seem to share a certain fear. Most are responding to the signals provided by others, unaware that those others are doing exactly the same thing. Of course, corrections might well come eventually, but sometimes they are late.

In the domain of social risks, "availability cascades" are responsible for many social beliefs.[14] A salient event, affecting people because

---

[11] Hirshleifer, *supra* note 9, at 204.

[12] John F. Burnham, Medical Practice à la Mode: How Medical Fashions Determine Medical Care, 317 *New England Journal of Medicine* 1220, 1221 (1987).

[13] See Sushil Bikhchandani et al., Learning from the Behavior of Others: Conformity, Fads, and Informational Cascades, 12(3) *J. Econ. Perspect.* 151, 167 (1998).

[14] See Timur Kuran and Cass R. Sunstein, Availability Cascades and Risk Regulation, 51 *Stan. L. Rev.* 683 (1999).

it is available, tends to be repeated, leading to cascade effects, as the event becomes available to increasingly large numbers of people. The point is amplified by the fact that fear-inducing accounts, with high emotional valence, are especially likely to spread.[15] There is a general implication here. Because different social influences can be found in different communities, local variations are inevitable, with different examples becoming salient in each. Hence such variations – between, say, New York and Ohio, or England and the United States, or between Germany and France – might involve coincidence or small or random factors, rather than large-scale cultural differences. Different judgments within different social groups, with different "available" examples, owe their origin to social processes of this sort. Indeed the different reactions to nuclear power in France and the United States can be explained in large part in this way. And when some groups concentrate on cases in which guns increased violence, and others on cases in which guns decreased violence, availability cascades are a large part of the reason. "Many Germans believe that drinking water after eating cherries is deadly; they also believe that putting ice in soft drinks is unhealthy. The English, however, rather enjoy a cold drink of water after some cherries; and Americans love icy refreshments."[16]

Consider in this regard a cross-national study of perceptions of risk associated with terrorism and SARS.[17] Americans perceived terrorism to be a far greater threat, to themselves and to others, than SARS; Canadians perceived SARS to be a greater threat, to themselves and to others, than terrorism. Americans estimated their chance of serious harm from terrorism as 8.27 percent, about four times as high as their estimate of their chance of serious harm from SARS (2.18 percent). Canadians estimated their chance of serious harm from SARS as 7.43 percent, significantly higher than their estimate for terrorism (6.04 percent). Notably, the figures for SARS were unrealistically high, especially for Canadians; the best estimate of the risk of contracting

[15] See Heath et al., *supra* note 8.

[16] See Joseph Henrich et al., Group Report: What Is the Role of Culture in Bounded Rationality? in *Bounded Rationality: The Adaptive Toolbox* 353–54, ed. Gerd Gigerenzer and Reinhard Selten (Cambridge, Mass.: MIT Press, 2001), for an entertaining outline in connection with food choice decisions.

[17] See Neal Feigenson et al., Perceptions of Terrorism and Disease Risks: A Cross-National Comparison, *U. Cin. L. Rev.* (forthcoming, 2005).

SARS, based on Canadian figures, was .0008 percent (and the chance of dying as a result less than .0002 percent). For obvious reasons, the objective risks from terrorism are much harder to calculate, but if it is estimated that the United States will suffer at least one terrorist attack each year with the same number of deaths as on September 11, the risk of death from terrorism is about .001 percent – a speculative number under the circumstances, but not an implausible place to start.

What accounts for the cross-national difference and for the generally exaggerated risk perceptions? Availability cascades provide a good answer. In the United States, risks of terrorism have (to say the least) received a great deal of attention, producing a continuing sense of threat. But there have been no incidents of SARS, and the media coverage has been limited to events elsewhere – producing a degree of salience, but far lower than that associated with terrorism. In Canada, the opposite is the case. The high degree of public discussion of SARS cases, accompanied by readily available instances, produced an inflated sense of the numbers – sufficiently inflated to exceed the same numbers from terrorism (certainly a salient risk in Canada, as in most nations post 9/11). In this case, as elsewhere, availability and cascade effects help to account for cross-national differences.

What accounts for people's perception of their risk of being infected with HIV? Why are some people, and some groups, entirely unconcerned about that risk, while other people and groups are nearly obsessed with it? A study of rural Kenya and Malawi suggests that social interactions play a critical role.[18] The authors find risk perception is a product of discussions that "are often provoked by observing or hearing about an illness or death."[19] People "know in the abstract how HIV is transmitted and how it can be prevented," but they are unclear "about the advisability and effectiveness of the changes in sexual behavior that are recommended by experts."[20] Perceptions of the risk of HIV transmission are very much a function of social networks, with pronounced changes in belief and behavior resulting from interactions with people expressing a high level of concern. The effects

---

[18] See Jere R. Behrman et al., Social Networks, HIV/AIDS, and Risk Perceptions (Feb. 18, 2003), available at ssrn.com.
[19] *Id.* at 10.   [20] *Id.* at 18.

of social networks are thus asymmetric, with substantial effects from having "at least one network partner who is perceived to have a great deal of concern about AIDS." The authors do not refer explicitly to cascade effects, but their findings are compatible with the suggestion that with respect to AIDS, risk perceptions are produced by just those effects.

We can better understand the important and much-discussed idea of "moral panics" in this light.[21] Sometimes societies, or subsets of societies, become suddenly fearful of some perceived moral threat – from religious dissidents, foreigners, immigrants, homosexuals, teenage gangs, and drug users. How do moral panics spread? Cascades provide much of the answer. Most people join moral panics not because they have independent reason to fear the moral threat, but because of the fear expressed by others. Many of us are likely to ask: How can so many people be wrong? Especially if the threat can be illustrated with an easily accessible example, one that seems to exemplify a general trend, we join the cascade. Social cascades are often moral panics. Fear, fueled by social influences, is responsible for them.

GROUP POLARIZATION

There is a closely related phenomenon. When like-minded people deliberate with one another, they typically end up accepting a more extreme version of the views with which they began.[22] This is the process known as *group polarization*. Consider a few examples:

- After discussion, citizens of France become more critical of the United States and its intentions with respect to economic aid.[23]
- A group of moderately profeminist women becomes more strongly profeminist after discussion.[24]
- After discussion, whites predisposed to show racial prejudice offer more negative responses to the question whether white racism is

---

[21] See Erich Goode and Nachman Ben-Yehuda, *Moral Panics: The Social Construction of Deviance* (Oxford: Blackwell, 1994).

[22] See Cass R. Sunstein, *Why Societies Need Dissent* (Cambridge, Mass.: Harvard University Press, 2003).

[23] Rupert Brown, *Prejudice: Its Social Psychology* 224 (Cambridge, Mass.: Blackwell, 1995).

[24] See David G. Myers, Discussion-Induced Attitude Polarization, 28 *Human Relations* 699 (1975).

responsible for conditions faced by African-Americans in American cities.[25]

- After discussion, whites predisposed not to show racial prejudice offer more positive responses to the same question, that is, they are more likely to find white prejudice to be the source of conditions faced by African-Americans in American cities.[26]
- Juries inclined to award punitive damages typically produce awards that are significantly higher than the awards chosen, before deliberation, by their median member.[27]
- Federal judges, appointed by Republican presidents, show extremely conservative voting patterns when sitting only with fellow Republican appointees – far more conservative than when sitting with at least one Democratic appointee. The same pattern holds for Democratic appointees, who show especially liberal voting patterns when sitting only with fellow Democratic appointees.[28]

Group polarization will inevitably occur in the context of fear. If several people fear global warming or terrorism, and speak to one another, their fear is likely to increase as a result of internal discussions. If other people believe that nuclear power is probably safe, their belief to that effect will be fortified after they speak with one another, to the point where they will believe that nuclear power is no reason for concern. If some groups seem hysterical about certain risks, and other groups treat those risks as nonexistent, group polarization is likely to be a reason. Hence group polarization provides another explanation for the different fears of groups, localities, and even nations. Internal discussions can make Berliners fearful of risks than do not bother New Yorkers, and vice versa; so, too, the citizens of London may fear a supposed danger that does not much bother the citizens of Paris – even if the danger is not greater in the former than in the latter.

There are four main explanations for group polarization, all of which have been extensively investigated.

[25] David G. Myers and George D. Bishop, The Enhancement of Dominant Attitudes in Group Discuission, 20 *J. Personality & Soc. Psych.* 386 (1971).

[26] See *id.*

[27] See Cass R. Sunstein, Reid Hastie, John W. Payre, David A. Schkade, and W. Kip Viscusi, *Punitive Damages: How Juries Decide* (Chicago: University of Chicago Press, 2002).

[28] See Cass R. Sunstein et al., Ideological Voting on Federal Courts of Appeals: A Preliminary Investigation, 90 *Va. L. Rev.* 301 (2004).

Persuasive arguments

The first explanation, emphasizing the role of persuasive arguments, is based on a common-sense intuition: any individual's position on an issue is partly a function of which arguments presented within the group seem convincing. People's judgments tend to move in the direction of the most persuasive and frequently defended position discussed by the group, taken as a collectivity. Because a group whose members are fearful will have a disproportionate number of arguments justifying their fear, discussion will typically move people toward greater fear. So, too, with a group whose members believe that a risk is inflated. If most people, in that group, discount the threat of global warming, then the balance of arguments will be in the direction of dismissing that threat. People will shift accordingly.

Social comparison

The second explanation, involving social comparison, begins with the claim that people want to be perceived favorably by other group members, and also to perceive themselves favorably. Once they hear what others believe, they adjust their positions in the direction of the dominant position. If most group members are seen as likely to punish expressions of fear, then members will take account of that fact, and adjust their statements accordingly. People may wish, for example, to seem to approve aggressive measures to protect against terrorism or global warming; hence their publicly stated views may shift when they see what other group members think. Group polarization is fueled by social influences that lead people to silence themselves in deference to the dominant position. Within groups, both fear and fearlessness can be a product of social comparisons.

Confidence breeds extremism

The third explanation begins by noting that people with extreme views tend to have more confidence that they are right, and that as people gain confidence, they become more extreme in their beliefs.[29]

---

[29] See Robert S. Baron et al., Social Corroboration and Opinion Extremity, 32 *J. Experimental Soc. Psych.* 537 (1996).

The basic idea here is simple: If you lack confidence, and are unsure what you should think, you will tend to moderate your views. But when other people share your view, you are likely to become more confident that you are correct – and hence to move in a more extreme direction. If people in a group tend in the direction of fear, that tendency will be fortified simply because the arguments for fear seems stronger as a result of group interactions. In a wide variety of experimental contexts, people's opinions have been shown to become more extreme simply because their view has been corroborated, and because they have become more confident after learning of the shared views of others.

Emotional contagion

Individuals are highly responsive to the emotions expressed by others.[30] Those surrounded by depressed people are more likely to become depressed; those surrounded by enthusiastic and energetic people are more likely to feel enthusiastic and energetic. The particular mechanisms behind emotional contagion are not fully understood, but fear is a prime example of an emotion that turns out to be contagious. It is therefore predictable that a group of frightened people will end up becoming still more fearful as a result of internal conversations.

Group polarization undoubtedly occurs in connection with the availability heuristic and probability neglect. Suppose, for example, that several people are discussing mad cow disease, or a recent wave of sniper attacks, or cases involving the kidnapping of young girls, or situations in which the government has wrongly ignored a serious foreign threat. If the particular examples are mentioned, they are likely to prove memorable. And if the group has a predisposition to think that one or another risk is serious, social dynamics will lead the group to believe that the example is highly revealing. An initial predisposition toward fear is likely to be aggravated after collective deliberations. Within groups, a tendency toward fear breeds its own amplification.

[30] See Elaine Hatfield, John T. Cacioppo, and Richard L. Rapson, *Emotional Contagion* (Cambridge: Cambridge University Press, 1994).

Consider in this light the 2004 report of the United States Senate Select Committee On Intelligence, which contended the Central Intelligence Agency's predisposition to find a serious threat from Iraq led it to fail to explore alternative possibilities or to obtain and use the information that it actually held.[31] Falling victim to group polarization in the particular context of fear, the agency showed a "tendency to reject information that contradicted the presumption" that Iraq had weapons of mass destruction.[32] This claim is a remarkable echo of one that followed the 2003 investigation of failures at NASA, in which the Columbia Accident Investigation Board explicitly attributed the accident to NASA's unfortunate culture, one that does too little to elicit information. In the Board's words, NASA lacks "checks and balances"[33] and pressures people to follow a "party line."[34] The result was a process of polarization that led to a dismissal of serious risks.

MEDIA, INTEREST GROUPS, AND POLITICIANS

Thus far the discussion has involved interactions among individuals, all treated as equals. But it should be clear that in the real world, some voices are more important than others, especially when availability and salience are involved. In particular, the behavior and preoccupations of the media play a large role. Many perceived "epidemics" are in reality no such thing, but instead a product of media coverage of gripping, unrepresentative incidents. Attention to those incidents is likely to ensure availability and salience, promoting an inaccurately high estimate of probability and at the same time some degree of probability neglect. And in the face of close media attention, the demand for legal responses will be significantly affected. In the context of the Washington sniper attacks, intense media coverage was the central source of social fear, helping to ensure that large amounts of private and public resources were devoted to risk reduction.

A natural question, then, is why the media covers certain risks and not others. A clue comes from the following suggestion in 2002:

[31] Available at http://intelligence.senate.gov/.   [32] *Id.* at 6.
[33] Report of the Columbia Accident Investigation Board, available at http://www.nasa.gov/columbia/home/CAIB_Vol1.html, at 12.
[34] *Id.* at 102.

Whatever the criticisms, the reign of terror is boosting ratings for cable news networks. In fact, they are now at their highest levels since the Sept. 11, 2001, terrorist attacks. At the end of last week, Fox News Channel's average daily audience was up 27 percent from a month before; CNN's was up 29 percent; MSNBC's, up 24 percent.[35]

Hence the media's coverage reflects its economic self-interest. Gripping instances, whether or not representative, are likely to attract attention and to increase ratings. Often the result is to distort probability judgments. Hence there can be a vicious circle involving the availability heuristic and media incentives, with each aggravating the other, often to the detriment of public understanding.

Knowing the importance of media coverage, well-organized private groups work extremely hard to promote public attention to particular risks. Some of these groups are altruistic; others are entirely self-interested. The common tactic is to publicize an incident that might trigger both availability and salience. Terrorists themselves are the most extreme and vicious example, using high-visibility attacks to convince people that "they cannot be safe anywhere." But many illustrations are less objectionable and sometimes even benign. Consider the abandoned hazardous waste at Love Canal, used to promote hazardous waste cleanup, or the *Exxon Valdez* disaster, used by the Sierra Club and other environmental organizations to promote more stringent safeguards against oil spills. Showing at least a working knowledge of the availability heuristic, private groups seize on selected incidents and publicize them to make them generally salient to the public. In all of these examples, the use of particular instances might be necessary to move the public, and legislatures, in the right directions. Certainly the social processes that interact with salience and availability can promote reform where it is needed. But there is no assurance here, particularly if social influences are leading people to exaggerate a problem, or to ignore the question of probability altogether.

Politicians engage in the same basic project. By its very nature, the voice of an influential politician comes with amplifiers. When public officials bring an incident before the public, a seemingly illustrative

---

[35] Johanna Neuman, In a Sniper's Grip: Media's Role in Drama Debated, *Los Angeles Times*, Oct. 24, 2002, part 1, p. 16.

example is likely to spread far and wide. A legal enactment can itself promote availability; if the law responds to the problems associated with hazardous waste dumps, or "hate crimes," people might well come to see those problems as readily available. The terrorist attacks of September 11, 2001 would inevitably loom large no matter what President George W. Bush chose to emphasize. But the President, and his White House generally, referred to the attacks on countless occasions, frequently as a way of emphasizing the reality of seemingly distant threats and the need to incur significant costs to counteract them (including the 2003 Iraq war, itself fueled by presidential speeches including vivid narratives of catastrophic harm). And there is no doubt that the salience of these attacks played a large role in affecting political behavior – and that that role cannot be understood without reference to social influences.

PREDISPOSITIONS

All this does not provide the full picture. Beliefs and orientations are a product of availability, and social influences ensure both availability and salience. But as I have suggested, what is available is also a product of antecedent beliefs and orientations, both individual and social. In other words, availability is endogenous to, or a product of, individual predispositions.

Why do some people recall and emphasize incidents in which a failure to take precautions led to serious environmental harm? A likely reason is that they are predisposed to favor environmental protection. And why do some people recall and emphasize incidents in which environmental protection led to huge costs for little gain? A likely reason is that they are predisposed to oppose environmental controls. Here is an interaction between the availability heuristic and confirmation bias – "the tendency to seek information to confirm our original hypotheses and beliefs,"[36] a tendency that reviewers have found in the judgments, referred to above, of both the Central Intelligence Agency and NASA.

Of course, predispositions are not a black box, and they do not come from the sky. They have sources. Among their sources are

---

[36] See Elliott Aronson, *The Social Animal* 150 (New York: W. H. Freeman, 7th ed., 1995).

availability and salience. Hence there is complex set of interactions, with heuristics helping to constitute predispositions, which are in turn responsible for the real-world operation of heuristics. All this happens socially, not merely individually; and predispositions are not static. When people are in a group that is predisposed in a particular direction, the salient examples will be quite different from those that are salient in a group with an opposite predisposition. Here group polarization is especially important.

More generally, different cultural orientations play a large role in determining what turns out to be available. For example, the United States is highly diverse, and for some purposes, it is plausible to think of different regions and groups as having different cultures. Within African-American communities, the available instances are sometimes quite different from those that can be found within all-white communities. Across nations, the differences are even more striking, in part because different world-views play such a dominant role. And what is true for individuals is true for nations as well. Just as predispositions are, in part, a function of availability, so, too, availability is, in part, a function of predispositions. Social influences operate at both levels, affecting what is available and also moving predispositions in one or another direction. The problem is that both individuals and societies may be fearful of nonexistent or trivial risks – and simultaneously neglect real dangers.

My discussion of the problems caused by fear is essentially complete. We have seen that in its strongest form, the Precautionary Principle is incoherent and that it appears to give guidance only because of identifiable features of human cognition. We have seen as well that worst-case scenarios have a distorting effect on human judgment, often producing excessive fear about unlikely events. Social influences, including cascade effects and group polarization, both heighten and diminish fear. The result is a situation in which people often show baseless fear and confidence about situations that pose genuine danger.

At the individual and social level, what might be done to resolve these problems? If we are committed to a deliberative conception of democracy, we will be neither populists nor technocrats. Law and policy ought not to reflect people's blunders; democracies should not mechanically follow citizens' fears, or for that matter their fearlessness. Nor does anything here suggest the virtues of rule by a technocratic elite. As I have suggested, citizens make qualitative distinctions among quantitatively identical risks, and when their reflective values account for those qualitative distinctions, the judgments of citizens deserve respect.

Let us return to the subject of precautions.

PART II

Solutions

CHAPTER 5

Reconstructing the Precautionary Principle – and Managing Fear

I have been sharply critical of the Precautionary Principle, but no one doubts that it makes sense to take precautions. An appreciation of the salutary goals of the Precautionary Principle paves the way toward a reconstruction of the central idea, one that takes seriously the concerns of those who favor it. The reconstruction occurs along three dimensions. The first involves catastrophic risks. The second involves irreversible harms. The third involves margins of safety for risks that, while not potentially catastrophic, pose distinctive reasons for concern. After discussing the resulting principles, I explore how government might deal with both excessive and insufficient public fear.

CATASTROPHE

When citizens face catastrophic risks to which probabilities cannot be assigned, it makes sense for them to adopt an Anti-Catastrophe Principle. If regulators are operating under conditions of uncertainty, they might well do best to follow maximin, identifying the worst-case scenarios and choosing the approach that eliminates the worst of these. It follows that if aggressive measures are justified to reduce the risks associated with global warming, one reason is that those risks are potentially catastrophic and existing science does not enable us to assign probabilities to the worst-case scenarios.[1] Maximin is an appealing decision rule whenever uncertainty is present, but in the regulatory context, it is particularly important for extremely bad outcomes.

[1] See Richard Posner, *Catastrophe: Risk and Response* 50–58, 155–65 (New York: Oxford University Press, 2004).

To understand these claims, we need to back up a bit and to investigate maximin in more detail. Does it generally make sense to eliminate the worst-case scenario? Consider a reporter, now living in Los Angeles, who has been told that he can take one of two assignments. First, he can go to a nation, say Iraq, that is facing a large amount of terrorism. Second, he can go to Paris to cover anti-American sentiment in France. The Iraq assignment has, in his view, two polar outcomes: (a) he might have the most interesting and rewarding experience of his professional life, or (b) he might be killed. The Paris assignment has two polar outcomes of its own: (a) he might have an interesting experience, one that is also a great deal of fun, and (b) he might be lonely and homesick. It would hardly be senseless for the reporter to choose Paris, on the ground that the worst-case scenario, for that choice, is so much better than the worst-case scenario for Iraq.

But maximin is not always a sensible decision rule. Suppose that the reporter now has the choice of staying in Los Angeles or going to Paris; suppose, too, that on personal and professional grounds, Paris is far better. It would make little sense for him to invoke maximin in order to stay in Los Angeles on the ground that the plane to Paris might crash. Using an example of this kind, John Harsanyi contends that maximin should be rejected on the ground that it produces irrationality, even madness:

If you took the maximin principle seriously you could not ever cross the street (after all, you might be hit by a car); you could never drive over a bridge (after all, it might collapse); you could never get married (after all, it might end in a disaster), etc. If anybody really acted in this way he would soon end up in a mental institution.[2]

We might even use Harsanyi's argument to contest the use of maximin in the choice between Iraq and Paris. Shouldn't the reporter try to figure out the likelihood of being killed in Iraq, rather than simply identifying the worst-case scenario? Isn't maximin a form of probability neglect? Suppose that the risk of death, in Iraq, turns out to be 1/1,000,000, and that the choice of Iraq would be much better,

---

[2] See John C. Harsanyi, Morality and the Theory of Rational Behavior, in *Utilitarianism and Beyond* 40, ed. Amartya Sen and Bernard Williams (Cambridge: Cambridge University Press, 1982).

personally and professionally, than the choice of Paris. It is plausible to think that the reporter should choose Iraq rather than make the decision by obsessively fixating on the worst that might happen. So far, then, Harsanyi's criticism of maximin seems on firm ground.

But something important is missing from Harsanyi's argument and even from the reporter's analysis of the choice between Los Angeles and Paris: Risks are on all sides of the relevant situations. If the reporter stayed in Los Angeles, he might be killed by a member of a street gang, and hence the use of maximin does not justify the decision to stay in the United States. And contrary to Harsanyi's argument, maximin doesn't really mean that people shouldn't cross streets, drive over bridges, and get married. The reason is that refusing to do those three things has worst-case scenarios of its own (including death and disaster). In fact, Harsanyi is making exactly the same mistake as the scientists who fear that the Precautionary Principle would not have permitted airplanes or antibiotics. To implement maximin, or an injunction to take precautions, we need to identify all relevant risks, not a subset.

Nonetheless, the more general objection to maximin holds. If probabilities can be assigned to the various outcomes, it does not make sense to follow maximin when the worst case is highly improbable and when the alternative option is both much better and much more likely. It follows that our reporter would do well to reject maximin, and to go to Paris, even if the worst-case scenario for Paris is worse than that for Los Angeles *if* the realistically likely outcomes are much better in Paris. I am not suggesting that in order to be rational, the reporter must calculate expected values, multiplying imaginable outcomes by probability and deciding accordingly. Life is short; people are busy; and it is far from irrational to create a margin of safety to protect against disaster. But if the likelihood of a really bad outcome is really small, maximin is foolish.

But is it always? As I have suggested, it can make a great deal of sense under circumstances of uncertainty rather than risk. Suppose that the situation in Paris is such that the reporter cannot assign probabilities to an awful death there, because a communicable disease is spreading at an unknown rate; if so, he might sensibly choose to stay in Los Angeles. In a highly illuminating effort to recast the Precautionary Principle,[3] Stephen Gardiner invokes John Rawls' argument that when "grave risks" are involved, and when probabilities cannot be assigned to the occurrence of those risks, maximin is the appropriate decision rule, at least if the chooser "cares very little, if anything, for what he might gain among the minimum stipend that he can, in fact, be sure of by following the maximin rule."[4] Adapting Rawls' claims about distributive justice to the environmental setting, Gardiner urges that maximin, and hence a "core" Precautionary Principle, is justified (1) in the face of potentially catastrophic outcomes, (2) where probabilities cannot be assigned, and (3) where the loss, from following maximin, is a matter of relative indifference.

Gardiner adds, sensibly, that to justify maximin, the threats that are potentially catastrophic must satisfy some minimal threshold of plausibility. If they can be dismissed as unrealistic, then maximin should not be followed. Gardiner believes that the problem of global warming can be usefully analyzed in these terms and that it presents a good case for the application of maximin.

This argument seems to me on the right track, but its conclusion, as stated, risks triviality, above all because of condition (3). If individuals and societies can eliminate an uncertain danger of catastrophe for essentially no cost, then of course they should eliminate that risk. But the real world rarely presents problems of this form. (When it does, by all means follow maximin!) In real disputes, the elimination of uncertain dangers of catastrophe imposes both costs and risks. In the context of global warming, for example, it is implausible to say that regulatory choosers can or should care "very little, if anything," for what might be lost by following maximin. If we followed maximin for global warming, we would spend a great deal to reduce greenhouse gas emissions, and the result would almost certainly be higher prices for gasoline and energy, probably producing increases in unemployment and poverty.

Does Gardiner's argument provide help beyond the trivial cases? I believe that if properly recast, it does, for one simple reason: Condition (3) is too stringent and should be abandoned. Even if the costs of following maximin are significant, and even if choosers care a great

---

[3] See Stephen Gardiner, A Core Precautionary Principle (unpublished manuscript, 2004).
[4] See John Rawls, *A Theory of Justice* (Cambridge, Mass.: Harvard University Press, 1971).

deal about incurring those costs, it makes sense to follow maximin when they face uncertain dangers of catastrophe. The hardest question here is: How much cost does it make sense to incur in the service of maximin? Consider an easy case: The catastrophic dangers associated with global warming could be eliminated if every nation contributed $2 million to a fund to combat that risk. Surely that cost would be acceptable. And indeed it has been argued that global warming presents catastrophic risks whose probability cannot be specified with any confidence, that the costs of limiting emissions are far better understood, and that for these reasons, aggressive precautions might well be justified in principle.[5]

Consider a very different case: The catastrophic dangers associated with global warming could be eliminated only if every nation contributed enough resources to reduce standards of living by 50 percent worldwide, with a corresponding increase in global poverty. If global warming really does pose an uncertain danger of total catastrophe, the formal logic of maximin argues in favor of this extraordinary reduction in worldwide standards of living; but it is not clear that following that logic would be reasonable. To incur costs of this magnitude, we might want to insist that the danger of catastrophe rise above a minimal threshold – that there be a demonstrable probability, and a not-so-low one, that the catastrophic risk will occur. It would seem far more sensible to take less costly steps now and to engage in further research, attempting to learn enough to know more about the probability that the catastrophic outcomes will occur.

To appreciate this point, and a more general problem with maximin, imagine an individual or society lacking the information that would permit the assignment of probabilities to a *series* of hazards with catastrophic outcomes; suppose that the number of hazards is twenty, or a hundred, or a thousand. Suppose, too, that such an individual or society is able to assign probabilities (ranging from 1 percent to 90 percent) to an equivalent number of other hazards, with outcomes that range from bad to very bad, but never catastrophic. Suppose, finally, that every one of these hazards can be eliminated at a cost – a cost that is high, but that does not, once incurred, inflict harms that

---

[5] See W. David Montgomery and Anne E. Smith, Global Climate Change and the Precautionary Principle, 6 *Hum. & Ecol. Risk Assess.* 399 (2000).

count as very bad or catastrophic. The maximin principle suggests that our individual or society should spend a great deal to eliminate each of the twenty, or hundred, or thousand potentially catastrophic hazards. But once that amount is spent on even one of those hazards, there might be nothing left to combat the very bad hazards, even those with a 90 percent chance of occurring. In the face of a large number of hazards, some in the domain of risk and others in the domain of uncertainty, maximin seems inconsistent with intelligent priority setting. We could even imagine that a poorly informed individual or society would be condemned to real poverty and distress, or even worse, merely by virtue of following maximin.[6]

I cannot attempt to sort through these complexities here. But I do suggest that the Anti-Catastrophe Principle has a definite place in both life and law, applying to uncertain dangers of catastrophe, at least when the costs of reducing those dangers are not huge and when incurring those costs does not divert resources from more pressing problems. The Anti-Catastrophe Principle is not the Precautionary Principle; it is far narrower than that. But it nonetheless deserves to play a role in regulatory choices, including those that involve global warming – plausibly by calling for significant (but not hugely costly) steps now, accompanied by further research to obtain a better understanding of the likelihood of real disaster.

Four qualifications are important. *First*, the Anti-Catastrophe Principle must be attentive to the full range of social risks; it makes no sense to take steps to avert catastrophe if those very steps would create catastrophic risks of their own. If a preemptive war, designed to reduce the risks of terrorism from one source, would increase those

---

[6] This objection derives indirect support from the empirical finding that when asked to decide on the distribution of goods and services, most people reject the two most widely discussed principles in the philosophical literature: average utility, favored by Harsanyi, and Rawls' difference principle (allowing inequalities only if they work to the advantage of the least well off). Norman Frohlich and Joe A. Oppenheimer, *Choosing Justice: An Experimental Approach to Ethical Theory* (Berkeley: University of California Press, 1992). Instead, people choose average utility with a floor constraint – that is, they favor an approach that maximizes overall well-being, but subject to the constraint that no member of society may fall below a decent minimum. Insisting on an absolute welfare minimum to all, they maximize over that floor. Their aversion to risk leads them to a pragmatic threshold in the form of the floor. The analogy is not precise, but something similar may be at work in the context of precautions against risks. A sensible individual, or society, would not want to use maximin if it forced them to go below a decent floor of well-being.

very risks from another source, then the Anti-Catastrophe Principle is indeterminate. *Second,* use of the principle should be closely attentive to the idea of cost-effectiveness, which requires regulators to choose the least costly means of achieving their ends. In the context of global warming, there are many methods by which to reduce the relevant risks. Both nations and international institutions should choose those methods that minimize costs. The same is true for efforts to combat terrorism. *Third,* distributional considerations matter. The principle should be applied in a way that reduces extreme burdens on those least able to bear them. For global warming, there is a particular need to ensure that citizens of poor nations are not required to pay a great deal to contribute to the solution of a problem for which those in wealthy nations are most responsible. If an antiterrorism policy would impose special burdens on members of racial and religious minority groups – consider racial profiling – it is worth considering other policies that reduce or eliminate those burdens. *Fourth,* costs matter as such. The extent of precautions cannot reasonably be divorced from their expense. In cases of the kind I am discussing, where the worst-case scenario is truly catastrophic and when probabilities cannot be assigned, a large margin of safety makes a great deal of sense.

IRREVERSIBLE HARMS: AN AMBIVALENT NOTE

The Precautionary Principle is often invoked in cases involving risks of irreversible harm.[7] As we have seen, the term "irreversible" appears in numerous descriptions of what the principle is designed to avoid. The intuition here is both straightforward and appealing: More steps should be taken to prevent harms that are effectively final than to prevent those that can be reversed at some cost. If an irreversible harm is on one side, and a reversible one on the other, an understanding of "option value" suggests that it is worthwhile to spend a certain amount to preserve future flexibility, by paying a premium to avoid the irreversible harm.

But there is a serious problem with an emphasis on irreversibility, and it lies in the ambiguity of the basic idea. Any death, of any living

---

[7] For a valuable and somewhat technical discussion see Christian Gollier and Nicolas Treich, Decision-Making under Scientific Uncertainty: The Economics of the Precautionary Principle, 27 *J. Risk & Uncertainty* 77 (2003).

creature, is irreversible, and those who invoke irreversibility do not intend the notion of irreversible harm to apply to each and every mortality risk. What is true for living creatures is true for rocks and refrigerators, too; if these are destroyed, they are destroyed forever. And because time is linear, every decision is, in an intelligible sense, irreversible. If I play tennis at 11 a.m. today, that decision cannot be reversed, and what might have been done at that time will have been permanently lost. If the government builds a new highway in upstate New York in May, that particular decision will be irreversible, even though the highway can be replaced or eliminated. Whether a particular act is "irreversible" depends on how it is characterized; if we characterize it narrowly, to be precisely what it is, any act is literally irreversible by definition.

Those who are concerned about irreversibility have something far more particular in mind. They mean something like a large-scale alteration in environmental conditions, one that imposes permanent, or nearly permanent, changes on those subject to them. But irreversibility in this sense is not a sufficient reason for a highly precautionary approach. At a minimum, the irreversible change has to be for the worse, and it must also rise to a certain level of magnitude. A truly minuscule change in the global temperature, even if permanent, would not justify expensive precautions if it is benign or if it imposes little in the way of harm.

The idea of irreversibility is really important for two reasons. The first, referred to in chapter 1, draws on the analogy to stock options, and suggests that it is worthwhile to spend resources on (bounded) precautions to wait for more information to emerge before incurring a substantial and irreversible loss. The second and more fundamental reason involves the relationship between irreversibility and catastrophic harm. If a loss that seems catastrophic can actually be prevented or stopped at reasonable cost, it is not catastrophic at all; if it is literally irreversible, or extremely costly to reverse, then the Anti-Catastrophe Principle comes directly into play. For those who believe that the loss of a species is a tragedy, protection of endangered species is an effort to avoid a kind of catastrophe. The point is not that the death of individual animals is reversible; it is not. The point is that on a widely held view, extinction counts as a catastrophic loss, whereas the death of species members does not. We might conclude that whether an irreversible loss deserves real attention, sufficient to trigger the Anti-Catastrophe Principle or any special kind of precaution, turns on its magnitude, not on the mere fact of irreversibility.

MARGINS OF SAFETY

Margins of safety are hardly limited to catastrophic risks; they are reasonable in many contexts. But how should we select margins of safety?

The first step is to notice that regulators, no less than ordinary citizens, should pay attention both to the probability of harm and to its magnitude. If the magnitude of the harm is high, then regulators need not require as much evidence that it is probable. A 1/10,000 risk of 10,000 deaths must be taken very seriously. Whether or not the outcome qualifies as catastrophic, it is appropriate to weigh both probability and magnitude.

This simple point helps to distinguish cases of sensible and senseless use of the Precautionary Principle. On the senseless side: There has been no good reason for invocation of the principle in the context of cancer risks said to be associated with cellphones. For each cellphone user, the risk of harm is exceedingly low or possibly even nonexistent.[8] On the sensible side: The risks associated with low levels of arsenic in drinking water (50 parts per billion) were certainly high enough to make it reasonable for the United States to impose further regulation (a ceiling of 10 parts per billion) under the rubric of precaution.

Alternatively, suppose that science currently allows us to group the outcomes into rough, general categories of probability – with, for example, low harm being 30 percent likely, moderate harm being 40 percent likely, serious harm being 35 percent likely, and catastrophic harm being 5 percent likely. Let us suppose, too, that we will learn an increasing amount over time. If so, we might elect to take certain steps now, on the basis of a principle of "Act, then learn." The steps we now take would not be the same as those that we would take if the worst outcomes were more probable, but they should be designed so

---

[8] See Adam Burgess, *Cellular Phones, Public Fears, and a Culture of Precaution* (Cambridge: Cambridge University Press, 2004).

as to permit us to protect against the worst outcomes if we eventually learn that they are actually likely.[9] On this view, an understanding of what we do not know means not that regulators should do little, but that they should act in stages over time, adopting precautions that amount to a kind of insurance against the chance that the harm will be higher than we currently project in light of our current knowledge of both probability and magnitude.

But an understanding of probability and magnitude is not nearly enough. At a minimum, it is also necessary to identify the appropriate regulatory tool. A high probability of a serious harm might justify a flat ban on the product or process in question – what we might call a Prohibitory Precautionary Principle. By contrast, a low probability of a less serious harm might support further research or information disclosure. For many risks, it makes sense to follow an Information Disclosure Precautionary Principle – one that requires those who create risks to disclose that fact to the public. An understanding of the probability of the risk, its magnitude, and the menu of regulatory tools goes a long way toward the specification of good options. For every such option, a margin of safety might be selected in accordance with the existing evidence and the magnitude of the risk if it comes to fruition.

Even at this stage, however, the analysis remains badly incomplete. It is also necessary to know about the risks and costs that would be introduced by the chosen tool. If precautions would be costless, they should by all means be taken. Consider the appealing notion of "prudent avoidance," calling for avoidance of even speculative hazards when avoidance comes at a small cost. But if precautions would introduce a serious probability of a significant risk, then they are forbidden by the very idea of precaution. I have emphasized the importance of a wide viewscreen for thinking about dangers, one that asks both regulators and ordinary citizens to consider the problems produced by reducing one of a set of possible risks. But this idea is not fatal to the notion of margins of safety; it merely requires regulators to identify the particular risks that are receiving special concern, and to explain why margins of safety are appropriate for those risks.

[9] Montgomery and Smith, *supra* note 5, at 409–10. See also Scott Farrow and Hiroshi Hayakawa, Investing in Safety: An Analyical Precautionary Principle, 33 *J. Safety Research* 165 (2002).

Suppose, for example, that the risk of getting cancer from sunbathing is not trivial, and that the cost of risk reduction consists of using sunscreen or staying out of the sun for some part of every day. A margin of safety is hard to contest. Or suppose that the risk of a terrorist attack in airports cannot be dismissed, and that the costs of risk reduction consist of the security measures that have become standard in the United States in the aftermath of the attacks of 9/11. On plausible assumptions, those costs are well worth incurring, even though they are far from trivial. Compare the American-led war to remove Saddam Hussein from Iraq. Reasonable people could justify that war on "margin of safety" grounds. The very high costs, in terms of both human life and money, might have been worth incurring if we attend only to the risks, to the people of Iraq, that were associated with the continuation of Saddam's horrific regime. But some reasonable people feared that the war itself would contribute to risks of terrorism, above all by fueling anti-American sentiment and thus making it easier to recruit terrorists and to inspire them to murderous acts. When risks are on all sides, the idea of a "margin of safety" cannot by itself resolve the underlying disputes.

In any case the real question is not whether to have a margin of safety, but how big the margin of safety should be, and to which risks the margin should be applied. For the risks associated with terrorism, a huge margin of safety would call for a ban on air travel in the United States – a ban whose cost would obviously be too high (and one that would introduce multiple risks of its own). For the risks associated with air pollution and global warming, a ban on coal-fired power plants would be required if the margin of safety were set high enough – but at the present time, such a ban would simply be too expensive (and it would be far from risk free). For both individuals and societies, margins of safety are chosen with careful attention to the costs and risks that they produce.

THE ANALYTICS OF PRECAUTION

We should now be able to see that applications of the Precautionary Principle against particular risks can be described in terms of four important factors: (a) the level of uncertainty that triggers a regulatory response, (b) the magnitude of anticipated harm that justifies such a response, (c) the tools that will be chosen when the principle applies (tools such as disclosure requirements, technological requirements, or prohibitions), and (d) the margin of safety that applies in the face of doubt.[10]

No sensible person believes that an activity should be banned merely because it presents "some" risk of harm; in this sense, an absolutist version of the Precautionary Principle, while having occasional influence in practice,[11] lacks theoretical appeal even to its proponents.[12] Some threshold degree of evidence should be required for costly measures of risk avoidance, in the form of scientifically supported suspicion or suggestive evidence of significant risk. But the magnitude of the anticipated harm matters a great deal. The demand for scientific evidence should be reduced if the harm would be especially large if the risk came to fruition.

We can also identify a range of regulatory tools.[13] For example, a Funding More Research Precautionary Principle would say that if there is an even minimal reason for concern, the appropriate initial step would be to subsidize further research as a precautionary step.[14] The Information Disclosure Precautionary Principle would say that in the face of doubt, those who subject people to potential risks must disclose relevant information to those so subjected. The debate over labeling genetically modified organisms involves this form of the Precautionary Principle. An Economic Incentives Precautionary Principle would insist that in the face of doubt, those who impose a possible risk should be asked to pay a tax or a fee that corresponds to the public's best assessment of the cost of that risk. For every regulatory tool, there is a corresponding Precautionary Principle. Of course the idea of "margin of safety" can be understood in multiple different ways, with a continuum from a small margin, designed to counteract

---

[10] Compare Per Sandin, Dimensions of the Precautionary Principle, 5 *Hum. & Ecol. Risk Assess.* 889 (1999).

[11] See J. S. Gray, Statistics and the Precautionary Principle, 21 *Marine Pollution Bulletin* 174 (1990).

[12] Per Sandin et al., Five Charges against the Precautionary Principle, 5 *J. Risk Research* 287, 290–91 (2002).

[13] Richard B. Stewart, Environmental Regulatory Decisionmaking under Uncertainty, 20 *Res. L. & Econ.* 71, 76 (2002).

[14] See John D. Graham, Decision-Analytic Refinements of the Precautionary Prnciple, 4 *J. Risk Research* 127, 135–38 (2001).

speculative and noncatastrophic risks, to a large one, designed to insure against the worst imaginable cases.

A great deal of progress might well be made through attending to the various moving parts. An Information Disclosure Precautionary Principle would make best sense when there is some probability of harm, but it does not appear to be terribly high, and when the outcome would be far from catastrophic. A Prohibitory Precautionary Principle, with a large margin of safety, would be justified if the evidence of harm is clear and if the outcome would be particularly bad.

Consider in this light the partly sensible but frequently vague and confusing communication on the Precautionary Principle from the European Commission.[15] The communication urges that the principle "should be considered within a structured approach to the analysis of risk" that includes "risk assessment, risk management, risk communication." Hence measures based on the principle should not be blindly precautionary, but should be nondiscriminatory in application and consistent with similar measures previously taken. The Commission also insists that precautionary steps should be proportional to the chosen level of protection and "based on an examination of the potential benefits and costs of action or lack of action (including, where appropriate and feasible, an economic cost/benefit analysis)."

The idea of proportional response is a useful recognition of the fact that risk "can rarely be reduced to zero." (Rarely is surely an understatement.) The reference to cost-benefit analysis sensibly recognizes the relevance of "non-economic considerations," including public acceptability. But it is not so simple to combine cost-benefit analysis with the Precautionary Principle. What should be done if the anticipated costs of regulation exceed the anticipated benefits of regulation? Does the Commission mean to suggest that even in that case, action is justified in the interest of precaution? Always? Most of the time? An affirmative answer is suggested by the Commission's unhelpful contention "that the protection of health takes precedence over economic considerations."[16] This is unhelpful for two reasons. First, everything depends on degree; a very slight improvement in

[15] Communication from the Commission on the Precautionary Principle (Brussels, Feb. 2, 2000), available at http://europa.eu.int/comm/dgs/health_consumer_library/pub/pub07_en.pdf.
[16] *Id.* at 4.

public health would not justify an enormous expenditure of money. (Would a hundred million dollar expenditure be worthwhile to avoid a handful of minor health problems?) Second, large expenditures can themselves produce adverse health effects (as we saw in chapter 1). If government requires significant amounts to be spent on risk reduction, there is at least a risk of increases in unemployment and poverty – and both of these lead to increases in illnesses and deaths.

The Commission also emphasizes the importance of a "scientific evaluation of the potential adverse effects" when considering whether to act.[17] Indeed, recourse to the Precautionary Principle is said to presuppose "identification of potentially negative effects" alongside a "scientific evaluation" that shows inconclusive or imprecise data.[18] In this way, the Commission does not argue that the principle should be invoked without evidence. The Commission's communication leaves many open questions and I have raised a number of doubts about it. But insofar as it takes the Precautionary Principle to call for attention to potentially significant risks when the costs of control are not excessive or grossly disproportionate, it provides a plausible start.

The pieces are in place for an understanding of how to go beyond that start and to reconceive the Precautionary Principle outside of the context of uncertain risks of catastrophe. Margins of safety are sensibly used for risks that justify the most concern, at least if those margins do not themselves impose serious harm or create significant risks. If a product or activity produces real risks but offers no real benefits, there is a strong argument for banning it. The tasks are to identify the full universe of relevant risks, to specify the appropriate tools, and to impose margins of safety that are closely attuned both to the "target" risk and to the risks that are associated with reducing it. Sometimes those tasks are daunting, but in many cases a little attention to the central inquiries should go a long way toward resolving heavily contested questions for both ordinary citizens and nations.

MANAGING FEAR AND DISCLOSURE REQUIREMENTS

In the last decades, many people have been enthusiastic about the idea that producers of hazards should inform people of the underlying

---

[17] *Id.* at 13. [18] *Id.* at 14.

risks, so as to promote knowledge rather than ignorance and so as to allow for more informed choices. In the world of regulatory policy, information disclosure often seems better than either government inaction or command-and-control regulation, simply because it is less intrusive and allows people to choose as they wish. In the context of drugs and medical procedures, patients are often informed of low-probability events, including worst-case outcomes, even if the risk of disaster is exceedingly small. In general, isn't it best to tell people about the dangers that they face, whatever the likelihood of harm?

An understanding of the nature of fear raises cautionary notes about disclosure policies. Suppose, for example, that regulators propose to label goods that contain genetically modified foods, so as to ensure that consumers know that this is what they are buying. Or suppose that regulators require water companies to disclose to their customers the level of arsenic in their drinking water – a level that, in democratic societies, generally ranges from a high of 25 parts per billion to a low of 5 parts per billion. On reasonable assumptions, both of these steps may cause far more trouble than they are worth. The problem is not simply that people may well misunderstand risk disclosures, seeing the hazard as far greater than it is in fact. The problem is also that the disclosure may greatly alarm people, causing various kinds of harms, without giving them any useful information at all. If people neglect probability, they may fix, or fixate, on the bad outcome, in a way that will cause anxiety and distress but without altering behavior or even improving understanding. It would be better to tell people not only about the risk but also about the *meaning* of the probability information – for example, by comparing a risk to others encountered in ordinary life. But if the risk is low, and of the sort that usually does not trouble sensible human beings, is it really important to force disclosure of facts that will predictably cause high levels of alarm?

Of course there are difficult issues here about the relationship between respect for people's autonomy and concern for their welfare. On one view, people have a right to know the risks that they face. Perhaps disclosure of low-probability risks is justified on grounds of autonomy even if that disclosure would increase fear and distress. But if people are prone to neglect probabilities, and if we really are speaking of exceedingly improbable risks, it is by no means clear that the interest in autonomy justifies disclosure of information that will not be processed properly. At a minimum, any disclosure, if it is worthwhile, should be accompanied by efforts to enable people to put the risk in context.

This point very much bears on the civic responsibilities of those who disseminate information about risk, including public officials, the media, and those interested in moving regulatory law in one or another direction. In view of probability neglect and the operation of the availability heuristic, it is not difficult to produce large changes in public judgments, by dramatically increasing fear. A statement of worst-case scenarios can greatly alter both behavior and thought. Sometimes these changes are entirely justified as a way of reducing a kind of complacency, or fatalism, about real risks. But it is, to say the least, undesirable to take advantage of the psychological mechanisms to provoke public concern when the risks are statistically minuscule.

HEIGHTENING FEAR?

Suppose that government wants to encourage people to focus on risks that they are now ignoring. If so, it would do well to attempt not to provide information about probabilities, but to appeal to people's emotions and to attend to the worst case, above all by providing vivid narrative and clear images of alarming scenarios. For cigarette smoking, abuse of alcohol, reckless driving, and abuse of drugs, this is exactly what governments occasionally attempt to do. It should be no surprise that some of the most effective efforts to control cigarette smoking appeal to people's emotions, by making them feel that if they smoke, they will be dupes of the tobacco companies or imposing harms on innocent third parties;[19] some such efforts provide vivid images of illness or even death. Strategies of this kind can overcome unrealistic optimism – a common basis for inattention to risks that ought to justify serious concern.

Because of probability neglect, it should not be terribly difficult for government to trigger public fear. Terrorism is effective in part

---

[19] See Lisa K. Goldman and Stanton A. Glantz, Evaluation of Antismoking Advertising Campaigns, 279 *J.A.M.A.* 772 (1998).

for exactly that reason. But there are serious ethical issues here. Government ought to treat its citizens with respect; it should not treat them as objects to be channeled in government's preferred directions. It is plausible to insist that government ought not to manipulate or to trick people by taking advantage of their limitations in thinking about risk. A skeptic might think that the use of worst-case scenarios, or dramatic images of harm, consists of unacceptable manipulation. But so long as the government is democratically accountable and attempting to discourage people from running genuinely serious risks, there should be no objection in principle. Tobacco companies and others who want people to run risks, for economic or other purposes, try to engage people's emotions. So long as free speech is respected, government should be permitted to meet fire with fire. Of course the issue is not always simple. In the context of state lotteries, state governments use dramatic images of "easy street" in order to encourage people to spend money for tickets whose economic value is effectively zero. This strategy, exploiting probability neglect in the domain of hope, does raise ethical issues. My suggestion is only that if government seeks to trigger concerns about real risks, it is likely to do well if it appeals to people's emotions.

There is also a striking asymmetry between increasing fear and decreasing it: A vivid incident or a worst-case scenario can produce high levels of fear, but efforts at reassurance are far less likely to work. If people are now alarmed about a low-probability hazard, is there anything that government can do to dampen their concern? Government is unlikely to be successful if it simply emphasizes the low probability that the risk will come to fruition. The best approach may well be this: *Change the subject.* I have noted that discussions of low-probability risks tend to heighten public concern, even if those discussions consist largely of reassurance. Perhaps the most effective way of reducing fear of a low-probability risk is simply to discuss something else and to let time do the rest. Recall in this regard President Bush's effort, in the aftermath of the terrorist attacks of 9/11, not to emphasize that the statistical risks were low, but to treat flying as a kind of patriotic act, one that would prevent terrorists from obtaining victory. This effort probably did not reduce people's perception of the risk, but by focusing on the "meaning" of flying, it very likely altered their behavior.

TECHNOCRATS AND POPULISTS

But how should law and government respond to a public panic, based on an intense emotional reaction to a low-probability risk? Let us distinguish two possible positions. The *technocrat* would want to ignore public irrationality, and to respond to fear if and to the extent that it is anchored in reality. The *populist* would want to respond to public concerns, simply because they are public concerns. In my view, both positions are far too simple.

Suppose that we agree that government should not fall victim to probability neglect or otherwise excessive fears, and that it would be foolish, as a general rule, to spend a large amount of taxpayer resources to reduce risks that will never come to fruition. If so, a democratic society faces an obvious problem, for elected officers ordinarily face strong incentives to respond to excessive fear, perhaps by enacting legislation that cannot be justified by any kind of rational accounting. The best response involves education and information. Government ought not to capitulate to the public demand for regulation when there is no good reason for it.

The point suggests the importance of ensuring a large role for specialists in the regulatory process. If the public demand for regulation is likely to be distorted by unjustified fear, a major role should be given to more insulated officials who are in a better position to judge whether risks are real. Of course, specialists might be wrong. But if highly representative institutions, responding to public fear, are susceptible to error, then it is entirely appropriate to create institutions that will have a degree of insulation. Democratic governments should respond to people's values, not to their blunders.

But this claim raises some complexities of its own. Suppose that people are greatly concerned about a risk that has a small or even minuscule probability of occurring – shark attacks, or anthrax in the mail, or terrorism on airplanes. If government is confident that it knows the facts, and if people are far more concerned than the facts warrant, should the government respond, via regulation, to their concerns? Or should it ignore them, on the ground that the concerns are irrational? Consider the individual analogy first. Even if people's fear is itself irrational, it might well be rational for them to take account of that fear in their behavior. If I am afraid to fly, I might sensibly decline to do so, on the ground that my fear will make the experience quite dreadful – not only while flying but in anticipating it. If the fear exists, but if I cannot eliminate it, the most rational decision might be not to fly. Phobic people often do best to work around their phobias.

So, too, at the social level. Suppose, for example, that people are afraid of arsenic in drinking water, and that they demand steps to provide assurance that arsenic levels will not be hazardous. Suppose too that the risks from existing levels of arsenic are infinitesmal. Is it so clear that government should refuse to do what people want it to do? The fear is by hypothesis real. If people are scared that their drinking water is "not safe," they are, simply for that reason, experiencing a significant loss. In many domains, widespread fear helps produce an array of additional problems. It may, for example, make people reluctant to engage in certain activities, such as flying on airplanes or eating certain foods. The resulting costs can be extremely high; the mad cow disease scare is an example, producing many millions of dollars in losses. Why shouldn't government attempt to reduce fear, just as it attempts to produce other gains to people's well-being?

The simplest answer here is that if government is able to inform and educate people, it should do that instead. It should not waste resources on steps that will do nothing other than to reduce fear. But the simplest answer is too pat. Whether information and education will work is an empirical question. If these do not work, government should respond, just as individuals do, to fears that are real and by hypothesis difficult to eradicate. Suppose, for example, that government could cheaply undertake a procedure that would reduce a tiny risk to zero – and equally important, be seen to reduce the relevant risk to zero. It seems clear that government should take this step, which may be more effective and less expensive than education and information. Recall that fear is a real social cost, and it is likely to lead to other social costs. If, for example, people are afraid to fly, the economy will suffer in multiple ways; so, too, if people are afraid to send or to receive mail. The reduction of even baseless fear is a social good, not least because of the potentially enormous "ripple effects" associated with it.[20]

---

[20] See *The Social Amplification of Risk*, ed. Nick Pidgeon, Roger E. Kasperson, and Paul Slovic (New York: Cambridge University Press, 2003).

At the same time, there are some practical complications. If government attempts to reduce fear by regulating the activity that produces it, it might well intensify that very fear, simply by suggesting that the activity is worth regulating. As an analogue, return to the debate over whether the government should require genetically modified food to be labeled as such. Mandatory labels suggest a danger that might not exist. Sometimes the fear that accompanies probability neglect diminishes over time, as experience moves the activity or process from the cognitive category of "unsafe" to "safe." A regulatory approach might prevent this process (salutary when the risk really is low) from occurring. If so, inaction would be the preferred course.

Even if it is clear that government should respond, many questions remain. How and how much should government respond? The answer depends on the extent of the fear and the cost of the response. If people are extremely fearful, a substantial response is of course easier to justify. If the cost of response is very high, a refusal to respond might well make sense. We need to know how much good, and how much harm, would be done by the action in question. What I am emphasizing is that public fear is an independent concern, and it can represent a high cost in itself and lead to serious associated costs. If public fear cannot be alleviated without risk reduction, then government reasonably engages in risk reduction.

CHAPTER 6

Costs and Benefits

Cost-benefit analysis has become an increasingly popular tool for the assessment and management of social risks. Indeed, cost-benefit analysis is often urged as an alternative to the Precautionary Principle. Instead of blindly "taking precautions," it is argued, regulators should tally up the benefits of regulation and its costs, and choose the approach that maximizes net benefits. This approach is often justified on grounds of economic efficiency. On this view, regulators should proceed if the costs exceed the benefits, but not otherwise. I do not endorse this view. Efficiency is relevant, but it is hardly the only goal of regulation. Citizens in a democratic society might well choose to protect endangered species, or wildlife, or pristine areas, even if it is not efficient for them to do so. And if poor people stand to gain from regulatory protection, such protection might be worthwhile even if rich people stand to lose somewhat more.

I believe that the arguments made thus far establish a *cognitive* case for cost-benefit analysis – that is, an argument for cost-benefit analysis that does not depend on economic efficiency, but that stresses the possibility that an account of costs and benefits can respond to the problems that human beings face in thinking about risks. If the availability heuristic leads people to misestimate probabilities, then cost-benefit analysis can give them a more accurate sense of the actual harms against which protection is sought. If probability neglect makes people focus on worst-case scenarios, without thinking about their likelihood, then an emphasis on costs and benefits will provide a clearer sense of the stakes. If people neglect tradeoffs, then cost-benefit analysis is a natural corrective. For genetic modification of food, global warming, contaminated drinking water, and much more, it is important to see, as best we can, what would be gained and what would be lost by competing courses of action. Hence an accounting of costs and benefits is an important ingredient in the analysis of risks. It should be seen, not as an arithmetic straitjacket, but as a method for showing what is at stake. It is an important way of disciplining public fear – of creating a kind of System II corrective against System I heuristics and biases.

I do not contend that the cost-benefit analysis should control regulatory decisions. That analysis does not establish a rule by which choices must be made. Participants in a democratic society might choose to proceed even when the costs exceed the benefits – but if they do so, it should be after receiving the information that the cost-benefit analysis provides. And if regulators choose to impose costs that are disproportionately high in comparison to the expected benefits, they should explain why they have chosen to do that.

What, exactly, is the relationship between the Precautionary Principle and cost-benefit analysis? As we have seen, the European Commission has endorsed the Precautionary Principle but also stressed that cost-benefit analysis should play a role in its application. In so saying, the Commission contends that health has priority over mere money. I have complained that this is an almost comically unhelpful statement; if health would be promoted just a little, huge amounts of money ought not to be spent, partly because that money could be spent on other health problems, partly because large expenditures can cause health problems. I suggest that it would be better to endorse cost-benefit analysis while noting that precautions, especially against possible catastrophes, should play a role in its application. The chief advantage of cost-benefit analysis over the Precautionary Principle is that it provides a wide rather than narrow viewscreen.

Of course critics of cost-benefit analysis object that without precautions, analysts will neglect risks that will eventually turn out to be serious. The objection is convincing if the analysis of costs and benefits requires certainty and proof before counting benefits as such. But good analysts require neither certainty nor proof. They know that if there is a 1/1,000 chance of saving 50,000 lives, the expected value of regulation is fifty lives, not zero. They also know that citizens might want to build a margin of safety into regulation designed to protect against large harms with low probabilities, so that a 1/1,000 risk of 50,000 deaths might deserve more attention than a 1/100 risk of 5,000 deaths. Nothing in cost-benefit analysis can solve the evaluative questions. Those who use this tool do not reject the idea of "margins of safety." They attempt to assess costs and benefits in order to improve both individual and social cognition about risks.

I have elsewhere attempted to spell out the cognitive argument for cost-benefit analysis in some detail.[1] I want to focus here on another puzzle, one that is often raised by skeptics about cost-benefit analysis. What does cost-benefit actually entail? How can we possibly come up with monetary amounts for social risks? How do we value life and fear? My principal goal is to make some progress on these questions. I show that a simple idea underlies current practices. The idea is that *governments assign monetary values to risks by asking what monetary values ordinary people assign to risks.* I want to suggest that this idea has a great deal of appeal and coherence. But I also contend that current practices have two quite serious problems under the very theory that most plausibly justifies them. First, people do not see all statistically identical risks in the same way. People distinguish among 1/100,000 risks of dying from AIDS, an airplane crash, Alzheimer's disease, cancer, and a workplace accident. Second, different people, and different groups, evaluate risks differently from one another. Some people show an intense aversion to risks that other people face with equanimity. Old people do not think of risks in the same way that young people do; there are differences across lines of race, gender, and wealth as well. These objections do not cast doubt on the theory that underlies current practices; but they suggest that if the theory is right, current practices need to be changed fairly radically.

In short, I am going to try to take the current theory *very* seriously – more seriously, in fact, than do those who now use it. Of course, many people are deeply skeptical of that theory and believe that it provides a bad foundation for policies involving the environment and social risks.[2] I will turn to their arguments and the foundational issues in the next chapter. For now, let us begin with actual practices.

---

[1] See Cass R. Sunstein, *Risk and Reason* (Cambridge: Cambridge University Press, 2002).
[2] See Frank Ackerman and Lisa Heinzerling, *Priceless: On Knowing the Price of Everything and the Value of Nothing* (New York: New Press, 2004).

THE REAL WORLD OF COST-BENEFIT ANALYSIS:
WHAT AGENCIES DO AND WHY

It has now become standard for regulatory agencies to assign monetary values to human lives. In the United States, the Environmental Protection Agency uses a uniform value for a statistical life (VSL): $6.1 million.[3] Consider Table 6.1, which captures agency practices from 1996 through 2003. The initial question is how agencies generate monetary amounts of this kind. The answer comes from two kinds of evidence. The first and most important involves real-world markets, producing evidence of compensation levels for actual risks.[4] In the workplace and for consumer goods, additional safety has a price; market evidence is investigated to identify that price.[5] The second kind of evidence comes from contingent valuation studies, asking people how much they are willing to pay to reduce statistical risks.[6] The EPA's $6.1 million is a product of studies of actual workplace risks, attempting to determine how much workers are paid to assume mortality hazards.[7] The relevant risks usually are in the general range of 1/10,000 to 1/100,000. The calculation of VSL is a product of simple arithmetic. Suppose that workers must be paid $600, on average, to face a risk of 1/10,000. If so, the value of a statistical life would be said to be $6 million.

For at glimpse at some of the two dozen studies on which agencies currently rely, consider Table 6.2.[8] Of course many questions might be

---

[3] See 66 Fed. Reg. 6979, 7012 (Jan. 22, 2001). In its July 2003 regulation governing food labeling of trans fatty acids, the Food and Drug Administration used a VSL of $6.5 million, see 68 Fed. Reg. 41434, 41489 (July 11, 2003); in its March 13, 2003 proposed rule on dietary ingredients and dietary supplements, the same agency suggested a VSL of $5 million, see 68 Fed. Reg. 12158, 12229–30 (Mar. 13, 2003) (using this value to calculate the "value of a statistical life day").

[4] See W. Kip Viscusi, *Fatal Tradeoffs: Public and Private Responsibilities for Risk* (New York: Oxford University Press, 1992).

[5] A valuable and comprehensive overview can be found in W. Kip Viscusi and Joseph E. Aldy, The Value of a Statistical Life: A Critical Review of Market Estimates Throughout the World, 27 *J. Risk & Uncertainty* 5 (2003).

[6] See, e.g., James K. Hammitt and Jin-Tau Liu, Effects of Disease Type and Latency on the Value of Mortality Risk, 28 *J. Risk & Uncertainty* 73 (2004).

[7] See Viscusi, *supra* note 4.

[8] See Environmental Protection Agency, *Guidelines for Preparing Economic Analyses* 89 (Washington, D.C.: US EPA, 2000).

Table 6.1. *Agency Values of Life, 1996–2003*

Agency	Regulation and Date	Value of Statistical Life
Dept. of Transportation/Federal Motor Carrier Safety Administration	Safety Requirements for Operators of Small Passenger-Carrying Commercial Motor Vehicles Used in Interstate Commerce August 12, 2003, 68 FR 47860-01	$3 million
Dept. of Health & Human Services/FDA	Food Labeling: Trans Fatty Acids in Nutrition Labeling, Nutrient Content Claims, and Health Claims July 11, 2003, 68 FR 41434-01	$6.5 million
Dept. of Agriculture Food Safety & Inspection Service	Control of 1Listeria Monocytogenes in Ready-to-Eat Meat and Poultry Products June 6, 2003, 68 FR 34208-01	$4.8 million
Dept. of Health & Human Services/FDA	Labeling Requirements for Systemic Antibacterial Drug Products Intended for Human Use February 6, 2003, 68 FR 6062-01	$5 million
Office of Management & Budget	Report to Congress on the Costs and Benefits of Federal Regulations February 3, 2003, 68 FR 5492-01	$5 million
EPA	Control of Emissions from Nonroad Large Spark-Ignition Engines, and Recreational Engines (Marine & Land-Based) November 8, 2002, 67 FR 68242-01	$6 million
EPA	National Primary Drinking Water Regulations: Arsenic and Clarifications to Compliance and New Source Contaminants Monitoring January 22, 2001, 66 FR 6976-01	$6.1 million
EPA	Control of Air Pollution from New Motor Vehicles: Heavy-Duty Engine and Vehicle Standards and Highway Diesel Fuel Sulfur Control Requirements January 18, 2001, 66 FR 5002-01	$6 million
EPA	Control of Air Pollution from New Motor Vehicles: Tier 2 Motor Vehicle Emissions Standards and Gasoline Sulfur Control Requirements February 10, 2000, 65 FR 6698-01	$5.9 million

(cont.)

Table 6.1. *(cont.)*

Agency	Regulation and Date	Value of Statistical Life
EPA	Findings of Significant Contribution and Rulemaking on Section 125 Petitions for Purposes of Reducing Interstate Ozone Transport January 18, 2000, 65 FR 2674-01	$5.9 million
EPA	Final Standards for Hazardous Air Pollutants for Hazardous Waste Combustors September 30, 1999, 64 FR 52828-01	$5.6 million
EPA	National Primary Drinking Water Regulations: Disinfectants and Disinfection Byproducts December 16, 1998, 63 FR 69390-01	$5.6 million
Dept. of Transportation/FAA	Financial Responsibility Requirements for Licensed Launch Activities August 26, 1998, 63 FR 45592-01	$3 million
Dept. of Health & Human Services/FDA	Quality Mammography Standards October 28, 1997, 62 FR 55852-01	$2–3 million
Dept. of Health & Human Services/FDA	Regulations Restricting the Sale and Distribution of Cigarettes and Smokeless Tobacco to Protect Children and Adolescents August 28, 1996, 61 FR 44396-01	$2.5 million
Dept. of Agriculture/Food Safety & Inspection Service	Pathogen Reduction; Hazard Analysis and Critical Control Point (HACCP) Systems July 25, 1996, 61 FR 38806-01	$1.6 million
Dept. of Transportation/FAA	Aircraft Flight Simulator Use in Pilot Training, Testing, and Checking and at Training Centers July 2, 1996, 61 FR 34508-01	$2.7 million
Consumer Product Safety Commission	Requirements for Labeling of Retail Containers of Charcoal May 3, 1996, 61 FR 19818-01	$5 million
Consumer Product Safety Commission	Large Multiple-Tube Fireworks Devices March 26, 1996, 61 FR 13084-01	$3–$7 million

Table 6.2. *Value of Life Studies*

Study	Method	Value of Statistical Life
Kniesner and Leith (1991)	Labor market	$0.7 million
Smith and Gilbert (1984)	Labor market	$0.8 million
Dillingham (1985)	Labor market	$1.1 million
Marin and Psacharopoulos (1982)	Labor market	$3.4 million
V. K. Smith (1976)	Labor market	$5.7 million
Viscusi (1981)	Labor market	$7.9 million
Leigh and Folsom (1984)	Labor market	$11.7 million
Leigh (1987)	Labor market	$12.6 million
Garen (1988)	Labor market	$16.3 million

Source: United States Environmental Protection Agency, *Guidelines for Preparing Economic Analyses* 89 (Washington, D.C.: United States Printing Office, 2000).

raised about the use of these studies by government agencies.[9] Most obviously, the studies show significant variety in the crucial numbers, ranging from $0.7 million, in 1991 dollars, to $16.3 million. The EPA has adopted the $6.1 million figure on the ground that it represents the median in the relevant studies. But there is a risk of arbitrariness in fastening on that median figure, certainly if we lack reason to believe that the relevant study is the most accurate. In fact, a more general look at the VSL data produces further puzzles and wider ranges. Some studies find no compensating differentials at all, indicating a VSL of zero[10] – implausibly low, to say the least, for purposes of policy. Others find that nonunionized workers receive *negative* compensating differentials for risk, that is, they appear to be paid less because they face mortality risks.[11] Another study finds that African-Americans receive no significant compensating wage differential and hence that their particular VSL is zero.[12] On the other hand, it is possible to find studies finding a VSL not below the range in Table 6.1 but above it;

---

[9] See Richard W. Parker, Grading the Government, 70 *U. Chi. L. Rev.* 1345 (2003), and Robert H. Frank and Cass R. Sunstein, Cost-Benefit Analysis and Relative Position, 68 *U. Chi. L. Rev.* 323 (2001), for several such questions.

[10] See Peter Dorman and Paul Hagstrom, Wage Compensation for Dangerous Work Revisited, 52(1) *Industrial & Labor Relations Review* 116 (1998).

[11] Viscusi and Aldy, *supra* note 5, at 44.

[12] John D. Leeth and John Ruser, Compensating Wage Differentials for Fatal and Nonfatal Injury Risk by Gender and Race, 27 *J. Risk & Uncertainty* 257 (2003).

consider the finding that for people who choose jobs with low-level risks, the VSL is as much as $22 million.[13]

The most comprehensive review finds that most studies produce a range of between $3.8 million and $9 million.[14] This range is fairly compressed, in a way that disciplines agency decisions; for many regulations, the "bottom line" of the cost-benefit assessment will not be affected by a choice of $3.8 million or $9 million. But that range still leaves significant room for discretion, in a way that would have significant implications for policy and law. Consider the fact that the monetized value of a program that saves 200 lives would range from $760 million to $1.8 billion; consider also the fact that the EPA's highly publicized arsenic regulation would easily fail cost-benefit analysis with a $3.8 million VSL but easily pass with a $9 million VSL.[15] The simple point is that the variety of the outcomes raises questions about the reliability of any particular figure.

In addition, most of these studies on which EPA relies are based on data from the 1970s. Since that time, there has been significant growth in national income, in a way that suggests that any VSL derived from 1970s data is too low. Of course people with more money are willing to pay more, other things being equal, to reduce statistical risks. One study finds that at the beginning of the twentieth century, VSL was about $150,000 in current dollars – less than one-twentieth of the corresponding amount a century later.[16] On reasonable assumptions, the EPA's use of 1970s data has produced a significant undervaluation of the monetary value of the lives at stake, for the $6.1 million figure reflects no adjustment to account for changes in national real income growth.[17] In principle, the failure to undertake an adjustment is a serious mistake. The actual amount might be substantially higher.[18]

---

[13] Viscusi and Aldy, *supra* note 5, at 23.   [14] See *id.* at 18.

[15] See Sunstein, The Arithmetic of Arsenic, in *Risk and Reason* 153, *supra* note 1. The regulation was projected to cost about $200 million, and its monetized benefits, with a $6.1 million VSL, were around $190 million. It should be easy to see that a $3.8 million VSL would make the regulation impossible to defend – and a $9 million VSL would make it impossible to challenge.

[16] See Viscusi and Aldy, *supra* note 5, at 22.

[17] EPA has updated the relevant numbers for inflation, but it has not otherwise made adjustments.

[18] See Dora L. Costa and Matthew E. Kahn, The Rising Price of Nonmarket Goods, 93 *Am. Econ. Rev.* 227, 229 table 1 (2003) (suggesting likely current value of $12 million). For recent evidence that the current numbers are indeed too low, see W. Kip Viscusi, Racial Differences

Even more fundamentally, the relevant numbers deserve respect only if they are not a product of an absence of information and bounded rationality on the part of the people whose choices generate them. Suppose, for example, that workers do not know the risks that they face or that their decisions are a product of the availability heuristic or optimistic bias. If this is so, regulators should not use, for purposes of policy, a finding that workers are paid $60 to run a risk of 1/100,000; by hypothesis, that number does not reflect a rational tradeoff by informed workers. I will return to these points in the next chapter. Current practice is based on the assumption, not that all or even most workers make informed choices, but that market processes ensure the right "price" for various degrees of safety. Compare pricing for soap, cereals, and telephones: Most consumers do not have full information, and many use heuristics that lead them astray, but market competition produces a sensible structure of prices, at least most of the time.

Let us simply assume (without necessarily agreeing) that the relevant problems can be solved and that we can identify a number, call it $6 million, that really represents people's valuations. It should be clear that even if this were so, it is grossly misleading to make the following claim: *The value of a statistical life is $6 million*. It would be much more accurate to say that for risks of 1/10,000, the median willingness to pay (WTP), in the relevant population, is $600 – or that for risks of 1/100,000, the median WTP is $60. If true, these statements would, on assumptions to be explored, be extremely helpful for purposes of policy. But even at first glance, we can see that these numbers need not be taken to support a VSL that is independent of differences in probability. Suppose that people would be willing to pay $60 to reduce a risk of 1/100,000. From this it does not follow that people would be willing to pay $6 to eliminate a risk of 1/1,000,000, or $6,000 to reduce a risk of 1/1,000, or $60,000 to reduce a risk of

in Labor Market Values of a Statistical Life, 27 *J. Risk & Uncertainty* 239, 252 table 5 (2003) (hereinafter Viscusi, Racial Differences), finding values as high as $15.1 million in the case of white males. In the context of arsenic regulation, the EPA also noted in its sensitivity analysis that the appropriate adjustment would increase the VSL from $6.1 million to $6.7 million. 66 Fed. Reg. 6979, 7012 (Jan. 22, 2001). For recent evidence, suggesting that the current VSL is $4.7 million for a full sample, $7 million for blue-collar males, and $8.5 million for blue-collar females, see W. Kip Viscusi, The Value of Life: Estimates with Risks by Occupation and Industry, 42 *Ec. Inquiry* 29 (2004) (hereinafter Viscusi, Value of Life).

1/100. It is plausible to think that people's WTP to reduce statistical risks is nonlinear.[19] As the probability approaches 100 percent, people become willing to pay an amount for risk reduction that rises nonlinearly to 100 percent of their income; as the risk approaches 0 percent, WTP nonlinearly approaches zero. For a risk of 1 in 1 million, for example, many reasonable people would be willing to pay nothing, treating that risk as inconsequential.

Hence the claim that VSL is $6.1 million is merely a shorthand way of saying that people are willing to pay from $600 to $60 to eliminate risks of 1/10,000 to 1/100,000. Since this is the range for risks with which many agencies deal, the relevant evidence is highly informative. For current purposes, this point is the crucial one.

The problem – what I emphasize here – is that VSL will inevitably vary across both risks and persons. Let us begin with the variability of risks.

RISKS

I have noted that the evidence that underlies the $6.1 million figure comes from risks of accidents in the workplace – and that even if this evidence can be generalized, it would not justify a probability-independent VSL. But there is a point of greater practical importance. A 1/100,000 risk of dying in a workplace accident might well produce a different WTP from a 1/100,000 risk of dying of cancer from air pollution, which might in turn be different from the WTP to avoid a 1/100,000 risk of dying in an airplane as a result of a terrorist attack, and that number might in turn be different from a 1/100,000 risk of dying as a result of a defective snowmobile. The very theory that lies behind the US government's current use of VSL justifies a simple conclusion: *VSL should be risk-specific; it should not be the same across statistically equivalent risks.* The use of a single number produces significant blunders.

Data

Notice first that the very category of "workplace risks" conceals relevant differences. Every economy contains a range of occupations and

---

[19] See Richard Posner, *Catastrophe: Risk and Response* 166–71 (New York: Oxford University Press, 2004).

industries, and a uniform VSL should not be expected to emerge from each of them. Indeed, a recent study finds significant differences across both occupations and industries,[20] with blue-collar workers showing a higher VSL than others. It is inevitable that a wide range of values would emerge from studies that looked separately at machine operators, executive positions, sales, dental technicians, equipment cleaners, security guards, and secretaries – and undoubtedly diverse values could be found within each category.

In addition, many risks controlled by the EPA are qualitatively different from the workplace risks that EPA has used to generate its VSL. Two differences are particularly important. First, the workplace studies involve accidents rather than cancer, and cancer risks are often involved in the EPA's decisions. There is considerable evidence that the risks associated with cancer produce a higher WTP than other kinds of risk.[21] For example, Hammit and Liu find that in Taiwan, WTP to eliminate a cancer risk is about one-third larger than WTP to avoid a risk of a similar, chronic degenerative disease.[22] Some contingent valuation studies suggest that people are willing to pay twice as much to prevent a cancer death as an instantaneous death.[23] People seem to have a special fear of cancer, and they appear willing to pay more to prevent a cancer death than a sudden unanticipated death, or a death from heart disease.[24] The "cancer premium" might be produced by the "dread" nature of cancer. It is well established that dreaded risks produce special social concern, holding the statistical risk constant.

To be sure, existing evidence on this count is not unambiguous. One study of occupational exposures does not find a significantly higher VSL for cancer risks.[25] But that study assumes that occupational cancers account for 10–20 percent of all cancer deaths – an amount that is probably too high. If occupational exposures account

[20] Viscusi, Value of Life, *supra* note 18, 39–41.
[21] See Richard L. Revesz, Environmental Regulation, Cost-Benefit Analysis, and the Discounting of Human Lives, 99 *Colum. L. Rev.* 941, 962–74 (1999).
[22] See Hammitt and Liu, *supra* note 6.   [23] See *id.*
[24] See George S. Tolley et al., State-of-the-Art Health Values, in *Valuing Health for Policy* 339–40, ed. George S. Tolley and Robert Fabian (Chicago: University of Chicago Press, 1994).
[25] See Viscusi and Aldy, *supra* note 5, at 22. In the same vein, see Wesley A. Magat et al., A Reference Lottery Metric for Valuing Health, 42 *Management Science* 1118 (1996) (finding no difference between valuations of cancer death and auto accident death).

for 5 percent of all cancers – a more realistic number – then the VSL for cancer risks may be as high as $12 million, about double the amount the EPA now uses. In principle, the VSL figures should be risk-specific, and we know enough to suspect that cancer risks produce an unusually high VSL.

The second difference between workplace risks and the risks that concern the EPA is that the latter risks seem peculiarly involuntary and uncontrollable.[26] Unlike the risks of workplace accidents, most pollution risks are not assumed voluntarily in return for compensation.[27] If you live in a highly polluted city, it is not at all clear that you are receiving benefits in return for the risk. A great deal of literature suggests that involuntary, dread, uncontrollable, and potentially catastrophic risks produce unusually high levels of public concern.[28] If so, the numbers that derive from workplace accidents will substantially understate willingness to pay for regulatory benefits provided by the EPA and many other agencies.

The implications go well beyond the distinction between workplace accidents and environmental risks. For example, people appear to be willing to pay far more to produce safety in the air than to produce safety on the highways;[29] it follows that VSL should be higher for the Federal Aviation Administration than for the National Highway Traffic Safety Administration. Oddly, the former agency has an unusually low rather than an unusually high VSL.[30] Some diseases would produce a higher VSL than others. A 1/100,000 risk of death from Alzheimer's disease would almost certainly produce a higher VSL than 1/100,000 risk of death from a heart attack; 1/50,000 risk of an AIDS death would not produce the same VSL as a 1/50,000 risk of death from a defective brake system on an automobile; most people would pay more to reduce a risk of dying from slow-acting

---

[26] See Ackerman and Heinzerling, *supra* note 2.

[27] Of course, it is possible to question the idea that workplace risks are assumed voluntarily and in return for compensation. For example, many workers probably do not know the risks that they face. In addition, those who live in cities, or otherwise face apparently involuntary risks, could avoid those risks at a cost. The distinction I am drawing here is one of kind rather than degree. See Cass R. Sunstein, Bad Deaths, 14 *J. Risk & Uncertainty* 259 (1997).

[28] See Paul Slovic, *The Perception of Risk* (London: Earthscan, 2000).

[29] See Fredrik Carlsson et al., Is Transport Safety More Valuable in the Air? Working Papers in Economics, Gotenborg University, Department of Economics 84 (2002).

[30] See Table 6.1.

strokes than from strokes that kill outright. If we only had the tools to find it, there would be a distinctive population-wide median VSL for mortality risks of airplane accidents, of cancer from air pollution, of motor vehicle accidents, of defective toys, of cancer from water pollution.

In fact, studies have been done for seatbelt use, automobile safety, home fire detectors, and more, and they find a wide variety of numbers, with a VSL ranging from $770,000 (smoke detectors, based on data in the 1970s) to $9.9 million (fatality risks associated with safety belts and motorcycle helmets).[31] And within each of these categories, further distinctions would undoubtedly emerge. All cancer fatalities are not the same; informed people would surely make distinctions between those that involve long periods of suffering and those that do not. If we are really interested in basing VSL on WTP, a uniform number, treating all statistically identical mortality risks as the same, is obtuse.

Practice and voluntariness

These claims are not entirely foreign to current regulatory policy. In the context of arsenic regulation, the EPA was alert to some of them.[32] Hence its own analysis for arsenic suggested the need for an upward revision of 7 percent, because of the involuntariness and uncontrollability of the risk.[33] With this revision, along with the revision for income growth, the value of a statistical life would rise from $6.1 million to $7.2 million.[34] In fact there are reasons to suggest that this amount might be too low. Richard Revesz suggests that "the value of avoiding a death from an involuntary, carcinogenic risk should be estimated as four times as large as the value of avoiding an instantaneous workplace fatality."[35] If we take this approach, the VSL, in the context of arsenic, jumps from $6.1 million to $24.3 million. I am not arguing that $24.3 million is the correct number; I am suggesting only that VSL is almost certainly risk specific.

---

[31] Viscusi and Aldy, *supra* note 5, at 25.
[32] See Sunstein, The Arithmetic of Arsenic, in *Risk and Reason, supra* note 1.
[33] 66 Fed. Reg. 6979, 7014 (Jan. 22, 2001).   [34] *Id.*
[35] See Revesz, *supra* note 21, at 982.

It is important not to think that there is a rigid dichotomy between the involuntary/uncontrollable and the voluntary/controllable.[36] This is a continuum, without sharp divisions among various points, and hence it is a mistake to believe that risks can be neatly separated into the two categories. Are the risks of airplane travel uncontrollable? Many people think so, but the decision to fly is itself under human control. Are the risks from air pollution in Los Angeles involuntarily incurred? The answer might seem to be affirmative, but people have a choice whether or not to live in Los Angeles. Death from an asteroid appears to be a model case of involuntariness, at an opposite pole from hang-gliding. But why, exactly? In deciding whether a risk is faced involuntarily, or whether it is within personal control, the underlying issues seem to be twofold: first, whether those exposed to the risk are exposed knowingly; and second, whether it is costly or otherwise difficult for people to avoid the risk. When risks are approached in these terms, it is clear that some risks are worse than others, even if the probability of harm is identical. This point is enough to suggest that VSL cannot be uniform across risks.

PERSONS

Even when risks are identical, people are diverse in their values and their preferences. The $6.1 million itself is the median figure – it is the median of a set of means. But everyone agrees that in workplaces and elsewhere, individual WTP is highly variable. Some of the variability stems from different degrees of aversion to different risks. Diverse people have diverse fears. Some people are especially concerned to avoid the dangers associated with pesticides, whereas others focus on the risks of air travel; some of these differences are a product of beliefs (about existing risk levels), but others of tastes and values. So too, people who already face high levels of background risk should be expected to be willing to pay less to avoid an additional risk of 1/100,000 than those with low levels of background risk. People in a poor nation or a poor area, with low life expectancies, will show less concern with a 1/100,000 risk than people in a place with high life expectancies. If a relevant population faces thirty annual mortality

[36] See Sunstein, *supra* note 27.

risks of 1/10,000 or higher, it should show a lower VSL with respect to a new risk of 1/100,000 than a population whose background risks are less serious.[37] The difference between the VSL of people in wealthy nations and that of people in poor nations, taken up below, is partly a product of the fact that the latter group generally face far higher background risks.

WTP varies with age as well. We might well predict that other things being equal, older people will show a lower WTP and hence a lower VSL, simply because they have fewer years left. One study, for example, finds that the VSL of a 48-year-old is 10 percent lower than that of a 36-year-old; another finds that people under 45 have a VSL twenty times higher than people over 65.[38] A careful analysis suggests that VSL peaks around age 30, stays constant for about a decade, but declines from that point – so much so that the VSL for a 60-year-old is approximately half of that of people from 30 to 40.[39] These findings raise particular conundrums in the case of people under 18; how should government proceed if the people between infancy and 15 years of age show a tiny VSL, simply because they have little or no money? It is implausible to use a tiny VSL for them; but what number should be used, and why? Little progress has been made on this question,[40] with the American government using its ordinary, uniform number for children as for everyone else.[41] But if we put the vexing case of children to one side, then the prevailing theory suggests a lower VSL for those at the last stages of life than for those who have many decades to go – and that this difference ought to be reflected in regulatory policy.[42]

Along the same lines, many analysts have suggested that regulatory policy should focus not on statistical lives but on statistical life-years

---

[37] See Louis R. Eeckhoudt and James K. Hammitt, Background Risks and the Value of a Statistical Life, 23 *J. Risk & Uncertainty* 261 (2001).

[38] See Viscusi and Aldy, *supra* note 5, at 51. For contrary evidence, see Cass R. Sunstein, Lives, Life-Years, and Willingness to Pay, 104 *Colum. L. Rev.* 205 (2004).

[39] See Joseph E. Aldy and W. Kip Viscusi, Age Variations in Workers' Value of Statistical Life (2003), available at http://www.nber.org/papers/w10199.pdf.

[40] For an overview that turns out to be highly tentative and indeterminate, see Environmental Protection Agency, *Children's Health Valuation Handbook* (Washington, D.C.: US EPA, 2003).

[41] See *id.* at 3-12-3-13, referring to Environmental Protection Agency, *Guidelines for Preparing Economic Analyses* (Washington, D.C.: US EPA, 2000).

[42] See Sunstein, *supra* note 38.

(VSLY).[43] Suppose that they are right. If so, then the statistical lives of young people will be worth more than the statistical lives of older people. In 2003, the American government's interest in focusing on VSLY led to loud and vehement public objections to what, under one proposal, would seem to be a "senior death discount" – in accordance with which someone over 70 would be "worth" 58 cents on the dollar.[44] But assuming that people over 70 are willing to pay about 58 percent, on average, of what people under 70 are willing to pay, the theory that underlies current practice justifies exactly this disparity. If the theory is right, then a disparity between older people and younger people makes perfect sense to the extent that the WTP figures justify it.

Even more fundamentally, those with little to spare will show a far lower VSL than those who have plenty. WTP depends on ability to pay, and when ability to pay is low, WTP will of course be low as well. For this reason the VSL of people with an annual income of $50,000 will be lower than that of people with an annual income of $150,000. People in the former category might be willing to pay no more than $25 to reduce a risk of 1/100,000, where people in the latter group might be willing to pay as much as $100. If so, government should not require everyone to pay $100; its decision to do so would harm those unwilling to pay that amount, simply because it would require them to pay more than they think is worth their while. A uniform VSL, of the sort that government now uses, threatens to "overprotect" the poor, in a way that might well be harmful to them – and also threatens to underprotect the wealthy, in a way that is highly likely to be harmful to them. (I return to this controversial question in the next chapter.)

As a simple matter of fact, we would expect that unionized workers would receive more compensation for incurring risks – and studies almost always show a higher VSL for unionized workers, with amounts found to be as high as $12.3 million, $18.1 million, and even $44.2 million.[45] We would similarly expect to find large differences across nations, with VSL being higher in rich countries than in poor ones. And in fact, studies find a VSL as low as $200,000 for Taiwan, $500,000 for South Korea, and $1.2 million for India – but

---

[43] See *id.*   [44] See *id.*   [45] See Viscusi and Aldy, *supra* note 5, at 45.

Table 6.3. *VSL across Nations*

Nation and year of study	VSL (in 2000 US$)
Japan (1991)	$9.7 million
South Korea (1993)	$0.8 million
Canada (1989)	$3.9–4.7 million
India (1996/97)	$1.2–1.5 million
Taiwan (1997)	$0.2–0.9 million
Australia (1997)	$11.3–19.1 million
Hong Kong (1998)	$1.7 million
Switzerland (2001)	$6.3–8.6 million
United Kingdom (2000)	$19.9 million

Source: Drawn on the basis of W. Kip Viscusi and Joseph Aldy, The Value of a Statistical Life: A Critical Review of Market Estimates Throughout the World, 27 *J. Risk & Uncertainty* 5, 45 (2003).

$21.7 million for Canada and $19 million for Australia.[46] Consider, for purposes of illustration, Table 6.3.[47] Within the United States, wealthy populations should be expected to show a higher VSL than poorer populations. If a program is designed to combat health risks in wealthy suburbs, the VSL would be above the population-wide median; if the protected population is mostly in poor areas, the VSL would be below it. Currently agencies pay no attention to this possibility in undertaking cost-benefit analysis.

What about the more controversial categories of race and gender? Recent studies show big differences. Using workplace data from 1996 to 1998, Leeth and Ruser find that women's VSL ranges from $8.1 million to $10.2 million, whereas men's VSL is less than half that, ranging from $2.6 million to $4.7 million.[48] Leeth and Ruser find that Hispanic males show a slightly higher VSL than white males ($5 million to $3.4 million)[49] – and most strikingly, that African-Americans receive no compensation for workplace risks, producing a VSL of zero.[50] Using workplace data from 1992 through 1997, Viscusi also finds a significant disparity across racial lines, though his numbers are quite different from those found by Leeth and Ruser.[51] In

[46] See *id.* at 27–28.   [47] Drawn from *id.* at 26–27.
[48] See Leeth and Ruser, *supra* note 12, at 266.   [49] *Id.* at 270.
[50] *Id.* at 275.   [51] See Viscusi, Racial Differences, *supra* note 18, at 252.

Viscusi's study, the VSL is highest for white males and lowest for African-American males, with white females and African-American females falling between the poles. More particularly, Viscusi finds that the overall white VSL is $15 million, while the overall African-American VSL is $7.2 million.[52] For white females, the overall VSL is $9.4 million, compared to $18.8 million for white males; for African-American females, the overall VSL is $6.9 million, compared to $5.9 million for African-American males. Another study by Viscusi finds a VSL of $7 million for blue-collar males and $8.5 million for blue-collar females.[53]

The differences between Leeth and Ruser on the one hand and Viscusi on the other remain a puzzle. For my purposes, the central point is that demographic differences in VSL are entirely to be expected, and they are found in both studies.

THEORY AND PRACTICE

If we put the foregoing points together, we can see that there is not one VSL, but an exceptionally large number of VSLs. In fact, each of us has not one VSL but a number of them, targeted to each risk that each of us faces. A policy that truly tracks WTP would seek to provide each person with the level of protection for which he is willing to pay to reduce each risk. Tracking WTP is the goal that underlies current practice. Apart from the problem of administrability, that goal calls for a maximum level of individuation.

As a thought experiment, suppose that an all-knowing regulator could easily determine each person's WTP for each statistical risk that she faces – and perfectly match the level of regulatory protection to that WTP. In these circumstances, the regulator should give each person no more and no less than his WTP for each risk. (If people's WTP is low because they are poor, they might be subsidized; but they would not be forced to purchase goods for an amount in excess of their WTP. I will return to this point.) Under this approach, regulatory benefits would be treated the same as every other commodity that is traded on markets, including safety itself; consider the purchase of smoke alarms and Volvos. I have emphasized that most people

[52] *Id.*   [53] See Viscusi, Value of Life, *supra* note 18, at 39.

face extremely serious problems in dealing with risk, stemming both from an absence of information and from bounded rationality. The all-knowing regulator would overcome these problems and provide people with what they would want if they did not suffer from them.

If we could do this, then the current theory would be perfectly implemented. And if so, it would follow that with full individuation, overall WTP would be lower for poor people than for wealthy people, for African-Americans than for whites, and (possibly) for men than for women. But under this thought experiment, government would not discriminate against any group by deciding (for example) on a high VSL for programs with 95 percent whites and a lower VSL for programs with 55 percent blacks. The difference would be a product of aggregations of fully individual VSLs – aggregations of the kind that the most conventional markets, including those for automobiles and consumer goods, now provide. Relatively poor people, for example, have less-safe cars, on average, than relatively wealthy people.

Of course there are two practical problems with taking the thought experiment seriously. The first is that we do not know the WTP of every individual, and as a practical matter, it is not possible to find out. The second problem is that regulatory benefits are often collective goods – goods that cannot feasibly be provided to one without also being provided to many. In the context of air pollution, for example, it is not possible to provide cleaner air for some without providing cleaner air for many or all. In regulating air pollution and water pollution, individuation is simply not an option.

These problems are fatal objections to *full* individuation. But they are not fatal objections to *more* individuation. At a minimum, and while avoiding the most controversial issues, different social attitudes toward different risks might be made to count in cost-benefit analysis. For example, agencies might be encouraged to take account of existing research about cancer risks in their analyses, showing the numbers that emerge from different assumptions, resulting in increased estimates for cancer deaths. In addition, disparities in VSL findings might be mapped onto different agency estimates, producing reasonable rather than arbitrary differences across agencies. If, for example, the risks of death from workplace accidents produce a lower number than the risks of death from consumer products, then the Occupational Safety and Health Administration might have a lower VSL than the

Consumer Product Safety Administration. We could easily imagine a research program in which regulators try to elicit far more information on VSL across different risks. A movement in this direction need not raise troubling ethical questions.

It would be far more controversial to suggest that agencies should adopt different VSLs depending on whether the affected population is especially wealthy or especially poor. But at the very least, and without making arguably invidious distinctions, agencies should adjust VSL to changes in national wealth over time, producing a higher amount than would come from inflation adjustments alone. Or suppose, for example, that a regulation is designed to protect migrant farmworkers, expected to show a low VSL. Current studies in fact estimate the relationship between income and VSL,[54] allowing agencies to make suitable adjustments. And when the population is relatively wealthy, the agency might adopt a higher VSL.

For present purposes, I am not endorsing this approach; I am suggesting only that an approach of this kind is indicated by the theory that government now uses. Let us now turn to the larger questions that such an approach would make it necessary to answer. Is the current theory right? Where is it most vulnerable?

[54] See Viscusi and Aldy, *supra* note 5.

CHAPTER 7

Democracy, Rights, and Distribution

What is the argument for embodying people's actual willingness to pay (WTP) in regulatory policy? Why should anyone care about actual WTP at all? If we're trying to convert the reduction of danger into monetary equivalents, why is WTP even relevant? Don't people have the right to be free from (certain) risks, whatever their WTP? And what, most generally, is the relationship between deliberative democracy and cost-benefit analysis?

I hope that the discussion of fear has suggested the beginnings of an answer. Suppose that a regulation would cost $200 million annually and that it would save twenty lives – by, say, reducing the permissible level of arsenic in drinking water from 50 parts per billion to 10 parts per billion. (In fact these numbers are realistic for arsenic regulation.) If we refuse to convert the savings into monetary equivalents, we will have a hard time producing a coherent system of regulation. One policy might value a life at $10 million, another at $2 million, another at $40 million, another at $200,000. Of course different valuations would be justified if they stemmed from the nature of the risk or the affected population – and of course we need an account that justifies one assignment of monetary equivalents rather than another. But without some kind of effort to use monetary equivalents, randomness and incoherence – and susceptibility to powerful private interest groups – are likely. I have emphasized that the bottom-line numbers are not decisive. But to increase the coherence of programs that would otherwise be a product of some combination of fear, neglect, and interest-group power, monetary equivalents at least produce useful information.

Skeptics might observe at this point that for many risks, we are unable to estimate the magnitude of the risk with any precision.

In the context of toxic substances, for example, extrapolations about harm at low levels are often speculative. Even with epidemiological data about risks at high levels, the dose-response curves might be disputed. Do harms drop off rapidly as the dose declines? Is there a safe threshold, below which there is no risk at all? Might low exposures actually be beneficial to human health, as they sometimes have been shown to be? Science may allow only a range of possible outcomes. For other problems, including global warming, the range itself is debated. Perhaps we are operating under circumstances of uncertainty or even ignorance, making it impossible to have even a little confidence in a nonmonetized accounting of harms.

It would be a mistake to understate the formidable problems involved in the identification of likely harms from many social risks. The problem of terrorism defies cost-benefit accounting, and the same is true for many other dangers, both natural and man-made. But in many contexts, it is indeed possible to specify ranges of anticipated harms, and knowledge about how to do this is growing all the time. The use of cost-benefit analysis, in many parts of the world, attests to the feasibility of the enterprise. For present purposes, I am speaking only of situations in which reasonable ranges can be identified. What role should WTP play then?

EASY CASES

Let us begin with what I shall call the Easy Case for using WTP. For the sake of simplicity, assume a society in which people face multiple risks of 1/100,000 and in which every person is both adequately informed and willing to pay no more and no less than $60 to eliminate each of those risks. Assume, too, that the cost of eliminating these 1/100,000 risks is widely variable, ranging from close to zero for some to many billions for others. Assume, finally, that the cost of eliminating any risk is borne entirely by those who benefit from risk elimination. Under that (important) assumption, regulation imposes the equivalent of users' fees; for example, people's water bills will entirely reflect the costs of a policy that eliminates a 1/100,000 risk of getting cancer from arsenic in drinking water. If the per-person cost is $100, each water bill will be increased by exactly that amount.

With these assumptions, the argument for using WTP is both plausible and straightforward. Regulation amounts to a forced exchange; it tells people that they must purchase certain benefits for a certain amount. Why should government force people to pay for things that they don't want? If people are willing to pay only $60 to eliminate a risk of 1/100,000, why should government require them to pay $61 or more? By hypothesis, a forced exchange on terms that people dislike will make them worse off. Of course it would be possible to respond that in these circumstances, people should receive the benefit for free; a subsidy, rather than a forced exchange, would be in their interest. I will turn to this question below. Note for now that regulation is not a subsidy, because on the assumptions I am using, people are paying for the benefit that they receive.

At first glance, use of WTP and VSL, on those assumptions, is hard to contest. For purposes of evaluating regulation, it does not matter if the existing distribution of income is unjust or if poor people are, in an intelligible sense, coerced to run certain risks. The remedy for unjust distributions, and for that form of coercion, is not to require people to buy regulatory benefits on terms that they find unacceptable. Suppose that people are willing to pay only $20 to eliminate a 1/100,000 risk because they aren't rich; suppose too that if they had double their current wealth, they would be willing to pay $50. Even if this is so, government does people no favors by forcing them to pay the amount that they would pay if they had more money.

Now let us adopt somewhat less artificial assumptions and assume that the affected population is more like real-world populations – that (1) the relevant people show a high degree of variability in their WTP to avoid statistically equivalent risks and (2) individuals greatly differ in their desire to avoid different risks. Begin with variable assessments of risks: People are willing to pay no more than $50 to avoid a 1/100,000 risk of dying in a car crash, but they are willing to pay up to $100 to avoid a 1/100,000 risk of dying of cancer. Should government pay attention to their WTP? I think that it should, at least if (as in the Easy Case) people are going to be paying for the benefits that they are receiving. If government uses a WTP for both risks of $75, it will force people to pay more than they want to avoid the risks associated with car crashes – and less than they want to avoid risks of cancer. Why should government do that? And if the argument is convincing in this example, it should apply in numerous cases in which WTP and VSL vary across risks.

Now turn to individual differences. Should government pay attention to the fact that different people are willing to pay different amounts to avoid statistical risks? At first glance, the answer is yes; differences are appropriate here as well. If people in New York are willing to pay more to reduce arsenic risks than people in Montana, then regulators should attend to that fact – at least if the relevant people are properly informed. Here as elsewhere, government does not help people by requiring them to pay more than they want for social goods. If different people have different tastes and tolerances for risk, government should recognize that fact.

Indeed we can see that use of WTP, under the stated assumptions, is rooted in two different kinds of considerations. The first involves welfare; the second involves individual autonomy. I have emphasized that from the standpoint of welfare, people should not be forced to pay more for risk reduction than they see fit, because their own choices are a good guide to their own welfare (at least as a presumption; I raise complications in the next chapter). In addition, people should be permitted to use their resources as they like, simply because they ought to be treated with respect. Government does not respect people's autonomy if it tells them that they must spend their money on reducing a particular risk of 1/50,000, rather than on food, health care, housing, or recreation. Free citizens ought to be permitted to allocate their money as they choose.

This idea might be uncontroversial insofar as we are dealing with a population of citizens with diverse preferences and values. It will seem far more troubling insofar as the argument implies that government should use a higher WTP for rich people than for poor ones. Suppose, for example, that to reduce a risk of 1/50,000, people who earn a great deal are willing to pay more than twice the amount of people who earn much less. If WTP is what counts, regulators should take that point into account – and use a higher VSL for programs protecting rich people than for programs protecting poor people. The reason for the difference is not that poor people are less valuable than rich people. It is that no one, rich or poor, should be forced to pay more than they are willing to pay for the reduction of risks. Despite appearances, this idea embodies its own norm of equality. As in markets, so for policy: People should not be required to pay more than they would like for social goods.

If poor people are unwilling to pay much for the reduction of serious risks, the appropriate response is not a compelled purchase, but a subsidy. Suppose, for example, that each member of a group of relatively poor people, earning less than $30,000 annually, is willing to pay only $25 to eliminate a risk of 1/100,000 – about one-half, let us suppose, of the nation's population-wide median of $50. Should regulators require every citizen, including those in the relatively poor group, to pay $50? In principle, the government should force exchanges only on terms that people find acceptable, at least if it is genuinely concerned with their welfare and their autonomy. But perhaps regulators should provide poor people with risk reduction for free – making them safer and less frightened without forcing them to foot the bill. Often this is right; government should do this in many contexts. But my topic here is regulation, not subsidy, and for regulation, WTP has much to be said on its behalf.

Does the Easy Case, in which the beneficiaries of risk reduction pay for what they get, seem implausibly unrealistic? In many contexts, it certainly is. The costs of air pollution regulation are not fully borne by its beneficiaries.[1] But for workers' compensation regulation, the situation is very different. At least in the United States, nonunionized workers faced a dollar-for-dollar wage reduction, corresponding almost perfectly to the expected value of the benefits they received.[2] Because workers' compensation programs increase safety, they effectively require workers to pay, in salary reduction, for what they receive in improved health. For drinking water regulation, something similar is involved. The cost of regulations is passed on to consumers in the form of higher water bills. Hence the Easy Case finds a number of real-world analogues.

OBJECTIONS

There are several possible objections to my argument in favor of the use of WTP in the Easy Case. They point to some important

---

[1] Matthew E. Kahn, The Beneficiaries of Clean Air Act Regulation, 24 *Regulation* 34 (2001).
[2] Price V. Fishback and Shawn Everett Kantor, *A Prelude to the Welfare State* (Chicago: University of Chicago Press, 2000).

qualifications, and in some circumstances, they provide reasons to rethink the straightforward argument.

Adaptive preferences, deprivation, and "miswanting"

The first objection would emphasize the possibility that people's preferences have adapted to existing opportunities, including deprivation.[3] Perhaps people show a low WTP for environmental goods, including health improvements, simply because they have adjusted to environmental bads, including health risks. Perhaps people's WTP reflects an effort to reduce cognitive dissonance through the conclusion that risks are lower than they actually are.[4] To generalize the objection, perhaps people suffer from a problem of "miswanting";[5] they want things that do not promote their welfare, and they do not want things that would promote their welfare. If this is so, then WTP loses some of its underlying justification; people's decisions do not actually improve their welfare.[6] And if government can be confident that people are not willing to pay for goods from which they would greatly benefit, then government should abandon WTP.

In some contexts, this objection raises serious problems for neoclassical economics and for unambivalent enthusiasm for freedom of choice. Autonomy is implicated in addition to welfare. Suppose that people do not want risk reduction because they believe risk to be inevitable, or because their preferences have adapted to dangerous and unfair conditions. If so, people's preferences do not reflect their autonomy. In other words, the idea of autonomy requires not merely respect for whatever preferences people happen to have, but also social conditions that allow preferences to be developed in a way

---

[3] See Jon Elster, *Sour Grapes* (Cambridge: Cambridge University Press, 1983); Matthew Adler and Eric A. Posner, Implementing Cost-Benefit Analysis when Preferences Are Distorted, 29 *J. Legal Stud.* 146 (2000).

[4] See George A. Akerlof, *An Economic Theorist's Book of Tales* 123, 123–37 (Cambridge: Cambridge University Press, 1984).

[5] Daniel T. Gilbert and Timothy D. Wilson, Miswanting: Some Problems in the Forecasting of Future Affective States, in *Feeling and Thinking: The Role of Affect in Social Cognition* 178, ed. Joseph P. Forgas (Cambridge: Cambridge University Press, 2000); Timothy D. Wilson and Daniel T. Gilbert, Affective Forecasting, 35 *Advances in Experimental Soc. Psych.* 345 (2003).

[6] For general discussion, see Daniel Kahneman, A Psychological Perspective on Economics, 93(2) *Am. Econ. Rev. (Papers & Proc.)* 162 (2003); Daniel Kahneman et al., Back to Bentham? Explorations of Experienced Utility, 112 *Q.J. Econ.* 375, 379–80 (1997).

that does not reflect coercion or injustice. With respect to some risks, the relevant preferences are nonautonomous; consider the fact that many women face a risk of male violence under circumstances in which they believe that little can be done and hence adapt.

This point has implications for many questions of risk policy. In the context of ordinary regulation, however, it has more theoretical than practical interest. Typically we are speaking of steps that would reduce low-level mortality risks (say, 1/100,000). Much of the time, there is no reason to believe that the use of informed WTP (say, $100) is a product of adaptive preferences. When there is such a reason, the judgment about the Easy Case must be revised.

Inadequate information and bounded rationality

A closely related objection would point to an absence of information and to bounded rationality. As I have stressed throughout, people have a difficult time in dealing with low-probability events. If people are not aware of what they might gain by regulation, their WTP will be too low. Perhaps the availability heuristic will lead them to underestimate certain risks. If people cannot recall a case in which some activity produced illness or death, they might conclude that the risk is trivial even if it is large. Or perhaps the same heuristic, and probability neglect, will lead people to exaggerate risks, producing a WTP that is wildly inflated in light of reality. And if people are unable to understand the meaning of ideas like "1 in 50,000," or to respond rationally to evidence of statistical risks, then there are serious problems with relying on WTP. In imaginable circumstances, this is a real difficulty for the use of WTP and VSL.

Or perhaps people's WTP reflects excessive discounting of future health benefits. If workers are ignoring the future, or applying an implausibly high discount rate to future gains and losses, then there is a good argument for putting their WTP to one side. In the context of global warming, for example, the temporally distant nature of the harm might well lead to insufficient concern with a potentially catastrophic risk. The same is true for less dramatic risks that people face in their daily lives. Young smokers probably give too little attention to the health harms caused by smoking. Those who choose a poor diet and little exercise often fail to consider the long-term effects of their behavior. Self-control problems are an important part of bounded rationality, and if a low WTP shows a failure to give adequate attention to the future, then there is reason not to use WTP.

All of this is possible. In many cases, however, WTP is not a result of inadequate information and bounded rationality is not leading people to err. If it is, appropriate adjustments should be made.

Rights

A quite different objection would point to people's rights. Perhaps people have a right not to be subjected to risks of a certain magnitude, and the use of WTP will violate that right. In fact, it is fully reasonable to say that whatever their WTP, human beings should have a right not to be subject to risks above a particular level. Imagine, for example, that poor people live in a place where they face a 1/20 annual risk of dying from water pollution; it makes sense to say that the government should reduce that risk even if people are willing to pay only $1 to eliminate it and the per-person cost is $2. The only qualification is that in practice, rights are resource dependent. What rights people are able to claim, against their government, are a product of the amount of available money, and hence people's legitimate arguments for protection are inevitably affected by the level of resources in the society. But let us simply assume here that risks above a certain level should count as violative of rights.

We might add that people have a right not to be subjected to an intentional or reckless imposition of harm, whatever their WTP. If a company subjects the citizens of a town to a high danger, and it does so maliciously or without the slightest concern for their welfare, the rights of those citizens have been violated, even if their WTP is low. Well-functioning legal systems make wrongdoers pay for the injuries they inflict. Indeed, some such systems impose strict liability for harms.

As an abstract claim about people's rights, these objections are entirely correct. Something has gone badly wrong if people are exposed to serious risks and if their low WTP prevents them from doing anything in response. Things are even worse if government uses their low WTP to justify inaction in the face of those risks.

It would be ludicrous to suggest that WTP is determinative of the appropriate use of government subsidies; a redistributive policy hardly tracks people's WTP. (Would it make sense to say that government will give poor people a check for $100 only if they are willing to pay $100 for that check?) And in many cases people are subject to risks whose magnitude is an unquestionable violation of their rights.

In many cases, however, rights of this kind are not involved; we are speaking here of statistically small risks. Even if rights are involved, the proper response is not to force people to buy protection that they do not want, but to provide a subsidy that will give them the benefit for free or enable them to receive the benefit at what is, for them, an acceptable price. I have emphasized that government should provide certain goods via subsidy. For the Easy Case, the question is one of regulation under the stated assumptions. So long as that is the question, use of WTP does not violate anyone's rights.

What about wrongdoers? It is right to insist that a company should be held accountable when it has intentionally or recklessly exposed people to harm, even if those who are harmed have a low WTP. (I do not attempt to justify this conclusion here; it can be supported by reference to either utilitarian or deontological considerations, and hence an incompletely theorized agreement can be obtained on its behalf.) We can go much further. A sensible legal system might well choose to force companies to internalize the costs of their activities by requiring them to pay for the harms they have caused, even if there has been neither intentional nor reckless wrongdoing. Within tort theory, there is an active debate on this question, and here, too, it is possible to support liability by reference to a range of theoretical positions.[7] But my subject is regulation, not compensation via the tort system. Certainly regulators should forbid the intentional or reckless infliction of harm. But it would be odd to say that people have a right to be required to pay more for risk reduction than they are willing to pay, at least if they are adequately informed. If people are willing to pay only $25 to eliminate a risk of 1/100,000, a reference to their "rights" cannot plausibly justify the conclusion that government should impose a regulation that costs them $75.

---

[7] See Richard A. Epstein, A Theory of Strict Liability, 2 *J. Legal Stud.* 151 (1973); Richard Posner, *Economic Analysis of Law* 38–45 (New York: Aspen Publishers, 6th ed., 2003).

Democracy vs. markets

An independent objection would stress that people are citizens, not merely consumers; it would urge that regulatory choices should be made after citizens have deliberated with one another about their preferences and values. The argument against forced exchanges treats people as consumers; it sees their decisions about safety as the same as their decisions about all other commodities. For some decisions, this approach is badly misconceived. I have suggested that a good constitutional system is a deliberative democracy, not a maximization machine. Many social judgments should be made by citizens engaged in deliberative discussion with one another rather than by aggregating the individual choices of consumers.

Consider some examples:

- In the context of racial and sex discrimination, sensible societies do not aggregate people's WTP. The level of permissible discrimination is not set by using market evidence or contingent valuation studies to see how much people would be willing to pay to discriminate (or to be free from discrimination). Even if discriminators would be willing to pay a lot to avoid associating with members of racial minority groups, such discrimination is banned. Through political processes, citizens have decided that certain forms of discrimination are illicit, whatever people's WTP.

- The prohibition on sexual harassment does not emerge from asking anything about WTP. Many harassers would be willing to pay something for the privilege, perhaps a great deal – in imaginable circumstances, more than their victims would be willing to pay to prevent harassment. Nonetheless, harassment is forbidden, and WTP is irrelevant.

- The protection of endangered species is not chosen on the basis of aggregated WTP. Whether and when to protect members of endangered species is a moral question to be resolved through democratic discussion, not through exercises in consumer sovereignty. Some people might be willing to pay a significant amount to harm endangered species, at least if that harm is necessary to undertake development activities. Their WTP is not taken to be part of the legal assessment of what they are permitted to do.

- Laws that forbid cruelty to animals, and that impose affirmative duties of protection on human beings, stem not from anything involving WTP, but from moral commitments. When laws require animals to be protected against unjustified suffering, it does not matter that those who are regulated (university laboratories, for example) would be willing to pay a significant amount to avoid the regulation. Of course, the cost of the regulatory burden might play some role in deciding whether to impose it. But the underlying moral judgment is rooted in a belief in the avoidance of suffering that does not essentially turn on WTP.

Emphasizing the limits of any approach that takes "preferences" to be the foundation of regulatory policy, Amartya Sen emphasizes that "discussions and exchange, and even political arguments, contribute to the formation and revision of values."[8] Sen urges that in the particular context of environmental protection, solutions require us "to go beyond looking only for the best reflection of existing individual preferences, or the most acceptable procedures for choices based on those preferences."[9]

These claims are both fundamental and correct. They point to some serious limitations on the use of WTP. But it is important not to read such objections for more than they are worth. In trading off safety and health in our own private lives, we do not have static values and preferences. Much of the time, our choices are a product of reflection, even if we are simply acting as consumers. Reflection and deliberation, including deliberation with other people, are hardly absent from the market domain. To be sure, moral questions are not to be resolved by aggregating private willingness to pay. Sometimes people's preferences, even though backed by WTP, are morally off-limits, and policy should not take account of them. In addition, people are sometimes unwilling to pay a great deal for goods that have strong moral justifications; animal welfare is an example. In these circumstances, the market model is inapplicable and WTP tells us very little.

But what about the Easy Case? Do these arguments suggest that government should override individual choices about how much to spend to eliminate low-level risks, even when those choices are adequately informed? For environmental protection generally, it is indeed

---

[8] Amartya Sen, *Rationality and Freedom* 287–89 (Cambridge, Mass.: Harvard University Press, 2003).
[9] *Id.* at 289.

important to go beyond "the best reflection of existing individual preferences." But this point does not mean that people should be required to pay (say) $100 to eliminate mortality risks of 1/100,000 when they are willing to pay only $75. If people's WTP reflects an absence of information or insufficient deliberation, then it is important for other people, in government as elsewhere, to draw their attention to that fact. And in some cases, a low WTP might be overridden on the ground that it is rooted in errors, factual or otherwise. But these points should not be taken as a general objection to my conclusion about the Easy Case, and to suggest that government should force people to reduce statistical risks at an expense that they deem excessive.

Very low probabilities and catastrophic risks

Suppose that everyone in the United States faces an annual death risk of 1/10,000,000 – and that this risk, if it comes to fruition, will kill every person in the country. The expected number of annual deaths is twenty-six, which would produce expected annual costs in excess of $158 million, assuming a VSL of $6.1 million. But if we attempt to elicit each individual's WTP to avoid a risk of 1/10,000,000, we might well produce a number very close to zero. How much would you be willing to spend to avoid a risk of 1/10,000,000? If you say "nothing," you might well be like most people. And if most people really are like that, our supposed risk of 1/10,000,000, applicable to everyone in the United States, yields both twenty-six expected annual fatalities and expected annual costs very close to zero – an especially odd result in light of the fact that there is a 1/10,000,000 risk not simply that *each* American will die, but that *every* American will die.[10]

This does seem to be an anomaly. For one thing, is it really sensible to conclude that the prevention of twenty-six deaths is worth nothing, or close to it? An affirmative answer might be suggested by a perspective that is entirely based on people's WTP. But assigning a value near zero, for the prevention of dozens of deaths, seems quite implausible. In cases of this kind, there is a serious problem with using WTP.

---

[10] For a valuable discussion, see Richard A. Posner, *Catastrophe: Risk and Response* 165–70 (New York: Oxford University Press, 2004).

Actually this conclusion understates the problem. In the case at hand, the risk is potentially catastrophic. As I have said, if the 1/10,000,000 chance comes through, every American will be dead. Even if people show a WTP near zero to face a risk of that size, it does not seem right to think that the nation should spend almost nothing to prevent it. The point has a general bearing on precautions against low probability risks of catastrophe: Some degree of precaution is justified even if WTP numbers do not justify them. Part of the problem with those numbers is that if individual behavior is consulted, it will not reflect a "catastrophe premium" or "extermination premium" that would almost certainly emerge if it were possible to test for it. People might be willing to pay nothing to avoid a risk of 1/100,000,000 that they themselves face; but if they were told that this risk faces every person in their nation, and that if it comes to fruition all would die, they might come up with a significantly higher figure. Perhaps we could produce those higher numbers if we asked the correct question. But part of the problem is that WTP is not an adequate measure of social responses to catastrophes – perhaps because people are not familiar with making choices about risks of that sort.

I believe that this is a sound objection to the use of a (low or near-zero) VSL in the context of catastrophic risks, even if the WTP numbers justify that VSL. As Richard Posner has demonstrated,[11] this is an important point when government is considering how to respond to small risks of catastrophic harm. But notice that the objection has built-in limitations. It does not apply to the overwhelming number of cases in which VSL is actually used. In those cases, we are dealing with risks of 1/10,000 to 1/100,000, and no large-scale catastrophe is at issue. Here, then, is a limitation on the use of WTP, but the domain of the objection is restricted.

Third party effects

A final objection would point to effects on third parties. If outsiders would be harmed, and if their welfare is not being considered, then the WTP calculus is seriously incomplete. Suppose, for example, that

[11] See *id.*

workers are paid $60 to face a risk of 1/100,000 – but that when that risk comes to fruition, friends and family members are hurt as well. Their own loss is not considered. Isn't this a problem?

This point creates a general and badly neglected problem for WTP as it is currently used: Agencies consider people's WTP to eliminate statistical risks without taking account of the fact that others – especially family members and close friends – would also be willing to pay something to eliminate those risks. John might be willing to pay $25 to eliminate his own risk of 1/100,000, but his wife Jane might be willing to pay $25 to eliminate John's risk too; if we add the WTP, on John's behalf, of John's friends and relatives, the total WTP might soon exceed $100. This point is a real problem for existing uses of WTP.

But in the Easy Case, we are stipulating that there are no third-party effects. The argument for using WTP, on the stated assumptions, is that government should not force people to buy goods that are not worthwhile for them. At least at first glance, this argument is sound with respect to statistical risks of the kind on which I am focusing here. When third-party effects are involved, existing practice generates numbers that are far too low. The appropriate response is to increase the numbers.

DEMOGRAPHIC DIFFERENCES, INTERNATIONAL DIFFERENCES

Rich and poor

Suppose that poor people are willing to pay only $20 to eliminate a statistical risk of 1/100,000, but that wealthy people are willing to pay $60. It would follow that the VSL would be lower for poor people than for wealthy people – and that a regulatory policy that focuses on WTP would provide a higher VSL for wealthy people ($6 million) than for poor people ($2 million). Is this unjust or unfair to poor people? On the current assumptions, it is not. As I have stressed, government should not force poor people to buy more than their WTP to eliminate statistical risks. Forced exchanges of this kind do poor people no good and some harm. (Of course, subsidies must be analyzed differently.)

It is tempting to justify a uniform VSL, one that does not distinguish between rich and poor, on the ground that it embodies a form of "risk equity," treating every person as no more and no less than one and redistributing resources in the direction of poor people. But this is an error. A uniform WTP, taken (let us suppose) from a population-wide median, does not really produce redistribution toward the poor, any more than any other kind of forced exchange. If government wants to help poor people, it should make them less poor; it should not require poor people to buy goods at the prices that rich people are willing to pay for them. Government does not require people to buy Volvos, even though Volvos would reduce statistical risks. If government required everyone to buy Volvos, it would not be producing desirable redistribution. It would not be helping poor people at all. A uniform VSL has some of the same characteristics as a policy that requires people to buy Volvos.

Rich countries, poor countries

The point has significant implications for global risk regulation. I have suggested that people in poor nations show a lower VSL than people in wealthy nations. Building on evidence of this kind, some assessments of the effects of global warming value the lives of the rich more highly than those of the poor, and hence find far higher monetized costs from deaths of people in rich countries than from deaths of people in poor countries.[12] In its Second Report in 1995, the International Panel on Climate Change calculated that a life in an industrialized country was worth $1.5 million, while a life in a developing country was worth only $150,000.[13] These assessments have been highly controversial. John Broome, for example, notes that under this approach, an American life is worth ten or twenty Indian lives, a judgment that he deems "absurd."[14] Hence some analysts,

---

[12] See http://www.ipcc.ch/pub/reports.htm.   [13] See *id.*
[14] See John Broome, Cost-Benefit Analysis and Population, 29 *J. Legal Stud.* 953, 957 (2000), noting that this conclusion is a product of what Broome rejects, "a money-metric utility function to represent a person's preferences," *id.* In the Easy Cases, I suggest that a money-metric utility function is not absurd, and it is not quite that in the hard cases either; see below. See also the discussion of the International Panel on Climate Change, *Climate Change 2001*, available at http://www.grida.no/climate/ipcc_tar/wg3/302.htm: "The VSL is generally lower in poor countries than in rich countries, but it is considered unacceptable by many

including the International Panel, have opted for a worldwide VSL of $1 million, a choice that seems quite arbitrary and potentially harmful to people in rich nations and poor ones alike.

To be sure, there is absurdity as well as crudeness in the distinction between lives in industrialized nations ($1.5 million) and lives in developing countries ($150,000). The problem raises important dilemmas, and a uniform number may not be helpful to anyone. Let us explore some of the complexities here.

Abstract values?

What are the monetized costs of (say) 10,000 worldwide deaths from global warming, deaths that include (say) 9,000 people from poor countries and 1,000 from wealthy ones? The discussion thus far suggests that there is no sensible abstract answer to these questions; we have to know what the answer is *for*. If a general question is asked, outside of any particular context, about the monetary value of a stated number of deaths in 2020, it is best unanswered (except perhaps with laughter). The appropriate assessments of VSL, and variations across countries, depend on their intended use. If the disparate numbers are meant to identify the actual monetary values of human lives, and to suggest that people in Canada are "worth" much more than people in Argentina or that poor people are "worth" less than rich ones, they are ludicrous as well as offensive.

We can go further. Suppose that the disparate numbers are meant to suggest the appropriate amount that donor institutions, private and public, should spend to reduce mortality risks. If so, they make no sense at all. Let us stipulate that a poor person in a poor nation would be willing to pay $1 to eliminate a risk of 1/10,000, whereas a wealthy person in a wealthy nation would be willing to pay $100 to eliminate that same risk. It would be ludicrous to take this fact to

analysts to impose different values for a policy that has to be international in scope and decided by the international community. In these circumstances, analysts use average VSL and apply it to all countries. Of course, such a value is not what individuals would pay for the reduction in risk, but it is an 'equity adjusted' value, in which greater weight is given to the WTP of lower income groups. On the basis of EU and US VSLs and a weighting system that has some broad appeal in terms of government policies towards income distribution, . . . the average world VSL [is estimated] at around 1 million Euros (approximately US$1 million at 1999 exchange rates)."

show that an international agency should devote its resources to the rich nation rather than the poor one. To see the point, suppose that you are asked to choose between two programs:

(A) Program A would eliminate (at a stated cost to you of $500) a 1/10,000 risk faced by fifty poor people in Costa Rica, each willing to pay $2 to eliminate that risk.

(B) Program B would eliminate (also at a stated cost of $500) a 1/10,000 risk faced by fifty wealthy people in Berlin, each willing to pay $350 to eliminate that same risk.

Other things being equal, it is absurd to think that you should prefer to save the Berliners, even though their VSL is far higher. In fact, Program A has much higher priority, because it would help people who are facing extreme deprivation. What is true at the individual level is true across nations as well.

VSL in poor countries

Now let us ask, not what donor institutions should do, but what governments should do. Imagine that the government in a poor nation is deciding on appropriate policy to reduce workplace risks. At least under the Easy Case assumptions I have made thus far, such a government would do well to begin by using the admittedly low WTP of its own citizens. If citizens in that nation show a WTP of $2 to eliminate risks of 1/10,000, then their government does them no favors by requiring them to pay $50 or $10. This is the sense in which VSL properly varies across nations, and in which citizens of poor nations have a lower VSL than citizens of wealthy ones. The claim is hardly that people in poor countries are "worth less" than people elsewhere. The claim is intensely pragmatic; it is that regulators, in Easy Cases, *use* a higher VSL in rich countries, because that is the best way to respect people's autonomy and to make them better off.

The point has strong implications for international labor standards. It is tempting to suggest that workers in poor countries, for example China and India, should receive the same protection as those in the United States. Why should a worker in Beijing be subject to significantly higher death risks than a worker in Los Angeles? As a matter of basic principle, there is no good answer to this question. But as a matter of regulatory policy, the answer is straightforward.

The distribution of global income is what it is, with people in Beijing having far less money than people in Los Angeles. So long as this is so, a system that gives Chinese workers the same protection as American workers is not in the interest of Chinese workers – assuming, as we are doing, that the cost of that protection is borne by workers themselves. Requiring Chinese workers to have the same protection as Americans amounts to a forced exchange on terms that Chinese workers reject. The idea that workers in poor nations should have the "same" protection as workers in wealthy nations is an error, rooted in a moral heuristic involving the equal worth of all human lives – a heuristic that usually works well but that also misfires.

Note, once again, that the argument for using WTP does not imply any satisfaction with the existing distribution of wealth. We might believe that the existing distribution is unjust and that it should be dramatically changed. In fact this is what I believe. The problem with forced exchanges is that they do nothing to alter existing distributions. Instead, they make poor people worse off, requiring them to use their limited resources for something that they do not want to buy.

HARDER CASES: DISTRIBUTION AND WELFARE

There is an obvious artificiality in the assumptions that underlie the Easy Case. Most important, people do not always bear the full social costs of the regulatory benefits they receive. Sometimes they pay only a fraction of those costs – or possibly even nothing at all. When this is so, the analysis is much more complicated. In the context of air pollution regulation, for example, there is a complex set of distributional effects, and on balance, poor people, and members of minority communities, appear to be net gainers.[15] An efficiency analysis, based on WTP, might not produce an adequate account of the welfare effects of air pollution regulation. If poor people are receiving major benefits, their welfare gains might dwarf the welfare losses faced by those who are paying – and use of WTP will not adequately capture that fact. The reason that poor people's WTP is low is not that they are not gaining from the program; they are gaining a lot. Their WTP is low simply because they don't have much money.

---

[15] See Kahn, *supra* note 1.

It is no insult to their autonomy to give them a benefit for which they pay only a fraction. On balance, a program that delivers large benefits to the poor, and imposes diffuse costs on other people, might well promote social welfare.

Suppose that in certain cases this conclusion is wrong and that the relevant programs reduce social welfare, taken in the aggregate sense. Even if this is so, an account of welfare effects might not end the question of what to do, because the distributional gains are important to consider. If poor people gain a great deal, the program might be worthwhile even if wealthier people lose even more; recall that government should not be seen as an aggregating machine. Hence the use of WTP raises more complexities when the beneficiaries pay for only a fraction of the cost of the benefit that they receive. Let me spell out these points with an example.

Imagine that the beneficiaries of a proposed drinking water regulation are willing to pay only $80 to eliminate a risk of 1/50,000 in drinking water; that the per-person cost of eliminating a 1/50,000 risk is $100; but that for every dollar of that cost, the beneficiaries actually pay only 70 cents. The beneficiaries are, in that case, left $10 better off than they would have been had they paid the full amount that they are willing to pay. The remaining 30 cents on the dollar might be paid by water companies themselves, in the form of reduced profits, or by employees of the water companies, in the form of reduced wages and fewer jobs. In this example, the costs of the regulation exceed the benefits; it is inefficient. But by hypothesis, the regulation makes its beneficiaries better off. If the WTP criterion is used, the fact that the monetized costs exceed the monetized benefits is decisive. But the analysis of this case is far harder than in the Easy Cases. Mightn't the regulation be justified on balance? On what assumption should the WTP numbers be decisive?

The assumption must be that economic efficiency is the goal of government, at least in the context of regulation – that in order to know what to do, we should aggregate the benefits and costs of regulation, and act if and only if the benefits exceed the costs. When using the WTP numbers, government is acting as a maximization machine, aggregating all benefits and costs as measured by the WTP criterion. But this is a highly contestable and in my view preposterous understanding of what government should be doing. In fact it represents a shift from the relatively uncontroversial Pareto criterion, asking whether there is a way of making at least one person better off without making anyone worse off, to a version of the far more controversial Kaldor-Hicks criterion,[16] which assesses policy by asking this question: Are the gainers winning more than the losers are losing? The Kaldor-Hicks criterion is sometimes described as potential Pareto superiority, because it asks whether, in principle, the winners could compensate the losers and a surplus could be left over. The difficulty, of course, is that Pareto superiority is merely potential. Some people really are losing and others are gaining.

In the harder cases, the gainers are gaining less (in monetary terms) than the losers are losing (in monetary terms) – and hence the regulation is said to be unjustified. Under the assumptions I have given, the regulation is indeed inefficient by definition: Its social cost is higher than its social benefit. But is the regulation unjustified? This is not at all clear. The first problem is that WTP is measuring gains and losses in monetary terms, rather than in welfare terms. It is possible that those who gain, in the harder cases, gain more welfare than the losers lose; WTP does not answer that question. The second problem is distributional. Suppose that in terms of overall welfare, the regulation is not desirable; it makes aggregate welfare lower rather than higher. But suppose, too, that those who benefit are less advantaged than those who lose. If, for example, those who are willing to pay $80 are disproportionately poor, and those who pay the remainder are disproportionately wealthy, the regulation might be justified despite the welfare loss.

There is a standard response. If redistribution is what is sought, then it should be produced not through regulation but through the tax system, which is a more efficient way of transferring resources to those who need help.[17] At least as a general rule, this response is right. It would be better to give money directly to the poor than to

[16] It is only a version of that criterion, because it is measuring welfare in monetary equivalents. A direct assessment of welfare, if it were possible, might show that the regulation in question is justified on Kaldor-Hicks grounds.

[17] See, e.g., Louis Kaplow and Steven Shavell, Why the Legal System Is Less Efficient than the Income Tax in Redistributing Income, 23 *J. Legal Stud.* 667, 667 (1994) ("[R]edistribution through legal rules offers no advantage over redistribution through the income tax and typically is less efficient"); Steven Shavell, A Note on Efficiency vs. Distributional Equity

attempt to produce redistribution through the much cruder tool of regulation. But suppose that redistribution is not going to happen through the tax system. If so, then the regulation in the harder cases cannot be ruled off-limits despite its inefficiency.

HARDER CASES AS EASY ONES?

Is there a reason to treat the harder cases as identical to the easy ones? Is this absurd? A possible reason for treating the harder cases as the easy ones is optimistic: Maybe everything will balance out in the end. Maybe no group will be systematically helped or hurt, and the tax system will be used to produce appropriate redistribution. In the real-world cases, we might also think that a direct inquiry into welfare, bypassing WTP, would be extremely difficult or perhaps even impossible to operationalize. And if distributional considerations were deemed relevant, interest-group warfare might be the consequence, rather than distribution to those who particularly need and deserve help. More modestly, we might conclude that agencies should generally pursue efficiency, using VSL as the foundation for decision, but should allow distributional findings to cut the other way – saying, for example, that when poor people stand to gain a great deal, regulation will go forward even if it is not justified by cost-benefit analysis. What I am suggesting here is that an assessment of the anticipated effects of various alternatives is an important part of sensible decision making; that anticipated benefits should be turned into monetary equivalents; that WTP provides a place not to end but to start; and that an understanding of distributional effects might well change the conclusion, producing or forbidding regulatory controls precisely because of their effects on the most vulnerable members of society.

Let us return in this light to VSL. In the Easy Case, the resulting redistribution is almost certainly perverse, because forced exchanges, under the stated assumptions, are highly likely to harm the people

in Legal Rulemaking, 71 *Am. Econ. Rev. (Papers & Proc.)* 414, 414 (1981) (describing how income tax can compensate for inefficient liability rules and redistribute income); David A. Weisbach, Should Legal Rules be Used to Redistribute Income? 70 *U. Chi. L. Rev.* 439, 439–40 (2003) ("[T]he tax system is a better tool for redistribution of income than legal rules").

who are being coerced. But in the harder cases, it cannot be said that the beneficiaries of regulation will be harmed if government uses a number that exceeds their actual VSL. Everything depends on the distributional effects of the regulation. If its beneficiaries are well off, a high VSL will produce perverse redistribution if those who lose are toward the bottom of the economic ladder. We could imagine this result, for example, with a pollution program that protects those who visit expensive recreational areas. But if the beneficiaries are poor, and if the costs are born by the wealthy, a high VSL will be in the interest of those who need help. Air pollution programs, providing special protection for those in cities, is an example. We can therefore reject the confident view of economically inclined analysts who believe that accurate VSLs, based on actual WTP, should always be the basis of regulatory policy. But we can also reject the confident view of skeptics who believe that a uniform WTP, refusing to make distinctions among persons, is best on distributive grounds.

Return in this light to the use of VSL in poor nations. Suppose that in such nations, VSL turns out to be $100,000. If governments use a VSL of $6 million, on the theory that their citizens should not be valued less than those of wealthy nations, social harm will almost inevitably result. In the Easy Cases, the forced exchanges will be ludicrously harmful to the people they are supposed to help. Even in the hard cases, where the beneficiaries pay only a fraction of the cost, such a nation will be spending far too much of its money on risk reduction (or more precisely, on reducing the particular risks that happen to get onto the regulatory agenda). The resulting levels of regulation would almost certainly have adverse effects on wages and employment levels. (In these circumstances it is unsurprising that workers in wealthy nations, not in poor ones, often clamor the loudest for greater protection of workers in poor nations; workers in wealthier nations would be the principal beneficiaries of such regulation, which would protect them against competition from those in poorer nations. Workers in the poorer nations might well be big losers.) The inefficiency of an extremely high VSL will be felt acutely and in many forms. But if the costs of risk reduction will be paid by third parties – for example, wealthy nations – then the people in that poor country will be helped even if risk reduction is based on an excessive VSL. Of course, they would almost certainly be helped more if they were given cash rather than in-kind benefits. But if cash redistribution is not possible, regulatory benefits, provided for free or for a fraction of their cost, remain a blessing.

GLOBAL WARMING

How, then, should global institutions, like the International Panel on Climate Change, assess the monetary costs of risks faced by people all over the world? As I have suggested, the answer turns on the purpose of the assessment – on what issue the answer is supposed to be addressing. There is no good acontextual way of calculating the aggregate costs of global climate change by 2050; actually that is a ludicrous question, because it does not have any point. A far more sensible question is whether it would make sense for any particular nation to accept a particular way of responding to the problem, such as the Kyoto Protocol.[18] At the national level, an assessment of the costs and benefits of the Kyoto Protocol is not much different from an assessment of the costs and benefits of any other regulation.

For the United States, the likely costs of the Kyoto Protocol seem to exceed its likely benefits. The anticipated costs are $325 billion,[19] an amount that might be worthwhile if the anticipated benefits, for the United States, were in the ballpark of that number. But the overall benefits of the Kyoto Protocol are small, simply because the mandatory emissions reduction would make only a slight dent in global warming – in part because the Kyoto Protocol does not affect the rapidly growing emissions in developing countries.[20] In the United States alone, the benefits almost certainly do not justify the costs.[21] The picture for the world as a whole is more mixed, with Europe anticipated to be a net gainer.[22] But even for the world, the Kyoto Protocol appears to impose costs in excess of benefits – and this is so even if improbable catastrophic risks are taken into account. The only qualification here is that the science of global warming is greatly

---

[18] See William D. Nordhaus and Joseph Boyer, *Warming the World: Economic Models of Global Warming* 168 (Cambridge, Mass.: MIT Press, 2000): "Finally, the Kyoto Protocol has significant distributional consequences . . . The lion's share of the costs are borne by the United States. Indeed, the United States is a net loser while the rest of the world on balance benefits from the Kyoto Protocol."

[19] See *id*. at 161.   [20] *Id*. at 152.   [21] *Id*. at 130–21.   [22] *Id*. at 162.

disputed, and if we agree that this is a realm of uncertainty rather than risk, and if worst-case scenarios are emphasized, then the Kyoto Protocol might be justified as a sensible impetus toward technological innovation and far more dramatic reductions.

For wealthy nations, of course, the argument for contributing to the reduction of global warming is strengthened by the fact that the harms of global warming will be felt disproportionately in poor nations – and also by the fact that wealthy nations have done by far the most to produce the situation that makes global warming a serious problem. Hence it is reasonable to say that the United States should join international agreements to combat global warming even if that particular nation loses more than it gains. The problem with the Kyoto Protocol is that on what seem to be the most reasonable estimates, it combines extremely high global costs with relatively low global benefits, even if the problem of global warming is taken quite seriously.[23] A central reason is that the atmospheric concentrations of greenhouse gases have a *cumulative* effect. Carbon dioxide, the leading greenhouse gas, can stay in the atmosphere for hundreds of years. Hence even dramatic reductions in current emissions will only slow the rate of increase; it will not "reduce" global warming.

A sensible approach, going beyond the Kyoto Protocol, would control emissions in developing countries as well as others, so as to increase the overall benefits, and also would use emissions trading and other strategies to reduce the overall costs. Through these routes it should be possible to produce worthwhile agreements to address climate change.[24] If a worldwide treaty included comprehensive systems for tradable emissions rights, the economic cost of the system of controls would be reduced by many billions of dollars. Hence it would make sense to adopt an approach that, as compared with the Kyoto Protocol, both increases the benefits of regulation and decreases its cost. To the extent that emissions controls in developing countries would impose a significant burden, wealthy nations should help foot the bill.

Should more radical steps be taken? Should wealthy nations do something on their own? Richard Posner makes the dramatic

[23] See *id.*
[24] See Richard B. Stewart and Jonathan B. Wiener, *Reconstructing Climate Policy* (Washington, D.C.: AEI Press, 2003).

suggestion that the United States should aggressively regulate carbon emissions with a stiff carbon tax, simply in order to stimulate technological innovation that will ultimately produce extremely significant reductions – which is what, in his view, should be seen as the ultimate goal.[25] Posner contends that the potential risks of global warming are exceptionally serious and certainly catastrophic, and that in light of current scientific knowledge, those risks cannot be dismissed as highly improbable. Like many others, Posner claims that global warming presents a problem of uncertainty. If Posner is right on this point, his suggestion is entirely plausible.

But I believe that it has two problems. The first is that we need to know more about the effects of a stiff carbon tax. A study done at the Wharton School, for example, projected extremely high costs for the United States from the Kyoto Protocol[26] – including a loss of 2.4 million jobs and $300 billion in the nation's GDP, with an average annual cost of $2,700 per household, including a 65 cent per gallon increase in the price of gasoline and a near-doubling of the price of energy and electricity. These numbers are almost certainly inflated, especially in light of the technological innovations that would undoubtedly drive expenses down. But Posner seems to be proposing far more expensive controls than those contemplated by the Kyoto Protocol, and hence he is suggesting extremely costly regulation, with a series of adverse effects, above all for poor people, who cannot easily bear significant increases in energy prices. The expense might be worth incurring if Posner is right in contending that the catastrophic outcomes cannot be said to be highly trivial. But my own reading of the evidence is that Posner is not right – that the truly catastrophic outcomes are most unlikely to come to fruition. International action should indeed be taken on global warming, but aggressive technology-forcing, by the United States alone, is not simple to justify. It would be far better to start with cautious agreements that would build toward more aggressive reductions as technologies advance.

I am hardly a specialist on the underlying evidence, and I am not attempting here to resolve any particular controversy. My major suggestions are that within nations, diverse VSL are perfectly sensible,

[25] See Posner, *supra* note 10.
[26] See http://www.api.org/globalclimate/wefastateimpacts.htm.

and that answers to questions about valuation must be closely attuned to the purposes for which those questions are being asked.

The discussion of cost-benefit analysis has covered a great deal of ground, and it will be useful to conclude with the major themes. The principal point of that analysis is to give a more concrete sense of what is actually at stake, in a way that responds to both excessive and insufficient fear. At a minimum, it is important to present a nonmonetized account of the expected effects of both inaction and regulatory alternatives. These effects should be converted into monetary equivalents, not to create any kind of arithmetic straitjacket, but to discipline the analysis and to promote coherence. WTP provides a place to start, especially in the Easy Cases, but it should not be taken as decisive. Margins of safety ought to be used to protect against the most troublesome risks. And if disadvantaged people have a great deal to gain from one or another option, it would make sense to select that option even if the cost-benefit analysis suggests otherwise.

CHAPTER 8

Libertarian Paternalism

with Richard Thaler

To engage in cost-benefit analysis, regulators need to know a great deal. Often they won't know enough to produce an analysis in which they can have any confidence. What might they do instead? Sometimes an Anti-Catastrophe Principle makes a lot of sense, but its domain is restricted (fortunately). My goal in this chapter is to sketch an alternative approach, one that is especially designed for cases in which people are insufficiently fearful, but that also has potential applications in cases in which people's fear is excessive.

OF SAVINGS AND CHOICES

Begin with two studies of savings behavior:

- Hoping to increase savings by workers, several employers have adopted a simple strategy. Instead of asking workers to elect to participate in a 401(k) (i.e., savings for retirement) plan, workers will be assumed to want to participate in such a plan, and hence they will be enrolled automatically unless they specifically choose otherwise. This simple change in the default rule has produced dramatic increases in enrollment.[1]
- Rather than changing the default rule, some employers have provided their employees with a novel option: *Allocate a portion of future wage increases to savings*. Employees who choose this plan are free to opt out at any time. A large number of employees have

---

[1] See James J. Choi et al., Defined Contribution Pensions: Plan Rules, Participant Choices, and the Path of Least Resistance, 16 *Tax Policy & the Economy* 67, 70 (2002); Brigitte C. Madrian and Dennis F. Shea, The Power of Suggestion: Inertia in 401(k) Participation and Savings Behavior, 116 *Q.J. Econ.* 1149, 1149–50 (2001).

agreed to try the plan, and only a few have opted out. The result has been significant increases in savings rates.[2]

Libertarians embrace freedom of choice, and so they deplore paternalism. Paternalists are thought to be skeptical of unfettered freedom of choice and to deplore libertarianism. According to the conventional wisdom, libertarians cannot possibly embrace paternalism, and paternalists abhor libertarianism. The idea of libertarian paternalism seems to be a contradiction in terms.

If we keep in view the two studies just described, however, the conventional wisdom starts to dissolve. It is possible to propose a form of paternalism, libertarian in spirit, that should be acceptable to those who are firmly committed to freedom of choice. Indeed, libertarian paternalism provides a basis for both understanding and rethinking a number of areas of contemporary law, including those aspects that deal with worker welfare, consumer protection, and the family.[3] In many domains, people lack clear, stable, or well-ordered preferences. What they choose is strongly influenced by details of the context in which they make their choice, for example, default rules, framing effects (that is, the wording of possible options), and starting points. These contextual influences render the very meaning of the term "preferences" unclear.

Consider the question whether to undergo a risky medical procedure. When people are told, "Of those who undergo this procedure, 90 percent are still alive after five years," they are far more likely to agree to the procedure than when they are told, "Of those who undergo this procedure, 10 percent are dead after five years."[4] What, then, are the patient's "preferences" with respect to this procedure? Repeated experiences with such problems might be expected to eliminate this framing effect, but doctors, too, are vulnerable to it. Or return to the question of savings for retirement. It is now clear that

---

[2] See Richard H. Thaler and Shlomo Benartzi, Save More Tomorrow: Using Behavioral Economics to Increase Employee Saving, 112 *J. Polit. Econ.* S164 (2004).

[3] The defense of libertarian paternalism is closely related to the arguments for "asymmetric paternalism," illuminatingly discussed in Colin Camerer et al., Regulation for Conservatives: Behavioral Economics and the Case for "Asymmetric Paternalism," 151 *U. Pa. L. Rev.* 1211 (2003). Camerer et al. urge that governments should consider a weak form of paternalism – a form that attempts to help those who make mistakes, while imposing minimal costs on those who are fully rational. *Id.* at 1212.

[4] See Donald A. Redelmeier, Paul Rozin, and Daniel Kahneman, Understanding Patients' Decisions: Cognitive and Emotional Perspectives, 270 *J.A.M.A.* 72, 73 (1993).

if an employer requires employees to make an affirmative election in favor of savings, with the default rule devoting 100 percent of wages to current income, the level of savings will be far lower than if the employer adopts an automatic enrollment program from which employees are freely permitted to opt out. Can workers then be said to have well-defined preferences about how much to save? This simple example can be extended to many situations.

As the savings problem illustrates, the design features of both legal and organizational rules have surprisingly powerful influences on people's choices. Libertarian paternalists contend that such rules should be chosen with the explicit goal of improving the welfare of the people affected by them. The libertarian aspect of these strategies lies in the straightforward insistence that, in general, people should be free to opt out of specified arrangements if they choose to do so. To borrow a phrase, libertarian paternalists urge that people should be "free to choose."[5] Hence they do not defend any approach that blocks individual choices. The paternalistic aspect consists in the claim that it is legitimate for private and public institutions to attempt to influence people's behavior even when third-party effects are absent. In this understanding, a policy therefore counts as "paternalistic" if it attempts to influence the choices of affected parties in a way that will make choosers better off. In some cases individuals make inferior decisions in terms of their own welfare – decisions that they would change if they had complete information, unlimited cognitive abilities, and no lack of self-control. Hence libertarian paternalism promises to be responsive to both excessive and insufficient fear.

Libertarian paternalism is a relatively weak and nonintrusive type of paternalism, because choices are not blocked or fenced off. In its most cautious forms, libertarian paternalism imposes trivial costs on those who seek to depart from the planner's preferred option. But the approach nonetheless counts as paternalistic, because private and public planners are not trying to track people's anticipated choices, and are self-consciously attempting to move people in welfare-promoting

---

[5] See Milton Friedman and Rose Friedman, *Free to Choose: A Personal Statement* (New York: Harcourt Brace Jovanovich, 1980). To be sure, it would be possible to imagine a more robust understanding of libertarianism, one that attempts to minimize influences on free choice, or to maximize unfettered liberty of choice. But as discussed below, influences on freedom of choice are often impossible to avoid.

directions. Some libertarians will have little or no trouble with an endorsement of paternalism for private institutions; their chief objection is to paternalistic law and government. But the same points that support welfare-promoting private paternalism apply to government as well. It follows that there is a real problem with the dogmatic anti-paternalism of many observers of law and policy. This dogmatism is based on a combination of a false assumption and two misconceptions.

The false assumption is that almost all people, almost all of the time, make choices that are in their best interest or at the very least are better, by their own lights, than the choices that would be made by third parties. This claim is either tautological, and therefore uninteresting, or testable. It is best taken as testable and false, indeed obviously false. In fact, no one believes it on reflection. Suppose that a chess novice were to play against an experienced player. Predictably the novice would lose precisely because he made inferior choices – choices that could easily be improved by some helpful hints. More generally, how well people choose is partly an empirical question, one whose answer is likely to vary across domains. As a first approximation, it is reasonable to say that people make better choices in contexts in which they have experience and good information (say, choosing ice cream flavors) than in contexts in which they are inexperienced and poorly informed (say, choosing among medical treatments or investment options).

The first misconception is that there are viable alternatives to paternalism. In many situations, an organization or agent *must* make a choice that will affect the behavior of some other people. There is, in those situations, no alternative to a kind of paternalism – at least in the form of an intervention that affects what people choose. People's preferences, in certain domains and across a certain range, are influenced by the choices made by planners. The point applies to both private and public actors, and hence to those who design legal rules as well as to those who serve consumers. As a simple example, consider an area (usually!) far afield from the particular issue of fear: the cafeteria at some organization. The cafeteria must make a multitude of decisions, including which foods to serve, which ingredients to use, and in what order to arrange the choices. Suppose that the director of the cafeteria notices that customers have a tendency to choose more of the items that are presented earlier in the line. How should the director decide in what order to present the items? To simplify, consider some alternative strategies that the director might adopt in deciding which items to place early in the line:

1. She could make choices that she thinks would make the customers best off, all things considered.
2. She could make choices at random.
3. She could choose those items that she thinks would make the customers as obese as possible.
4. She could give customers what she thinks they would choose on their own.

Option 1 appears to be paternalistic, but would anyone advocate options 2 or 3? Option 4 is what many anti-paternalists would favor, but it is much harder to implement than it might seem. Across a certain domain of possibilities, consumers will often lack well-formed preferences, in the sense of preferences that are firmly held and preexist the director's own choices about how to order the relevant items. If the arrangement of the alternatives has a significant effect on the selections the customers make, then their true "preferences" do not formally exist.

Of course, market pressures will impose a discipline on the choices of those cafeteria directors who face competition. If there are many cafeterias, a cafeteria that offers healthy but terrible-tasting food is unlikely to do well. Market-oriented libertarians might urge that the cafeteria should attempt to maximize profits, selecting menus in a way that will increase net revenues. But profit maximization is not the appropriate goal for cafeterias granted a degree of monopoly power – for example, those in schools, dormitories, or some companies. And even those cafeterias that face competition will find that some of the time, market success will come not from tracking people's preferences, but from providing goods and services that turn out, in practice, to promote their welfare, all things considered. Consumers might be surprised by what they end up liking; indeed, their preferences might change as a result of consumption. And in some cases, the discipline imposed by market pressures will nonetheless allow the director a great deal of room to maneuver, because people's preferences are not well formed across the relevant domains.

The lesson for fear is clear. If people are fearful when they ought not to be, a private institution might structure the relevant options in a way that will steer people away from decisions that capitulate to unjustified fear. For example, hospitals might frame options in a way that will lead people to choose medical procedures that are clearly best, even if a small probability of failure might frighten some patients and lead them to less promising options. (There is a warning here about the popular idea of patient autonomy: Some patients will be excessively influenced by hearing that of 10,000 people who have a certain operation, one or two have serious complications.) And if people are not fearful when they have reason to be, a private institution should make arrangements that will steer people away from situations that impose real risks. In the domain of savings, for example, employers might protect people against their own disregard of the long term.

This will not satisfy those libertarians who will happily accept this point for private institutions, but who object to government efforts to influence choice in the name of welfare. Skepticism about government might be based on the fact that governments are disciplined less or perhaps not at all by market pressures. Or such skepticism might be based on the belief that parochial interests will drive government planners in their own preferred directions, by structuring situations so that citizens will do what regulators (or powerful private interests) want. For government, the risks of mistake and overreaching are real and sometimes serious. But governments, no less than cafeterias (which governments frequently run), have to provide starting points of one or another kind; this is not avoidable. As we shall see, they do so every day through the rules of contract and tort, in a way that inevitably affects some preferences and choices. In this respect, the anti-paternalist position is unhelpful – a literal nonstarter.

The second misconception is that paternalism always involves coercion. As the cafeteria example illustrates, the choice of the order in which to present food items does not coerce anyone to do anything, yet one might prefer some orders to others on grounds that are paternalistic in the sense that the term is used here. Would anyone object to putting the fruit and salad before the desserts at an elementary school cafeteria if the result were to increase the consumption ratio of apples to candy? Is this question fundamentally different if the customers are adults? Since no coercion is involved, some types of paternalism should be acceptable to even the most ardent libertarian. To those antilibertarians who are suspicious of freedom of choice and would prefer to embrace welfare instead, the response is that it is often possible for paternalistic planners to make common cause with their libertarian adversaries by adopting policies that promise to promote welfare but that also make room for freedom of choice. To confident planners, the response is that the risks of confused or ill-motivated plans are reduced if people are given the opportunity to reject the planner's preferred solutions.

Once it is understood that some organizational decisions are inevitable, that a form of paternalism cannot be avoided, and that the alternatives to paternalism (such as choosing options to make people worse off) are unattractive, we can abandon the less interesting question of whether to be paternalistic or not, and turn to the more constructive question of how to choose among the possible choice-influencing options.

THE RATIONALITY OF CHOICES

The presumption that individual choices should be respected is often based on the claim that people do an excellent job of making choices, or at least that they do a far better job than third parties could possibly do.[6] But there is little empirical support for this claim, at least if it is offered in this general form. Consider the issue of obesity. Rates of obesity in the United States are now approaching 20 percent, and over 60 percent of Americans are considered either obese or overweight. There is overwhelming evidence that obesity causes serious health risks, frequently leading to premature death.[7] It is quite fantastic to

---

[6] It is usually, but not always, based on this claim. Some of the standard arguments against paternalism rest not on consequences but on autonomy – on a belief that people are entitled to make their own choices even if they err. Thus John Stuart Mill, *On Liberty* (1859), in *Utilitarianism, On Liberty, Considerations on Representative Government* 69, ed. H. B. Acton (London: J. M. Dent & Sons, 1972), is a mix of autonomy-based and consequentialist claims. The principal concern here is with welfare and consequences, though as suggested below, freedom of choice is sometimes an ingredient in welfare. Respect for autonomy is adequately accommodated by the libertarian aspect of libertarian paternalism, as discussed below.

[7] See, for example, Eugenia E. Calle et al., Body-Mass Index and Mortality in a Prospective Cohort of U.S. Adults, 341(15) *New Eng. J. Med.* 1097 (1999) (discussing increased risk of death from all causes among the obese). See also National Institute of Diabetes and Digestive and Kidney Diseases, *Understanding Adult Obesity*, NIH Pub. No. 01-3680 (Oct 2001),

suggest that everyone is choosing the optimal diet, or a diet that is preferable to what might be produced with third-party guidance. Of course, rational people care about the taste of food, not simply about health, and it would be foolish to claim that everyone who is overweight is necessarily failing to act rationally. It is the strong claim that all or almost all Americans are choosing their diet *optimally* that seems untenable. What is true for diets is true as well for much other risk-related behavior, including smoking and drinking, which produce over 500,000 premature deaths in the United States each year.[8] In these circumstances, people's choices cannot reasonably be thought, in all domains, to be the best means of promoting their well-being. Indeed, many smokers, drinkers, and overeaters are willing to pay for third parties to help them choose better consumption sets.

On a more scientific level, research by psychologists and economists over the past three decades has raised questions about the rationality of many judgments and decisions that individuals make. We have seen that people use heuristics that lead them to make systematic blunders, and they make different choices depending on the framing of the problem.[9] They also fail to make forecasts that are consistent with Bayes' rule,[10] exhibit preference reversals (that is, they prefer

online at http://www.niddk.nih.gov/health/nutrit/pubs/unders.htm#Healthrisks (visited May 10, 2003) (noting links between obesity and cancer, diabetes, heart disease, high blood pressure, and stroke).

[8] See Cass R. Sunstein, *Risk and Reason* 8–9 (Cambridge: Cambridge University Press, 2002), relying on J. Michael McGinnis and William H. Foege, Actual Causes of Death in the United States, 270 *J.A.M.A.* 2207 (1993). For an interesting discussion, see Jonathan Gruber, Smoking's "Internalities," 25(4) *Regulation* 52, 54–55 (2002/3) (finding a disconnect between smokers' short-term desire for self-gratification and their long-term desire for good health, and suggesting that cigarette taxation can help smokers exercise the self-control needed to act on behalf of their long-term interests).

[9] See Colin F. Camerer, Prospect Theory in the Wild: Evidence from the Field, in *Choices, Values, and Frames* 288, 294–95, ed. Daniel Kahneman and Amos Tversky (Cambridge: Cambridge University Press, 2000); Eric J. Johnson et al., Framing, Probability Distortions, and Insurance Decisions, in *id.* at 224, 238. Note also the emerging literature on people's inability to predict their own emotional reactions to events, a literature that might well bear on the uses of libertarian paternalism. See Timothy D. Wilson and Daniel T. Gilbert, Affective Forecasting, 35 *Advances in Experimental Soc. Psych.* 345 (2003).

[10] See David M. Grether, Bayes' Rule as a Descriptive Model: The Representativeness Heuristic, 95 *Q.J. Econ.* 537 (1980). Bayes' rule explains how to change existing beliefs as to the probability of a particular hypothesis in the light of new evidence. See Jonathan Baron, *Thinking and Deciding* 109–15 (Cambridge: Cambridge University Press, 3d ed., 2000) (giving a mathematical explanation and examples of the rule's application).

A to B *and* B to A),[11] and suffer from problems of self-control.[12] It is possible to raise questions about some of these findings and to think that people may do a better job of choosing in the real world than they do in the laboratory. But studies of actual choices reveal many of the same problems, even when the stakes are high.[13] Recall that the decision to buy insurance for natural disasters is a product not of a systematic inquiry into either costs or benefits, but of recent events.[14] If floods have not occurred in the immediate past, people who live on flood plains are far less likely to purchase insurance. Findings of this kind do not establish that people's choices are usually bad or that third parties can usually do better. But they do show that some of the time, people do not choose optimally even when the stakes are high.

In any case, the issue here is not blocking choices, but developing strategies that move people in welfare-promoting directions while also allowing freedom of choice. Evidence of bounded rationality and problems of self-control is sufficient to suggest that such strategies

[11] See Richard H. Thaler, *The Winner's Curse: Paradoxes and Anomalies of Economic Life* 79–91 (New York: Free Press, 1992). In the legal context, see Cass R. Sunstein et al., Predictably Incoherent Judgments, 54 *Stan. L. Rev.* 1153 (2002).

[12] See Shane Frederick, George Loewenstein, and Ted O'Donoghue, Time Discounting and Time Preference: A Critical Review, 40 *J. Econ. Lit.* 351, 367–68 (2002).

[13] For evidence that heuristics and biases operate in the real world, even when dollars are involved, see Werner F. M. De Bondt and Richard H. Thaler, Do Security Analysts Overreact?, 80(2) *Am. Econ. Rev.* 52 (1990) (demonstrating that security analysts overreact to market data and produce forecasts that are either too optimistic or too pessimistic); Robert J. Shiller, *Irrational Exuberance* 135–47 (Princeton, N.J.: Princeton University Press, 2000) (discussing anchoring and overconfidence in market behavior); Colin F. Camerer and Robin M. Hogarth, The Effects of Financial Incentives in Experiments: A Review and Capital-Labor-Production Framework, 19 *J. Risk & Uncertainty* 7 (1999) (finding that financial incentives have *never* eliminated anomalies or persistent irrationalities). See also Colin F. Camerer, *Behavioral Game Theory: Experiments in Strategic Interaction* 60–62 (Princeton, N.J.: Princeton University Press, 2003) (finding little effect from increased stakes in ultimatum games designed to test the hypothesis that people are self-interested, and adding, "If I had a dollar for every time an economist claimed that raising the stakes would drive ultimatum behavior toward self-interest, I'd have a private jet on standby all day").

[14] See Paul Slovic, Howard Kunreuther, and Gilbert F. White, Decision Processes, Rationality and Adjustment to Natural Hazards (1974), in Paul Slovic, *The Perception of Risk* 14 (London: Earthscan, 2000) (explaining that the availability heuristic "is potentially one of the most important ideas for helping us understand the distortions likely to occur in our perceptions of natural hazards"). See also Howard Kunreuther, Mitigating Disaster Losses through Insurance, 12 *J. Risk & Uncertainty* 171, 174–78 (1996) (explaining why individuals fail to take cost-effective preventative measures or voluntarily insure against natural disasters).

are worth exploring. Of course, many people value freedom of choice not as a way of promoting welfare but as an end in itself; such people should not object to approaches that preserve that freedom while also promising to improve people's lives.

IS PATERNALISM INEVITABLE?

A few years ago, the tax law was changed so that employees could pay for employer-provided parking on a pretax basis. Previously, such parking had to be paid for with after-tax dollars. The University of Chicago sent around an announcement of this change in the law and adopted the following policy: Unless the employee notified the payroll department, deductions for parking would be taken from pretax rather than post-tax income. In other words, the University of Chicago decided that the default option would be to pay for parking with pretax dollars, but employees could opt out of this arrangement and pay with after-tax dollars. Call this choice Plan A. An obvious alternative, Plan B, would be to announce the change in the law and tell employees that if they want to switch to the new pretax plan they should return some form electing this option. The only difference between the two plans is the default. Under Plan A the new option is the default, whereas under Plan B the status quo is the default.

How should the university choose between the two defaults? It is clear that every employee would prefer to pay for parking with pretax dollars rather than after-tax dollars. Since the cost savings are substantial (parking costs as much as $1,200 per year) and the cost of returning a form is trivial, standard economic theory predicts that the university's choice will not really matter. Under either plan, all employees would choose (either actively under Plan B or by default under Plan A) the pretax option. In real life, however, had the university adopted Plan B, it is reasonable to suspect that many employees, especially faculty members, would still have that form buried somewhere in their offices and would be paying substantially more for parking on an after-tax basis. In short, the default plan would have had large effects on behavior. Often that plan will be remarkably "sticky."

The conjecture that default plans affect outcomes is supported by numerous experiments documenting a "status quo" bias.[15] The existing arrangement, whether set out by private institutions or by government, is often robust. An illustration of this phenomenon comes from studies of automatic enrollment in 401(k) employee savings plans.[16] Most 401(k) plans use an opt-in design. When employees first become eligible to participate in the 401(k) plan, they receive some plan information and an enrollment form that must be completed in order to join. Under the alternative of automatic enrollment, employees receive the same information but are told that unless they opt out, they will be enrolled in the plan (with default options for savings rates and asset allocation). In companies that offer a "match" (the employer matches the employee's contributions according to some formula, often a 50 percent match up to some cap), most employees eventually do join the plan, but enrollments occur much sooner under automatic enrollment. For example, Madrian and Shea found that initial enrollments jumped from 49 percent to 86 percent,[17] and Choi and his coauthors found similar results.[18]

Should automatic enrollment be considered paternalistic? And if so, should it be seen as a kind of officious meddling with employee preferences? The best answers are yes and no respectively. If employers

---

[15] See Daniel Kahneman, Jack L. Knetsch, and Richard H. Thaler, The Endowment Effect, Loss Aversion, and Status Quo Bias: Anomalies, 5(1) *J. Econ. Perspect.* 193, 197–99 (1991); William Samuelson and Richard Zeckhauser, Status Quo Bias in Decision Making, 1 *J. Risk & Uncertainty* 7 (1988).

[16] See *supra* note 1 and accompanying text.

[17] See Madrian and Shea, *supra* note 1, at 1158–59.

[18] See Choi et al., *supra* note 1, at 76–77 (finding employee enrollment six months after hire at three companies increased after the adoption of automatic enrollment, from 26.4 percent to 93.4 percent, 35.7 percent to 85.9 percent, and 42.5 percent to 96 percent). In a separate phenomenon, the default rule also had a significant effect on the chosen contribution rate. See Madrian and Shea, *supra* note 1, at 1162–76. The default contribution rate (3 percent) tended to stick; a majority of employees maintained that rate even though this particular rate was chosen by around 10 percent of employees hired before the automatic enrollment. *Id.* at 1162–63. The same result was found for the default allocation of the investment: While fewer than 7 percent of employees chose a 100 percent investment allocation to the money market fund, a substantial majority (75 percent) of employees stuck with that allocation when it was the default rule. *Id.* at 1168–71. The overall default rate (participation in the plan, at a 3 percent contribution rate, investing 100 percent in the money market fund) was 61 percent, but only 1 percent of employees chose this set of options prior to their adoption as defaults. *Id.* at 1171–72.

think that most employees would prefer to join the 401(k) plan if they took the time to think about it and did not lose the enrollment form, then by choosing automatic enrollment, they are acting paternalistically in the sense that they are attempting to steer employees' choices in good directions. But since no one is forced to do anything, this steering should be considered unobjectionable even to committed libertarians. The employer must choose some set of rules, and either plan affects employees' choices. No law of nature says that in the absence of an affirmative election by employees, zero percent of earnings will go into a retirement plan. Because both plans alter choices, neither one can be said, more than the other, to count as a form of objectionable meddling.

Skeptical readers, insistent on freedom of choice, might be tempted to think that there is a way out of this dilemma. Employers could avoid choosing a default if they *required* employees to make an active choice, either in or out. Call this option *coerced choosing*. Doctors and regulators, dealing with people fearful or not so fearful of risks, might tell people that they have to choose for themselves. Undoubtedly coerced choosing is attractive in some settings, but a little thought reveals that this is not always the best solution. In fact, the very requirement that employees make a choice has a strong paternalistic element. Some employees (and patients) may not want to have to make a choice (and might make a second-order choice not to have to do so). Why should employers force them to choose?

Coerced choosing honors freedom of choice in a certain respect; but it does not appeal to those who would choose not to choose, and indeed it will seem irritating and perhaps unacceptable by their lights. In some circumstances, coerced choosing will not even be feasible. In some settings, it is simply too costly and time-consuming to ask every person to signal an individual judgment. In any case, an empirical question remains: What is the effect of coerced choosing? Choi et al. find that coerced choosing increases enrollments relative to the opt-in rule, though not by as much as automatic enrollment (opt-out).[19]

---

[19] Compare Choi et al., *supra* note 1, at 86 (noting that 78 percent of employees offered enrollment in a program committing to savings from future raises accepted, and 62 percent accepted and stayed in through three pay raises), with *id.* at 77 (showing enrollment rates in opt-out savings plans at three companies six months after hire at 93.4 percent, 85.9 percent, and 96.0 percent).

Other skeptics might think that employers can and should avoid paternalism by doing what most employees would want employers to do. On this approach, a default rule can successfully avoid paternalism if it tracks employees' preferences. Sometimes this is a plausible and good solution; as we have seen, current valuations of risk attempt to do precisely this. But what about cases in which many or most employees do not have stable or well-formed preferences, and what if employee choices are inevitably a product of the default rule? In such cases, it is meaningless to ask what most employees would do. The choices employees will make depend on the way the employer frames those choices. Employee "preferences," as such, do not exist in those circumstances.

Savings are a good example of a domain in which preferences are likely to be ill-defined. Few households have either the knowledge or inclination to calculate their optimal life-cycle savings rate, and even if they were to make such a calculation, its results would be highly dependent on assumptions about rates of return and life expectancies. In light of this, actual behavior is highly sensitive to plan design features.

GOVERNMENT

Enthusiasts for free choice might be willing to acknowledge these points and hence to accept private efforts to steer people's choices in what seem to be the right directions. Market pressures, and the frequently wide range of possible options, might be thought to impose sufficient protection against objectionable steering. But my emphasis has been on the inevitability of paternalism, and on this count, the same points apply to some choices made by governments in establishing legal rules.

Default rules

Default rules of some kind are inevitable, and much of the time those rules will affect preferences and choices. In the words of a classic article:

[A] minimum of state intervention is always necessary . . . When a loss is left where it falls in an auto accident, it is not because God so ordained it.

Rather it is because the state has granted the injurer an entitlement to be free of liability and will intervene to prevent the victim's friends, if they are stronger, from taking compensation from the injurer.[20]

If the law's entitlement-granting rules seem invisible, and to be a simple way of protecting freedom of choice, it is because they are being seen as so sensible and natural that they are not a legal allocation at all. But this is a mistake. When a default rule affects preferences and behavior, it has the same effect as employer presumptions about savings plans. This effect is often both unavoidable and significant. So long as people can contract around the default rule, it is fair to say that the legal system is protecting freedom of choice, and in that sense complying with libertarian goals.

Consumers, workers, and married people, for example, are surrounded by a network of legal allocations that provide the background against which agreements are made. As a matter of employment law, and consistent with freedom of contract, workers might be presumed subject to discharge "at will" (as in the United States) or they might be presumed protected by an implied right to be discharged only "for cause" (as in Europe). They might be presumed to have a right to vacation time, or not. They might be presumed protected by safety requirements, or the employer might be free to invest in safety as he wishes, subject to market pressures. In all cases, the law must establish whether workers have to "buy" certain rights from employers or vice versa. Legal intervention, in this important sense, cannot be avoided. The same is true for consumers, spouses, and all others who are involved in legal relationships. Much of the time, the legal background matters, even if transaction costs are zero, because it affects choices and preferences. Here, as in the private context, a form of paternalism is unavoidable.

In the context of insurance, and in a way that very much bears on fear, an unplanned, natural experiment showed that the default rule can be very "sticky."[21] New Jersey created a system in which the default insurance program for motorists included a relatively low premium and no right to sue. Purchasers were allowed to deviate from

[20] Guido Calabresi and A. Douglas Melamed, Property Rules, Liability Rules, and Inalienability: One View of the Cathedral, 85 *Harv. L. Rev.* 1089, 1090–91 (1972).
[21] See Camerer, *supra* note 9, at 294–95; Johnson et al., *supra* note 9, at 238.

the default program and to purchase the right to sue by choosing a program with that right and also a higher premium. By contrast, Pennsylvania offered a default program containing a full right to sue and a relatively high premium. Purchasers could elect to switch to a new plan by "selling" the more ample right to sue and paying a lower premium. In both cases, the default rule tended to stick. A strong majority accepted the default rule in both states, with only about 20 percent of New Jersey drivers acquiring the full right to sue, and 75 percent of Pennsylvanians retaining that right. There is no reason to think that the citizens of Pennsylvania have systematically different preferences from the citizens of New Jersey. The default plan is what produced the ultimate effects. Indeed, controlled experiments find the same results, showing that the value of the right to sue is much higher when it is presented as part of the default package.

In another example, a substantial effect from the legal default rule was found in a study of law student reactions to different state law provisions governing vacation time from firms.[22] The study was intended to be reasonably realistic, involving as it did a pool of subjects to whom the underlying issues were hardly foreign. Most law students have devoted a lot of time to thinking about salaries, vacation time, and the tradeoffs between them. The study involved two conditions. In the first, state law guaranteed two weeks of vacation time, and students were asked to state their median willingness to pay (in reduced salary) for two extra weeks of vacation. In this condition, the median willingness to pay was $6,000. In the second condition, state law provided a mandatory, nonwaivable two-week vacation guarantee, but it also provided employees (including associates at law firms) with the right to two additional weeks of vacation, a right that could be "knowingly and voluntarily waived." Hence the second condition was precisely the same as the first, except that the default rule provided the two extra weeks of vacation. In the second condition, students were asked how much employers would have to pay them to give up their right to the two extra weeks. All by itself, the switch in the default rule more than doubled the students' responses, producing a median willingness to accept of $13,000.

---

[22] See Cass R. Sunstein, Switching the Default Rule, 77 *N.Y.U. L. Rev.* 106, 113–14 (2002).

We can imagine countless variations. For example, the law might authorize a situation in which employees have to opt into retirement plans, or it might require employers to provide automatic enrollment and allow employees to opt out. Both systems would respect the freedom of employees to choose, and either system would be libertarian in that sense. In the same vein, the law might assume that there is no right to be free from age discrimination in employment, permitting employees (through individual negotiation or collective bargaining) to contract for that right. Alternatively, it might give employees a nondiscrimination guarantee, subject to waiver via contract. In all these cases, one or another approach is likely to have effects on the choices of employees. This is the sense in which paternalism is inevitable, from government no less than from private institutions.

Anchors

In emphasizing the absence of well-formed preferences, I am not speaking only of default rules. Consider the crucial role of "anchors," or starting points, in contingent valuation studies, an influential method of valuing regulatory goods such as increased safety and environmental protection.[23] Such studies, used when market valuations are unavailable, attempt to ask people their "willingness to pay" for various regulatory benefits. Because the goal is to determine what people actually want, contingent valuation studies are an effort to elicit, rather than to affect, people's values. Paternalism, in the sense of effects on preferences and choices, is not supposed to be part of the picture. But it is extremely difficult for contingent valuation studies to avoid constructing the very values that they are supposed to discover.[24] The reason is that in the contexts in which such studies

[23] See, for example, *Valuing Environmental Preferences*, ed. Ian J. Bateman and Kenneth G. Willis (Oxford: Oxford University Press, 1999). But see Peter A. Diamond and Jerry A. Hausman, Contingent Valuation Debate: Is Some Number Better than No Number? 8 *J. Econ. Perspect.* 45, 49–52 (1994) (arguing that contingent valuation surveys fail to accurately measure willingness-to-pay preferences with regard to public goods); Note, "Ask a Silly Question . . .": Contingent Valuation of Natural Resource Damages, 105 *Harv. L. Rev.* 1981 (1992) (criticizing contingent valuation in ascertaining natural resource damages, on grounds that it produces biased results that will lead to unfair liability burdens).

[24] See John W. Payne, James R. Bettman, and David A. Schkade, Measuring Constructed Preferences: Towards a Building Code, 19 *J. Risk & Uncertainty* 243, 266 (1999).

are used, people do not have clear or well-formed preferences, and hence it is unclear that people have straightforward "values" that can actually be found. Hence some form of paternalism verges on the inevitable: Stated values will often be affected, at least across a range, by how the questions are set up.

The most striking evidence to this effect comes from a study of willingness to pay to reduce annual risks of death and injury in motor vehicles.[25] The authors of that study attempted to elicit both maximum and minimum willingness to pay for safety improvements. People were presented with a statistical risk and an initial monetary amount, and asked whether they were definitely willing or definitely unwilling to pay that amount to eliminate the risk, or if they were "not sure." If they were definitely willing, the amount displayed was increased until they said that they were definitely unwilling. If they were unsure, the number was moved up and down until people could identify the minimum and maximum.

The authors were not attempting to test the effects of anchors; on the contrary, they were alert to anchoring only because they "had been warned" of a possible problem with their procedure, in which people "might be unduly influenced by the first amount of money that they saw displayed."[26] To solve that problem, the study allocated people randomly to two subsamples, one with an initial display of £25, the other with an initial display of £75. The authors hoped that the anchoring effect would be small, with no significant consequences for minimum and maximum values. But their hope was dashed. *For every level of risk, the minimum willingness to pay was higher with the £75 starting point than the maximum willingness to pay with the £25 starting point!* For example, a reduction in the annual risk of death by 4 in 100,000 produced a *maximum* willingness to pay of £149 with the £25 starting value, but a *minimum* willingness to pay of £232 with the £75 starting value (and a maximum, in that case, of £350). The most sensible conclusion is that people are sometimes uncertain about appropriate values, and whenever they are, anchors have an effect – sometimes a startlingly large one.

---

[25] See Michael Jones-Lee and Graham Loomes, Private Values and Public Policy, in *Conflict and Tradeoffs in Decision Making* 205, 208–12, ed. Elke U. Weber, Jonathan Baron, and Graham Loomes (Cambridge: Cambridge University Press, 2001).

[26] *Id.* at 210.

It is not clear how those interested in eliciting (rather than affecting) values might respond to this problem. Perhaps actual workplace data, of the sort that I have discussed in previous chapters, produces an adequate discipline on decisions, producing values that can actually be used. What is clear is that in the domains in which contingent valuation studies are provided, people often lack well-formed preferences, and starting points have important consequences for behavior and choice.

Framing

In the fear-pervaded context of medical decisions, framing effects are substantial. Apparently, most people do not have clear preferences about how to evaluate a procedure that leaves 90 percent of people alive (and 10 percent of people dead) after a period of years. A similar effect has been demonstrated in the area of obligations to future generations,[27] a much-disputed policy question. An influential set of studies finds that people value the lives of those in the current generation far more than the lives of those in future generations.[28] But it turns out that other descriptions of the same problem yield significantly different results.[29] Here, as in other contexts, it is unclear whether people actually have well-formed preferences with which the legal system can work.

The point applies in many domains. For example, people are unlikely to have context-free judgments about whether government should focus on statistical lives or statistical life-years in regulatory policy. Their judgments will be much affected by the framing of the question.[30] Here as elsewhere, preferences and values do not predate framing; they are a product of it.

---

[27] See Shane Frederick, Measuring Intergenerational Time Preference: Are Future Lives Valued Less?, 26 *J. Risk & Uncertainty* 39 (2003) (finding that imputed intergenerational time preferences can be dramatically affected by the specific question asked).

[28] See Maureen L. Cropper, Sema K. Aydede, and Paul R. Portney, Preferences for Life Saving Programs: How the Public Discounts Time and Age, 8 *J. Risk & Uncertainty* 243 (1994); Maureen L. Cropper, Sema K. Aydede, and Paul R. Portney, Rates of Time Preference for Saving Lives, 82 *Am. Econ. Rev.* 469, 472 (1992).

[29] See Frederick, *supra* note 27, at 50. ("Many of the elicitation procedures tested here indicate no substantial discounting of future lives.")

[30] See Cass R. Sunstein, Lives, Life-Years, and Willingness to Pay, 104 *Colum. L. Rev.* 205 (2004).

WHY EFFECTS ON CHOICE CAN BE HARD TO AVOID

Why, exactly, do default rules, starting points, and framing effects have such large effects? To answer this question, it is important to make some distinctions.

Suggestion

In the face of uncertainty about what should be done, people often rely on two related heuristics: do what most people do, or do what informed people do. (Divorcing spouses often follow that heuristic.) Choosers might think that the default plan or value captures one or the other. In many settings, any starting point will carry some informational content and will thus affect choices. When a default rule affects behavior, it might well be because it is taken to carry information about how sensible people usually organize their affairs. Notice that in the context of savings, people might have a mild preference for one or another course, but the preference might be overcome by evidence that most people do not take that course. Some workers might think, for example, that they should not enroll in a 401(k) plan and have a preference not to do so; but the thought and the preference might shift with evidence that the employer has made enrollment automatic. With respect to savings, the designated default plan apparently carries a certain legitimacy for many employees, perhaps because it seems to have resulted from some conscious thought about what makes most sense for most people.

Inertia

A separate explanation points to inertia.[31] Any change from the default rule or starting value is likely to require some action. Even a trivial action, such as filling in some form and returning it, can leave room for failures as a result of memory lapses, sloth, and procrastination. Many people wait until the last minute to file their tax return, even

---

[31] See Madrian and Shea, *supra* note 1, at 1171 (noting that, under automatic enrollment, individuals become "passive savers" and "do nothing to move away from the default contribution rate").

when they are assured of getting a refund. The power of inertia should be seen as a form of bounded rationality.

Endowment effect

A default rule might create a "pure" endowment effect. It is well known that people tend to value goods more highly if those goods have been initially allocated to them than if those goods have been initially allocated elsewhere.[32] And it is well known that, in many cases, the default rule will create an endowment effect. When an endowment effect is involved, the initial allocation, by private or public institutions, affects people's choices simply because it affects their valuations.

Ill-formed preferences

In many contexts, people's preferences are ill formed and murky. Suppose, for example, that people are presented with various options for insurance for serious risks, or for social security programs. They might be able to understand the presentation; there might be no confusion. But people might not have a well-defined preference for, or against, a slightly riskier plan with a slightly higher expected value. In these circumstances, their preferences might be endogenous to the default plan simply because they lack well-formed desires that can be accessed to overrule the default starting points. In unfamiliar situations, well-formed preferences are especially unlikely to exist. The range of values in the highway safety study is likely a consequence of the unfamiliarity of the context, which leaves people without clear preferences from which to generate numbers. The effects of framing on intergenerational time preferences attest to the fact that people do not have unambiguous judgments about how to trade off the interests of future generations with those of people now living.

---

[32] See generally Russell Korobkin, Status Quo Bias and Contract Default Rules, 83 *Cornell L. Rev.* 608 (1998); Richard H. Thaler, *Quasi Rational Economics* (New York: Russell Sage Foundation, 1991).

THE INEVITABILITY OF PATERNALISM

For present purposes, the choice among these various explanations does not greatly matter. The central point is that effects on individual choices can be unavoidable. Of course it is usually best not to block choices. But in an important respect the antipaternalist position is incoherent, simply because there is no way to avoid effects on behavior and choices. The task for the committed libertarian is, in the midst of such effects, to preserve freedom of choice. And because framing effects are inevitable, it is hopelessly inadequate to say that when people lack relevant information the best response is to provide it. In order to be effective, any effort to inform people must be rooted in an understanding of how people actually think. Presentation makes a great deal of difference: The behavioral consequences of otherwise identical pieces of information depend on how they are framed.

The point is a general one. In the face of health risks, some presentations of accurate information might actually be counterproductive, because people attempt to control their fear by refusing to think about the risk at all. In empirical studies, "some messages conveying identical information seemed to work better than others, and . . . some even appeared to backfire."[33] When information campaigns fail altogether, it is often because those efforts "result in counterproductive defensive measures."[34] Hence the most effective approaches go far beyond mere disclosure and combine "a frightening message about the consequences of inaction with an upbeat message about the efficacy of a proposed program of prevention."[35]

There are complex and interesting questions here about how to promote welfare. If information greatly increases people's fear, it will to that extent reduce welfare – in part because fear is unpleasant, in part because fear has a range of ripple effects producing social costs. The only suggestions here are that if people lack information, a great deal of attention needs to be paid to information processing, and that without such attention, information disclosure might well prove futile or counterproductive. And to the extent that those who design

[33] Andrew Caplin, Fear as a Policy Instrument, in *Time and Decision: Economic and Psychological Perspectives on Intertemporal Choice* 441, 443, ed. George Loewenstein, Daniel Read, and Roy Baumeister (New York: Russell Sage Foundation, 2003).
[34] *Id.* at 442.   [35] *Id.* at 443.

informational strategies are taking account of how people think and are attempting to steer people in desirable directions, their efforts will inevitably have a paternalistic dimension.

BEYOND THE INEVITABLE (BUT STILL LIBERTARIAN)

The inevitability of paternalism is clearest when the planner has to choose starting points or default rules. But if the focus is on people's welfare, it is reasonable to ask whether the planner should go beyond the inevitable, and whether such a planner can also claim to be libertarian. In the domain of employee behavior, there are many imaginable illustrations. Employees might be automatically enrolled in a 401(k) plan, with a right to opt out, but employers might require a waiting period, and perhaps a consultation with an adviser, before the opt-out could be effective. Richard Thaler and Shlomo Benartzi have proposed a method of increasing contributions to 401(k) plans that also meets the libertarian test.[36] Under the Save More Tomorrow plan, briefly described above, employees are invited to sign up for a program in which their contributions to the savings plan are increased annually whenever they get a raise. Once employees join the plan, they stay in until they opt out or reach the maximum savings rate. In the first company to use this plan, the employees who joined increased their savings rates from 3.5 percent to 11.6 percent in a little over two years (three raises). Very few of the employees who joined the plan dropped out. This is successful libertarian paternalism in action.

It should now be clear that the difference between libertarian and nonlibertarian paternalism is not simple and rigid. The libertarian paternalist insists on preserving choice, whereas the nonlibertarian paternalist is willing to foreclose choice. But in all cases, a real question is the cost of exercising choice, and here there is a continuum rather than a sharp dichotomy. A libertarian paternalist who is especially enthusiastic about free choice would be inclined to make it relatively costless for people to obtain their preferred outcomes. (Call this a *libertarian* paternalist.) By contrast, a libertarian paternalist who is especially confident of his welfare judgments would be willing to

---

[36] See Richard Thaler and Shlomo Benartzi, Save More Tomorrow: Using Behavioral Economics to Increase Employee Saving, 112 *J. Polit. Econ.* 164 (2004).

impose real costs on people who seek to do what, in the paternalist's view, would not be in their best interests. (Call this a libertarian *paternalist.*)

Rejecting both routes, a nonlibertarian paternalist would attempt to block certain choices. But notice that almost any such attempt will amount, in practice, to an effort to impose high costs on those who try to make those choices. Consider a law requiring drivers to wear seat belts. If the law is enforced, and a large fine is imposed, the law is nonlibertarian even though determined violators can exercise their freedom of choice – at the expense of the fine. But as the expected fine approaches zero, the law approaches libertarianism. The libertarian paternalism that we are describing and defending here attempts to ensure, as a general rule, that people can easily avoid the paternalist's suggested option.

ILLUSTRATIONS AND GENERALIZATIONS

In the domain of risk, many actual and proposed initiatives embody libertarian paternalism. Some of those provisions require disclosure of information; some of them shift the default rule; some of them preserve freedom of contract but impose procedural or substantive restrictions on those who seek to move in directions that seem, to the planner, to be contrary to their welfare.

Labor and employment law

Under the Age Discrimination in Employment Act (ADEA), employees are permitted to waive their rights at the time of retirement,[37] and hence the statutorily conferred right – to be free from age discrimination – does not reject the libertarian commitment to freedom of contract. But the employee is presumed to have retained that right unless there has been a "knowing and voluntary" waiver. To ensure that the waiver is knowing and voluntary, the ADEA imposes a range of procedural hurdles. Thus the waiver must specifically refer "to rights or claims arising under" the ADEA; the employee must be advised in writing to consult with an attorney before executing the agreement; the employee must be given "at least 21 days within

---

[37] 29 USC § 626(f)(1) (2000).

which to consider the agreement"; and the agreement must provide for a minimum of a seven-day post-execution revocation period. The ADEA has an unmistakable paternalistic dimension insofar as it switches the default rule to one favoring the employee and also creates a set of procedural barriers to insufficiently informed waivers. At the same time, the ADEA goes beyond the inevitable minimal level of paternalism by imposing those barriers, which significantly raise the burdens of waiver. But the ADEA preserves freedom of choice and thus satisfies the libertarian criterion.

Labor and employment law offers several other examples. The Model Employment Termination Act alters the standard American rule, which holds that employees may be discharged for no reason or for any reason at all.[38] Under the Model Act, employees are given the right to be discharged only for cause. But the Model Act complies with libertarian principles by allowing employers and employees to waive the right on the basis of an agreement, by the employer, to provide a severance payment in the event of a discharge not based on poor job performance. That payment must consist of one month's salary for every year of employment. This limitation on waiver is substantive and in that sense quite different from the procedural limitation in the ADEA; in this way it is less libertarian than it might be. But freedom of choice is nonetheless preserved.

An important provision of the Fair Labor Standards Act belongs in the same category.[39] Under that provision, employees may waive their right not to work for more than forty hours per week, but only at a governmentally determined premium (time and a half). Here, as under the Model Act, a substantive limitation is imposed on workers' rights to opt out of a default arrangement.

Consumer protection

In the law of consumer protection, the most obvious examples of libertarian paternalism involve "cooling-off" periods for certain decisions.[40] The essential rationale is that under the heat of the moment,

---

[38] See Model Employment Termination Act, reprinted in Mark A. Rothstein and Lance Liebman, *Statutory Supplement, Employment Law: Cases and Materials* 211 (New York: Foundation Press, 5th ed., 2003).

[39] See 29 USC § 207(f) (2000).

[40] See the valuable discussion in Camerer et al., *supra* note 3, at 1240–42.

consumers might make ill-considered or improvident decisions. Both bounded rationality and bounded self-control are the underlying concerns. A mandatory cooling-off period for door-to-door sales, of the sort imposed by the Federal Trade Commission in 1972,[41] provides a simple illustration. Under the Commission's rule, door-to-door sales must be accompanied by written statements informing buyers of their right to rescind purchases within three days of transactions. Some states also impose mandatory waiting periods before people may receive a divorce decree.[42] We could easily imagine similar restrictions on the decision to marry, and some American states have moved in this direction as well.[43] Aware that people might act impulsively or in a way that they will regret, regulators do not block their choices, but ensure a period for sober reflection. Note in this regard that mandatory cooling-off periods make best sense, and tend to be imposed, when two conditions are met: (1) people are making decisions that they make infrequently and for which they therefore lack a great deal of experience, and (2) emotions are likely to be running high. These are the circumstances – of bounded rationality and bounded self-control respectively – in which consumers are especially prone to make choices that they will regret.

Generalizations

It is now possible to categorize a diverse set of paternalistic interventions: minimal paternalism, coerced choices, procedural constraints, and substantive constraints.

Minimal paternalism
Minimal paternalism is the form of paternalism that occurs whenever a planner (private or public) constructs a default rule or starting point

---

[41] 16 CFR § 429.1(a) (2003).

[42] See, for example, Cal. Fam. Code § 2339(a) (requiring a six-month waiting period before a divorce decree becomes final); Conn. Gen. Stat. § 46b–67(a) (requiring a ninety-day waiting period before the court may proceed on the divorce complaint). For a general discussion, see Elizabeth S. Scott, Rational Decisionmaking about Marriage and Divorce, 76 *Va. L. Rev.* 9 (1990).

[43] See Camerer et al., *supra* note 3, at 1243 (citing state statutes that "force potential newlyweds to wait a short period of time after their license has been issued before they can tie the knot").

with the goal of influencing behavior. So long as it is costless or nearly costless to depart from the default plan, minimal paternalism is maximally libertarian. This is the form of paternalism that I have described as inevitable.

Coerced choices

Unsure of what choices will promote welfare, a planner might reject default plans or starting points entirely and force people to choose explicitly (the strategy of coerced choices). This approach finds an analogue in information-eliciting default rules in contract law, designed to give contracting parties a strong incentive to say what they want.[44] To the extent that planners force people to choose whether or not people would like to choose, there is a paternalistic dimension to their actions. "Choosing is good for both freedom and welfare," some appear to think, whether or not people agree with them!

Procedural constraints

A slightly more aggressive form of paternalism occurs when the default plan is accompanied by procedural constraints designed to ensure that any departure is fully voluntary and entirely rational. When procedural constraints are in place, it is not costless to depart from the default plan. The extent of the cost, and the aggressiveness of the paternalism, will of course vary with the extent of the constraints. The justification for the constraints will depend on whether there are serious problems of bounded rationality and bounded self-control. If so, the constraints are justified not on the ground that the planner disagrees with people's choices, but because identifiable features of the situation make it likely that choices will be defective. Such features may include an unfamiliar setting, a lack of experience, and a risk of impulsiveness.

Substantive constraints

A planner might impose substantive constraints, allowing people to reject the default arrangement, but not on whatever terms they choose. On this approach, the planner selects the terms along which

---

[44] See Ian Ayres and Robert Gertner, Filling Gaps in Incomplete Contracts: An Economic Theory of Default Rules, 99 *Yale L.J.* 87, 91 (1989).

the parties will be permitted to move in their preferred directions. The extent of the departure from libertarianism will be a function of the gap between the legally specified terms and the terms that parties would otherwise reach. Here, too, the justification for the constraint depends on bounded rationality and bounded self-control.

OBJECTIONS

Hard-line antipaternalists, and perhaps others, will have objections. Consider three possibilities.

The first is that libertarian paternalism starts down a very slippery slope. Once one grants the possibility that default rules for savings or cafeteria lines should be designed paternalistically, it might seem impossible to resist highly nonlibertarian interventions. Critics might envisage an onslaught of what seem, to them, to be unacceptably intrusive forms of paternalism in the face of excessive or insufficient fear, from requiring motorcycle riders to wear helmets, to mandatory waiting periods before consumer purchases, to bans on cigarette smoking, to intrusive health care reforms of many imaginable kinds. In the face of the risk of overreaching, might it not be better to avoid starting down the slope at all?

There are three responses. First, in many cases there is no viable alternative to paternalism in the weak sense, and hence planners are forced to take at least a few tiny steps down that slope. Recall that paternalism, in the form of effects on behavior, is frequently inevitable. In such cases, the slope cannot be avoided. Second, the libertarian condition, requiring opt-out rights, sharply limits the steepness of the slope. So long as paternalistic interventions can be easily avoided by those who seek to adopt a course of their own, the dangers emphasized by antipaternalists are minimal. Third, those who make the slippery slope argument are acknowledging the existence of a self-control problem, at least for planners. But if planners, including bureaucrats and human resource managers, suffer from self-control problems, then it is highly likely that other people do, too.

A second and different sort of objection is based on a deep mistrust of the ability of the planner (especially the planner working for the government) to make sensible choices. Even those who normally believe that everyone chooses rationally treat with deep skepticism any proposal that seems to hinge on rational choices by bureaucrats. Part of the skepticism is based on a belief that bureaucrats lack the discipline imposed by market pressures; part of it is rooted in the fact that individuals have the welfare-promoting incentives that are thought to come from self-interest; part of it is rooted in the fear that well-organized private groups like to move bureaucrats in their preferred directions. Of course, planners are human; they are boundedly rational and subject to the influence of objectionable pressures. Nevertheless, human planners are sometimes forced to make choices, and it is surely better to have them trying to improve people's welfare rather than the opposite. And by imposing a libertarian check on bad plans, regulators can create a strong safeguard against ill-considered or ill-motivated plans. To the extent that individual self-interest is a healthy check on planners, freedom of choice is an important corrective.

A third objection would come from the opposite direction. Enthusiastic paternalists, emboldened by evidence of bounded rationality and self-control problems, might urge that in many domains, the instruction to engage in libertarian paternalism is too limiting. At least if the focus is entirely or mostly on welfare, it might seem clear that in certain circumstances, people should not be given freedom of choice for the simple reason that they will choose poorly. Why should anyone insist on libertarian paternalism, as opposed to unqualified or nonlibertarian paternalism?

This objection raises complex issues of both value and fact, and there is no occasion to venture into difficult philosophical territory here. But there are three responses. First, planners are human, and so the real comparison is between boundedly rational choosers with self-control problems and boundedly rational planners facing self-control problems of their own. It is doubtful that the comparison can sensibly be made in the abstract. Second, an opt-out right operates as a safeguard against confused or improperly motivated planners, and, in many contexts, that safeguard is crucial even if it potentially creates harm as well. Third, nothing said here denies the possibility that significant costs should sometimes be imposed on those who seek to depart from the proposed course of action, or even that freedom of choice should sometimes be denied altogether. The only qualification is that when third-party effects are not present, the general presumption is in favor of freedom of choice, and that presumption should be rebutted only when individual choice is demonstrably inconsistent with individual welfare.

WELFARE, CHOICE, AND FEAR

The goal here has been to describe and to advocate libertarian paternalism – an approach that preserves freedom of choice while encouraging both private and public institutions to steer people in directions that will promote their own welfare. The central empirical claim has been that in many domains, people's preferences are labile and ill-formed, and hence starting points and default rules are likely to be quite sticky. In such domains, it is unhelpful to say that regulators should simply "respect preferences." What people prefer, or at least choose, is a product of starting points and default rules. For both private and public institutions, the goal should be to avoid random, inadvertent, arbitrary, or harmful effects and to produce a situation that is likely to promote people's welfare, suitably defined.

Often people's fears outrun reality; often people are unconcerned about quite serious risks. Unfortunately, many current decisions are a product of default rules whose behavior-shaping effects have never been a product of serious reflection. The most sensible correctives need not foreclose options, but they do give human well-being the benefit of the doubt. Libertarian paternalism is not only a conceptual possibility; it also provides a foundation for rethinking many areas of private and public law.

CHAPTER 9

Fear and Liberty

When a nation's security is threatened, are civil liberties at undue risk? If so, why? Consider a plausible account. In the midst of external threats, public overreactions are predictable. Simply because of fear, the public and its leaders will favor precautionary measures that do little to protect security but that compromise important forms of freedom. In American history, the internment of Japanese-Americans during World War II is perhaps the most salient example, but there are many more. Consider, for example, Abraham Lincoln's suspension of habeas corpus during the Civil War, restrictions on dissident speech during World War I, the Roosevelt Administration's imposition of martial law in Hawaii in 1941, and the Communist scares during the McCarthy period. Many people believe that some of the actions of the Bush Administration, in the aftermath of the September 11 attack, fall in the same basic category. Is it really necessary, under some sort of Precautionary Principle, to hold suspected terrorists in prison in Guantanamo? For how long? For the rest of their lives?

In explaining how public fear might produce unjustified intrusions on civil liberties, I shall emphasize two underlying sources of error: the availability heuristic and probability neglect. With an understanding of these, we are able to have a better appreciation of the sources of unsupportable intrusions on civil liberties. But there is an additional factor, one that requires a shift from psychological dynamics to political ones. In responding to security threats, government often imposes selective rather than broad restrictions on liberty. Selectivity creates serious risks. If the restrictions are selective, most of the public will not face them, and hence the ordinary political checks on unjustified restrictions are not activated. In these circumstances, public fear of national security risks might well lead to precautions that amount to excessive restrictions on civil liberties.

The implication for freedom should be clear. If an external threat registers as such, it is possible that people will focus on the worst-case scenario, without considering its (low) probability. The risk is all the greater when an identifiable subgroup faces the burden of the relevant restrictions. The result will be steps that cannot be justified by reality. The internment of Japanese-Americans during World War II undoubtedly had a great deal to do with probability neglect. A vivid sense of the worst case – of collaboration by Japanese-Americans with the nation's enemies, producing a kind of Pearl Harbor for the West Coast – helped to fuel a step that went far beyond what was necessary or useful to respond to the threat.

What is necessary, then, is a set of safeguards that will ensure against unjustified restrictions. In constitutional democracies, some of those safeguards are provided by courts, usually through interpretation of the Constitution. The problem is that courts often lack the information to know whether and when intrusions on civil liberties are justified. Civil libertarians neglect this point, tending to think that the interpretation of the Constitution should not change in the face of intense public fear. This view is implausible. The legitimacy of government action depends on the strength of the arguments it can muster in its favor. If national security is genuinely at risk, the arguments will inevitably seem, and will often be, much stronger. In the context of safety and health regulation generally, I have urged that cost-benefit analysis is a partial corrective against both excessive and insufficient fear. When national security is threatened, cost-benefit analysis is far less promising, because the probability of an attack usually cannot be estimated.

But this does not mean that courts cannot play a constructive role. I suggest three possibilities. *First*, courts should require restrictions on civil liberties to be authorized by the legislature, not simply by the executive. *Second*, courts should give special scrutiny to measures that restrict the liberty of members of identifiable minority groups, simply because the ordinary political safeguards are unreliable when the burdens imposed by law are not widely shared. *Third*, case-by-case balancing, by courts, might well authorize excessive intrusions into liberties – and hence clear rules and strong presumptions, for all their rigidity, might work better than balancing in the actual world.

BAD BALANCING: A SIMPLE ACCOUNT

An understanding of the dynamics of fear helps explain why individuals and governments often overreact to risks to national security. A readily available incident can lead people to exaggerate the threat. If the media focus on one or a few incidents, public fear might be grossly disproportionate to reality. And if one or a few incidents are not only salient but emotionally gripping as well, people might not think about probability at all. Both private and public institutions will overreact. This is almost certainly what happened in the case of the 2001 anthrax attacks in the United States, in which a few incidents led both private and public institutions to exaggerate a small threat. Of course, it is possible that such incidents are a harbinger of things to come. They might also disrupt a kind of public torpor, leading people to concern themselves with hazards that had been wrongly neglected. My only suggestion is that because of how human cognition works, this is hardly guaranteed; the increase in public fear might be unjustified.

Now suppose that in any situation, there is some kind of balancing between security and civil liberty. Suppose, that is, that the degree of appropriate intrusion into the domain of liberty is partly a function of the improved security that comes from the intrusion. The problem is that if people are more fearful than they ought to be, they will seek or tolerate incursions into the domain of liberty that could not be justified if fear were not disproportionate. Suppose that there is an optimal tradeoff among the relevant variables. If so, then the availability heuristic and probability neglect, combined with social influences, will inevitably produce a tradeoff that is less than optimal – one that unduly sacrifices liberty in the name of security. In the context of threats to national security, it is predictable that governments will infringe on civil liberties without adequate justification. History offers countless examples.[1] These are especially troublesome

---

[1] For America alone, see Geoffrey R. Stone, *Perilous Times* (New York: Norton, 2004).

applications of the Precautionary Principle, unnecessarily compromising freedom for the sake of an exaggerated risk.

WORSE BALANCING: SELECTIVE RESTRICTIONS

In the context of national security, and indeed more generally, a clear understanding of the possibility of excessive fear must make an important distinction. We can imagine restrictions on liberty that apply to all or most – as in, for example, a general increase in security procedures at airports, or a measure that subjects everyone, citizens and noncitizens alike, to special government scrutiny when they are dealing with substances that might be used in bioterrorism. By contrast, we can imagine restrictions on liberty that apply to some or few – as in, for example, restrictions on Japanese-Americans, racial profiling, or the confinement of enemy combatants at Guantanamo. When restrictions apply to all or most, it is reasonable to think that political safeguards provide a strong check on unjustified government action. If the burden of the restriction is widely shared, it is unlikely to be acceptable unless most people are convinced that there is good reason for it. For genuinely burdensome restrictions, people will not be easily convinced unless a good reason is apparent or provided. (I put to one side the possibility that because of the mechanisms I have discussed, people will think that a good reason exists even if it doesn't.) But if the restriction is imposed on an identifiable subgroup, the political check is absent. Liberty-reducing intrusions can be imposed even if they are difficult to justify.

These claims can be illuminated by a glance at the views of Friedrich Hayek about the rule of law. Hayek writes, "If all that is prohibited and enjoined is prohibited and enjoined for all without exception (unless such exception follows from another general rule) and if even authority has no special powers except that of enforcing the law, little that anybody may reasonably wish to do is likely to be prohibited."[2] Hence, "how comparatively innocuous, even if irksome, are most such restrictions imposed on literally everybody, as . . . compared

---

[2] Friedrich A. von Hayek, *The Constitution of Liberty* 155 (Chicago: University of Chicago Press, 1960).

with those that are likely to be imposed only on some!" Thus it is "significant that most restrictions on what we regard as private affairs, such as sumptuary legislation, have usually been imposed only on selected groups of people or, as in the case of prohibition, were practicable only because the government reserved the right to grant exceptions."

Hayek urges, in short, that the risk of unjustified burdens dramatically increases if they are selective and if most people have nothing to worry about. The claim is especially noteworthy in situations in which public fear is producing restrictions on civil liberties. People are likely to ask, with some seriousness, whether their fear is in fact justified *if* steps that follow from it impose burdensome consequence on them. But if indulging fear is costless, because other people face the relevant burdens, then the mere fact of "risk," and the mere presence of fear, will seem to provide a justification.

TRADEOFF NEGLECT AND LIBERTY

Return in this light to Howard Margolis' effort to explain why experts and ordinary people sharply diverge with respect to certain risks.[3] I have mentioned Margolis' suggestion that sometimes people focus only on the hazards of some activity, but not on its benefits, and therefore conclude, "better safe than sorry." This is sometimes the state of mind of those who favor precautions. But in other cases, the benefits of the activity are very much on people's minds, but not the hazards – in which case they think, "nothing ventured, nothing gained." In such cases, precautions seem literally senseless. In still other cases, both benefits and risks are "on-screen," and people assess risks by comparing the benefits with the costs. For infringements on civil liberties, a serious problem arises when the benefits of risk reduction are in view but the infringements are not; and this is inevitable in cases in which burdens are faced by identifiable subgroups.

It is only natural, in this light, that those concerned about civil liberties try to promote empathetic identification with those at risk or to make people fearful that they are themselves in danger. The goal is to place the relevant burdens or costs "on-screen," and hence

---

[3] See Howard Margolis, *Dealing With Risk* 71–143 (Chicago: University of Chicago Press, 1996).

to broaden the class of people burdened by government action, if only through an act of imagination. Thus Pastor Martin Niemöller's remarks about Germany in the 1940s have often been quoted by civil libertarians:

First they came for the socialists, and I did not speak out because I was not a socialist. Then they came for the trade unionists, and I did not speak out because I was not a trade unionist. Then they came for the Jews, and I did not speak out because I was not a Jew. Then they came for me, and there was no one left to speak for me.

In many situations, the apparent lesson of this tale is empirically doubtful. If "they" come for some, it does not at all follow that "they" will eventually come for me. Everything depends on the nature of "they" and of "me." But the tale is psychologically acute; it attempts to inculcate, in those who hear it, a fear that the risks of an overreaching government cannot be easily cabined.

The danger of unjustified infringement is most serious when the victims of the infringement can be seen as an identifiable group that is readily separable from "us." Stereotyping of groups significantly increases when people are in a state of fear; when people are primed to think about their own death, they are more likely to think and act in accordance with group-based stereotypes.[4] Experimental findings of this kind support the intuitive idea that when people are afraid, they are far more likely to tolerate government action that abridges the freedom of members of some "out-group." And if this is the case, responses to social fear, in the form of infringements on liberties, will not receive the natural political checks that arise when majorities suffer as well as benefit from them. The simple idea here is that liberty-infringing action is most likely to be justified if those who support that action are also burdened by it. In that event, the political process contains a built-in protection against unjustifiable restrictions. In all cases, it follows that government needs some methods for ensuring against excessive reactions to social risks, including unjustified intrusions on civil liberties.

---

[4] See William von Hippel et al., Attitudinal Process vs. Content: The Role of Information Processing Biases in Social Judgment and Behavior, in *Social Judgments* 251, 263, ed. Joseph P. Forgas, Kipling D. Williams, and William von Hippel (Cambridge: Cambridge University Press, 2003).

PROTECTING LIBERTY

It would be possible to take the arguments just made as reason for an aggressive judicial role in the protection of civil liberties, even when national security is threatened. But there are real complications here. Taking a page from the environmentalists' book, let us notice that the availability heuristic and probability neglect might be leading people not to overstate risks but to take previously overlooked hazards seriously – to pay attention to dangers that had not previously appeared on the public viewscreen. In the environmental context, the point seems right; readily available incidents help to mobilize people formerly suffering from torpor and indifference. The same cognitive processes that produce excessive fear can counteract insufficient fear.

The same might well be true of risks to national security. Indeed, lax airline security measures before 9/11 were undoubtedly a product of the "unavailability" of terrorist attacks. Availability bias, produced by the availability heuristic, is accompanied by unavailability bias, produced by the same heuristic: If an incident does not come to mind, both individuals and institutions should be expected to take insufficient precautions, even in the face of expert warnings (as were commonly voiced about the absence of serious security measures before the 9/11 attacks). Probability neglect can produce intense fear of low-probability risks. But when risks do not capture attention at all, they might be treated as zero, even though they deserve considerable attention. I have stressed that much of the time, public fear is bipolar: Either dangers appear "significant" or they appear not to exist at all. The mechanisms I have discussed help explain hysterical overreactions; but they can provide corrections against neglect as well.

There is also an institutional point. Courts are not, to say the least, in a good position to know whether restrictions on civil liberty are defensible. They lack the fact-finding competence that would enable them to make accurate assessments of the dangers. They are hardly experts in the question whether the release of a dozen prisoners at Guantanamo would create a nontrivial risk of a terrorist attack. It is quite possible that an aggressive judicial posture in the protection of civil liberties, amidst war, would make things worse rather than better. In any case, courts are traditionally reluctant to interfere with publicly supported restrictions on civil liberties; they do not like simply to "block" restrictions that have both official and citizen approval.[5] The remarkable decisions of the United States Supreme Court in 2004 mainly reflected a simple point: If people are being deprived of liberty, they have a right to a hearing to test the question whether they are being lawfully held.[6] This is a singularly important principle. But it is also a modest one.

I suggest that courts should and can approach the relevant issues through an institutional lens, one that pays close attention to the underlying political dynamics. There are three points here. The first and most important is that *restrictions on civil liberties should not be permitted unless they have unambiguous legislative authorization.* Such restrictions should not be permitted to come from the executive alone. The second point is that in order to protect against unjustified responses to fear, courts should be relatively more skeptical of intrusions on liberty that are not general and that burden identifiable groups. The third and final point is that constitutional principles should reflect second-order balancing, producing rules and presumptions, rather than ad hoc balancing. The reason is that under the pressure of the moment, courts are likely to find that ad hoc balancing favors the government, even when it does not.

THE PRINCIPLE OF CLEAR STATEMENT

For many years, Israel's General Security Service has engaged in certain forms of physical coercion, sometimes described as torture, against suspected terrorists. According to the General Security Service, these practices occurred only in extreme cases and as a last resort, when deemed necessary to prevent terrorist activity and significant loss of life. Nonetheless, practices worthy of the name "torture" did occur, and they were not rare. Those practices were challenged before the Supreme Court of Israel on the ground that they were inconsistent with the nation's fundamental law. The government responded that abstractions about human rights should not be permitted to overcome real-world necessities so as to ban a practice that was, in certain circumstances, genuinely essential to prevent massive deaths in an area

---

[5] See William Rehnquist, *All the Laws but One* (New York: Knopf, 1998).

[6] See *Hamdi v. Rumsfeld*, 124 S. Ct. 2633 (2004); *Rasul v. Bush*, 124 S. Ct. 2686 (2004).

of the world that was often subject to terrorist activity. According to the government, physical coercion was justified in these circumstances. A judicial decision to the opposite effect would be a form of unjustified activism, even hubris.

In deciding the case, the Supreme Court of Israel refused to resolve the most fundamental questions.[7] It declined to say whether the practices of the security forces would be illegitimate if expressly authorized by a democratic legislature. But the Court nonetheless held that those practices were unlawful. The Court's principal argument was that if such coercion were to be acceptable, it could not be because the General Security Service, with its narrow agenda, said so. At a minimum, the disputed practices must be endorsed by the national legislature, after a full democratic debate on the precise question. "[T]his is an issue that must be decided by the legislative branch which represents the people. We do not take any stand on this matter at this time. It is there that various considerations must be weighed."

It is worthwhile to pause over a central feature of this decision. Instead of resolving the fundamental issue, the Court relied on the inadequacy, from the democratic point of view, of a judgment by the General Security Service alone. To say the least, members of that organization do not represent a broad spectrum of society. It is all too likely that people who work with the General Security Service will share points of view and frames of references. When such people deliberate with one another, group polarization is likely to be at work; the participants will probably strengthen, rather than test, their existing convictions, very possibly to the detriment of human rights. A broader debate, with a greater range of views, is a necessary precondition for coercion of this sort. The Supreme Court of Israel required clear legislative authorization for this particular intrusion on liberty; it insisted that presidential action, under a vague or ambiguous law, would not be enough.

We can take this decision to stand for the general principle that the legislative branch of government must explicitly authorize disputed infringements on civil liberty. The reason for this safeguard is to ensure against inadequately considered restrictions – and to insist

---

[7] *Association for Civil Rights in Israel v. The General Security Service* (1999). Supreme Court of Israel: Judgment Concerning the Legality of the General Security Service's Interrogation Methods, 38 *I.L.M.* 1471 (1999).

that political safeguards, in the form of agreement from a diverse and deliberative branch of government, are a minimal precondition for intrusions on civil liberties. A special risk is that group polarization, within the executive branch, will lead to steps that have not been subject to sufficiently broad debate. Deliberation within the legislative branch is more likely to ensure that restrictions on liberty are actually defensible. Precisely because of its size and diversity, a legislature is more likely to contain people who will speak for those who are burdened, and hence legislative processes have some potential for producing the protection that Hayek identifies with the rule of law. In these ways, the requirement of a clear legislative statement enlists the idea of checks and balances in the service of individual rights – not through flat bans on government action, but through requiring two, rather than one, branches of government to approve.

By way of ironic comparison, consider the highly publicized 2002 memorandum on torture, written by the Office of Legal Counsel in the United States Department of Justice for the White House. The most remarkable aspect of the memorandum is its suggestion that as Commander-in-Chief of the Armed Forces, the President of the United States has the authority to torture suspected terrorists, so as to make it constitutionally unacceptable for Congress to ban the practice of torture. Where the Supreme Court of Israel held that clear legislative *authorization* is required to permit torture, the United States Department of Justice concluded that clear legislative *prohibition* is insufficient to forbid torture.[8] But the position of the Department of Justice was not well defended, and it is most unlikely that the Supreme Court, or an independent arbiter, would accept that position.

In the United States, a good model is provided by the remarkable decision in *Kent v. Dulles*,[9] decided at the height of the Cold War. In that case, the Supreme Court was asked to decide whether the Secretary of State could deny a passport to Rockwell Kent, an American citizen who was a member of the Communist Party. Kent argued that the denial was a violation of his constitutional rights and should be

---

[8] To be sure, the position of the Department of Justice was stated with a degree of tentativeness, with the suggestion that the congressional ban on torture "might" be unconstitutional in the context of battlefield interrogations; but the general impression is that the ban probably should be so regarded.

[9] *Kent v. Dulles*, 357 U.S. 116 (1958).

invalidated for that reason. The Court responded by refusing to rule on the constitutional question. Instead it said that at a minimum, any denial of a passport, on these grounds, would have to be specifically authorized by Congress. The Court therefore struck down the decision of the Secretary of State because Congress had not explicitly authorized the executive to deny passports in cases of this kind.

Kent v. Dulles has been followed by many cases holding that the executive cannot intrude into constitutionally sensitive domains unless the legislature has squarely authorized it to do so. What I am adding here is that because of the risk of excessive or unjustified fear, this is a salutary approach whenever restrictions on civil liberty follow from actual or perceived external threats. If congressional authorization is required, courts have a simple first question to ask in cases in which the executive branch is alleged to have violated civil liberties: Has the legislature specifically authorized that branch to engage in the action that is being challenged?

Of course requiring specific authorization is no panacea. It is possible that the legislature, itself excessively fearful, will permit the President to do something that cannot be justified in principle. It is also possible that the legislature will fail to authorize the executive to act in circumstances in which action is justified or even indispensable. What I am suggesting is that as a general rule, a requirement of legislative permission is a good way of reducing the relevant dangers – those of excessive and insufficient protections against security risks.

SPECIAL SCRUTINY OF SELECTIVE DENIALS OF LIBERTY

I have emphasized that public fear might well produce excessive reactions from Congress. The risk is especially serious when identifiable groups, rather than the public as a whole, are being burdened.

Consider in this regard an illuminating passage from a famous opinion by American Supreme Court Justice Robert Jackson:[10]

The burden should rest heavily upon one who would persuade us to use the due process clause to strike down a substantive law or ordinance. Even its provident use against municipal regulations frequently disables all government – state, municipal and federal – from dealing with the conduct in

---

[10] *Railway Express Agency v. New York*, 336 U.S. 106, 112–13 (1949) (Jackson, J., concurring).

question because the requirement of due process is also applicable to State and Federal Governments. Invalidation of a statute or an ordinance on due process grounds leaves ungoverned and ungovernable conduct which many people find objectionable.

Invocation of the equal protection clause, on the other hand, does not disable any governmental body from dealing with the subject at hand. It merely means that the prohibition or regulation must have a broader impact. I regard it as a salutary doctrine that cities, states, and the federal government must exercise their powers so as not to discriminate between their inhabitants except upon some reasonable differentiation fairly related to the object of regulation. This equality is not merely abstract justice. The framers of the Constitution knew, and we should not forget today, that there is no more effective practical guaranty against arbitrary and unreasonable government than to require that the principles of law which officials would impose upon a minority must be imposed generally. Conversely, nothing opens the door to arbitrary action so effectively as to allow those officials to pick and choose only a few to whom they will apply legislation and thus to escape the political retribution that might be visited upon them if larger numbers were affected. Courts can take no better measure to assure that laws will be just than to require that laws be equal in operation.

Justice Jackson is making two points here. The first is that when the Court rules (via the due process clause) that some conduct cannot be regulated at all, it is intervening, in a major way, in democratic processes, making that conduct essentially "unregulable." Consider, for example, a decision to the effect that certain security measures, applicable to everyone in (say) public spaces, are unacceptable because they intrude unduly into the realm of personal privacy. The second point is that when the Court strikes government action down on equality grounds, it merely requires the government to increase the breadth of its restriction, thus triggering political checks against unjustified burdens. Consider, for example, a decision to the effect that certain security measures, applicable only to people with dark skin, are unacceptable because they do not treat people equally.

With a modest twist on Jackson's argument, we can see a potential approach for courts faced with claims about unlawful interference with civil liberties. If the government is imposing a burden on the citizens as a whole, or on a random draw of citizens, then the appropriate judicial posture is one of deference to the government. (At least if free speech, voting rights, and political association are not involved; an exception for these rights makes sense in light of the fact that democratic processes cannot work well without them.) If government is intruding on everyone, it is unlikely to do so unless it has a good reason, one founded in something other than fear alone; recall Hayek's claims about the rule of law. But if the government imposes a burden on an identifiable subclass of citizens, a warning flag should go up. The courts should give careful scrutiny to that burden.

Of course these general propositions do not resolve concrete cases; everything turns on the particular nature of the constitutional challenge. But an appreciation of the risks of selectivity suggests the proper orientation. In the great *Korematsu* case,[11] challenging the internment of Japanese-Americans during World War II, the Court should have been far more skeptical of the government's justification. The reason is that the racist and selective internment was peculiarly immune from political checks on unjustified intrusions on liberty. Most Americans had nothing to fear from it. The same point holds for some aspects of the contemporary "war on terrorism." In the United States, many of the relevant restrictions have been limited to noncitizens, in a way that creates a real risk of overreaching; the most obvious examples are the detentions at Guantanamo Bay. Noncitizens cannot vote and they lack political power. If they are mistreated or abused, the ordinary political checks are unavailable.

When the legal texts leave reasonable doubt, courts should take a careful look at the legitimacy of the government's justifications for imposing burdens on people who are unable to protect themselves in the political process. Hence the Supreme Court should be applauded for its insistence that foreign nationals, challenging their detention, have a right of access to federal courts to contest the legality of what has been done to them.[12]

Compare in this regard one of President Bush's less circumspect remarks in defense of the idea that enemy combatants might be tried in special military tribunals. President Bush suggested that whatever

[11] *Korematsu v. United States*, 323 U.S. 214 (1944).
[12] See *Rasul v. Bush*, 124 S. Ct. 2686 (2004).

procedures are applied, the defendants will receive fairer treatment than they gave to murdered Americans on 9/11. The problem with this suggestion is that it begs the question, which is whether the defendants were, in fact, involved in the 9/11 attack. Here is an illustration of the extent to which fear, and the thirst for vengeance, can lead to unjustified infringements of civil liberties. Sadly, Attorney General John Ashcroft duplicated the error a few years later, suggesting that Supreme Court decisions in 2004 had given "new rights to terrorists," when a key question was whether the detainees were terrorists at all.

BALANCING AND SECOND-ORDER BALANCING

Thus far I have operated under a simple framework, supposing that in any situation, there is some kind of balancing between security and civil liberty – something like an optimal tradeoff. As the magnitude of the threat increases, the argument for intruding on civil liberties also increases. If the risk is great, government might, for example, increase searches in airports; ensure a constant police presence in public places, with frequent requests for identification; permit military tribunals to try those suspected of terrorist activity; hold detainees whom it suspects of terrorism; and allow the police to engage in practices that would not be permitted under ordinary circumstances.

Under the balancing approach, everything turns on whether the relevant fear is justified. What is the extent of the risk? If we believe that we should find a good tradeoff among the relevant variables, then excessive fear will inevitably cause a serious problem, by sacrificing liberty to protect security. This approach to the relationship between liberty and security is standard and intuitive, and something like it seems to me correct. But it is not without complications. There might be, for example, a "core" of rights into which government cannot intrude and for which balancing is inappropriate. Consider torture. Some people believe that whatever the circumstances, torture cannot be justified; even the most well-grounded public fear is insufficient to justify it. In one form, this argument turns on a belief that an assessment of consequences can never authorize this kind of intrusion. I believe that in this form, the argument is a kind of moral heuristic,[13]

---

[13] See Cass R. Sunstein, Moral Heuristics, *Behavioral and Brain Sciences* (forthcoming).

one that is far too rigid, even fanatical. Is it really sensible to ban torture when torture is the only means of protecting thousands of people from certain death? Suppose that a bomb is about to explode, killing thousands or hundreds of thousands of people, and that reasonable people believe that without torture, the bomb will indeed explode. Might not torture be morally permissible? Might it not be morally obligatory? The ban on torture can easily be seen as a moral heuristic, one that usually works well but that predictably misfires.

But another, more plausible form of the argument is rule utilitarian: A flat prohibition on torture, one that forbids balancing in individual cases, might be justified on the basis of a kind of second-order balancing. It might be concluded not that torture is never justified in principle, but that unless torture is entirely outlawed, government will engage in torture in cases in which it is not justified, that the benefits of torture are rarely significant, and that the permission to torture in extraordinary cases will lead, on balance, to more harm than good. I am not sure that this view is right, but it is entirely plausible. And if it is, we might adopt a barrier to torture, even when public fear is both extreme and entirely justified. Under most real-world circumstances, I believe that such a barrier is indeed justified.

Can other rights be understood similarly? Consider the area of free speech law in the United States, and the relationship between fear and restrictions on speech. In the Cold War, government attempted to regulate speech that, in its view, would increase the influence of Communism. The Smith Act, enacted in 1946, made it a crime for any person "to knowingly or willingly advocate, abet, advise, or teach the duty, necessity, desirability, or propriety of overthrowing or destroying any government in the United States by force or violence, or by the assassination of any officer of such government." In *Dennis v. United States*,[14] the government prosecuted people for organizing the Communist Party of the United States – an organization that was said to teach and advocate the overthrow of the United States government by force. The Court held that the constitutionality of the Smith Act would stand or fall on whether the speech in question "created a 'clear and present danger' of attempting or accomplishing the prohibited

---

[14] *Dennis v. United States*, 341 U.S. 494 (1951).

crime." In its most important analytic step, the Court concluded that the "clear and present danger" test did not mean that the danger must truly be clear and present. It denied "that before the Government may act, it must wait until the putsch is about to be executed, the plans have been laid and the signal is awaited." When a group was attempting to indoctrinate its members and to commit them to a course of action, "action by the Government is required."

Note the close relationship between the Court's analysis here, the Precautionary Principle, and President George W. Bush's doctrine of preemptive war. In the face of threats to national security, President Bush plausibly contended that if a country waits until the risk is "imminent," it may be waiting until it is too late; so, too, for those who invoke the Precautionary Principle. So, too, perhaps, for certain conspiracies, even conspiracies founded essentially on speech.

Following the distinguished Court of Appeals Judge Learned Hand, the *Dennis* Court said that the clear and present danger test involved a form of balancing, without an imminence requirement. "In each case [courts] must ask whether the gravity of the 'evil,' discounted by its improbability, justifies such invasion of free speech as is necessary to avoid the danger." The Court said that it would "adopt this statement of the rule." Having done so, the Court upheld the convictions. It recognized that no uprising had occurred. But the balancing test authorized criminal punishment in light of "the inflammable nature of world conditions, similar uprisings in other countries, and the touch-and-go nature of our relations with countries with whom [defendants] were in the very least ideologically attuned."

Dennis sees the clear and present danger test as one of ad hoc balancing, at least in cases that involve a potentially catastrophic harm; the Court might even be seen as accepting an Anti-Catastrophe Principle, perceiving the situation as one of uncertainty rather than risk. But many people have been skeptical of ad hoc balancing, which no longer reflects American constitutional law. Instead, the Supreme Court understands the idea of clear and present danger to require that the danger be both *likely* and *imminent*,[15] in a way that explicitly rejects precautionary thinking. This approach is quite different from

---

[15] See *Brandenburg v. Ohio*, 395 U.S. 444 (1969).

Judge Hand's balancing test. It does not ask courts to discount the evil by its probability – an approach that would permit speech regulation if an extremely serious evil has (say) a 20 percent chance of occurring. And even if a risk has a 70 percent chance of occurring, and is therefore "likely," regulation of speech is unacceptable unless the risk is imminent. Indeed, regulation is impermissible even if the risk of serious harm cannot plausibly be calculated. The government must, in short, wait until the harm is both likely to occur and about to occur – a view pressed by many who object to "preemptive war" and who say that a nation may not make war on another unless the threat is indeed "imminent."

How should we compare a balancing approach with one that requires both likelihood and imminence? At first glance, the *Dennis* approach seems much better, at least on consequentialist grounds. If a risk is only 10 percent likely to occur, but if 100,000 people will die in the event that the risk comes to fruition, government should not simply stand by until it is too late. In the environmental context, balancing is surely preferable to a rule that would require both likelihood and imminence. For global warming, we ought not to wait until the serious harm is upon us. So, too, for security measures meant to reduce the risk of crime or terrorism. It is worthwhile to invest significant resources if the evidence suggests a real risk, even if the most serious harms are less than likely to occur.

What, then, can be said in favor of the requirements of likelihood and imminence? Perhaps we distrust any balancers. Perhaps the requirements are a response to a judgment that in the real world, the *Dennis* approach will produce excessive regulation of speech. If our balancing is entirely accurate, we should balance. But where speech is unpopular, or when people are frightened of it, government might well conclude that "the gravity of the 'evil,' discounted by its probability," justifies regulation even if it does not. For all these reasons, the requirements of likelihood and imminence have reasonable institutional justifications, having to do with the incentives and attitudes of government officials and citizens themselves.

In the context of speech, there are independent considerations. Public disapproval of the content of speech – of the ideas that are being offered – might result in a judgment that speech is likely to cause harm even if the real motivation for censorship is less harm than disagreement with the underlying ideas.[16] And if the harm is not imminent, further discussion, rather than censorship, is the proper remedy. As long as there is time for public discussion and debate, more talk is usually the best response to speech that seems to create a risk of harm. The imminence requirement is a recognition of this idea. In this light, the clear and present danger test, requiring both likelihood and imminence, reflects a kind of second-order balancing, one that distrusts on-the-spot judgments about risks and harms and that puts on government an unusually high burden of proof. So defended, the test does not reject the idea of balancing in principle, or insist that the protection of liberty does not vary with the extent of the threat to security. The test merely recognizes that our balancing is likely to go wrong in practice – and that we need to develop safeguards against our own bad balancing, especially when public fear will predictably lead us astray.

As I have suggested, a general prohibition of torture can be understood in similar terms. The argument need not be that torture can never be defended by reference to consequences; if the only way to prevent catastrophe is to torture a terrorist, perhaps torture is justified. A more sensible justification for banning torture is that a government that is licensed to torture will do so when torture is not justified – and that the social costs of disallowing torture do not, in the end, come close to the social benefits. I am not suggesting that this judgment is necessarily correct. In imaginable circumstances, torture is indeed justifiable. All I am arguing is that aggressive protection of civil liberties and civil rights is often best defended as a safeguard against mass fear or hysteria that would lead to steps that cannot really be justified on balance. In a sense, sensible governments "overprotect" liberties, compared to the level of protection that liberties would receive in a system of (optimal) case-by-case balancing. Because optimal balancing is not likely to occur in the real world, rule-based protection is a justifiable second best.

Aggressive protection of free speech has been justified on the ground that courts should take a "pathological perspective" – one suited for periods in which the public, and hence the judiciary, will be tempted to allow indefensible restrictions under the heat of the

---

[16] For a great deal of evidence, see Stone, *supra* note 1.

moment.[17] The argument is that free speech law builds up strong, rule-like protections, eschewing balancing and sometimes protecting speech that ought not to be protected. The goal of the "pathological perspective" is to create safeguards that will work when liberty is under siege and most at risk. The pathological perspective creates an obvious problem: It might be that when liberty is under siege, public necessity requires it to be. Hence the pathological perspective runs the risk of overprotecting liberty. But if the argument here is correct, there is reason to believe that public fear, heightened by worst-case scenarios, will result in selective burdens on those who are unable to protect themselves. In such cases, constitutional law operates best if it uses not balancing but rules or presumptions – allowing government to compromise liberty only on the basis of a compelling demonstration of necessity.

FEAR AND FREEDOM

My goal here has been to uncover some mechanisms that can lead a fearful public to invoke a kind of Precautionary Principle that produces unjustified intrusions on civil liberties. The availability heuristic and probability neglect often lead people to treat risks as much greater than they are in fact, and hence to accept risk-reduction strategies that do considerable harm and little good. When the burdens of government restrictions are faced by an identifiable minority rather by the majority, the risk of unjustified action is significantly increased. The internment of Japanese-Americans during World War II is only one salient example. Hence precautions can be worse than blunders; they can be both cruel and unjust.

What can be done in response? I have suggested three possibilities. First, courts should not allow the executive to intrude on civil liberties without explicit legislative authorization. Second, courts should be relatively deferential to intrusions on liberty that apply to all or most; they should be far more skeptical when government restricts the liberty of a readily identifiable few. Third, courts should avoid ad hoc balancing of liberty against security; they should develop principles

---

[17] See Vincent Blasi, The Pathological Perspective and the First Amendment, 85 *Colum. L. Rev.* 449 (1985).

that reflect a kind of second-order balancing, attuned to the risk of excessive fear.

These three strategies are unlikely to provide all of the protection sought by civil libertarians. But when the risks to national security are real, courts are properly reluctant to be as aggressive as in ordinary times. When those risks are real, some infringements on freedom are both inevitable and desirable. The task is to develop approaches that counteract the risk that public fear will lead to unjustified restrictions, without authorizing freedom-protecting institutions to adopt a role for which they are ill suited.

.. *Concluding Note: Fear and Folly*

By its very nature, fear is selective. Some people are afraid to fly but not to drive. Others are afraid of medication but not of the risks associated with avoiding medication. We might fear the risks of insufficient exercise but neglect the danger of excessive exposure to the sun. We might fear the risks of terrorism but neglect the risks of smoking. Unfortunately, it is not possible to take strong precautions against all risks. Those who seem most fearful, and most determined to avoid danger, often increase risks through their very efforts to eliminate danger.

On these counts, nations are the same as ordinary people. When governments claim to be taking precautions, they might well be increasing risks rather than reducing them. Any preemptive war – and the 2003 war against Iraq in particular – can turn out to be an example. So, too, with environmental restrictions that control genetically modified food, or lead companies to use less safe substitutes, or dramatically increase the price of energy.

For these reasons I have criticized the Precautionary Principle, at least if the idea is taken as a plea for aggressive regulation of risks that are unlikely to come to fruition. That idea is literally incoherent, simply because regulation itself can create risks. If the Precautionary Principle seems to offer clear guidance, it is only because human cognition and social influences make certain hazards stand out from the background. When, for example, a particular incident is "available," in the sense that it comes readily to mind, people tend to be a lot more worried than they need to be. They may well take excessive precautions against the most available risks. And if no vivid example is associated with a particular risk, people may well be fearless – and expose themselves to real danger.

The selectivity of fear is aggravated by probability neglect, through which intense emotions lead people to focus on worst-case scenarios without taking account of the likelihood that they will occur. Probability neglect is a serious problem, because it leads to badly misplaced priorities. Social influences multiply that problem. If fearful people speak and listen mostly to one another, their fear will be heightened, regardless of reality. And if fearless people talk to each other about the unjustified zealotry of those who are worried about global warming, asbestos, or occupational disease, they will become still more fearless – even if the underlying hazards are serious.

What can be done by way of response? Sensible regulators manage fear through education and information. Cost-benefit analysis is an exceedingly helpful tool, simply because it provides an understanding of the stakes – of what is to be gained and what is to be lost from regulatory interventions. If an environmental regulation would cost a great deal and do little to improve public health or the environment, there is no reason to adopt it. At the same time, the outcome of cost-benefit analysis should not be decisive. Perhaps those who would benefit from regulation are poor, whereas those who would pay are wealthy; if so, regulation might be justified whatever cost-benefit analysis says. I have also emphasized that people are citizens, not merely consumers, and their reflective judgments might lead them to favor policies that do not track cost-benefit balancing. Moreover, the Precautionary Principle has a legitimate place when people face a potentially catastrophic risk to which probabilities cannot be assigned. Hence I have suggested that an Anti-Catastrophe Principle deserves to play a role in regulatory policy.

Libertarian paternalism is an exceptionally promising approach to the dual problems of excessive and insufficient fear. In countless domains, both private and public institutions can steer people in better directions without eliminating freedom of choice. Sometimes our choices lead us in directions that make our lives go worse. Often our preferences are a product of starting points and default rules. With better beginnings, people can be helped to make better choices by their own lights.

When public fear is excessive, it is likely to produce unjustified infringements on liberty. In democratic nations in the twentieth century, public fear has led to unjustified imprisonment, unreasonable intrusions from the police, racial and religious discrimination, official abuse and torture, and censorship of speech. In short, fear can led to human rights violations of the most grotesque kind. The danger to liberty is heightened if an identifiable group is burdened by the infringements, leaving the majority unrestricted. In these circumstances, courts can take three useful steps. First, they can require the legislature specifically to authorize any intrusions on liberty. Second, they can carefully scrutinize restrictions that burden the identifiable few. Third, they can adopt rules and principles that protect against the danger that freedom will be on the losing end of any "balance."

Fear is an ineradicable part of human life. Often it points us in the right directions. Nations, no less than individuals, pay attention to it. But in democratic societies, governments do not capitulate to the fears of their citizens, or pretend that a general idea of precaution can provide helpful guidance. Democratic governments care about facts as well as fears. Because they respect liberty and self-government, and because they want to improve human lives, they listen closely to what people have to say. But for the same reasons, they take careful steps to ensure that laws and policies reduce, and do not replicate, the errors to which fearful people are prone.

Index

Printed in the United States
50724LVS00001B/13-30

9 780521 848237